MW00560584

Beyond Liberalism

Beyond Liberalism

Toward a Purpose-Guided Democracy

Michael K. Briand

 PRAEGER™

An Imprint of ABC-CLIO, LLC

Santa Barbara, California • Denver, Colorado

Library of Congress Cataloging-in-Publication Data

Names: Briand, Michael K. (Michael Keith), author.
Title: Beyond liberalism : toward a purpose-guided democracy / Michael K. Briand.
Description: Santa Barbara, California : Praeger, [2019] | Includes bibliographical
   references and index.
Identifiers: LCCN 2019013678 (print) | LCCN 2019017881 (ebook) |
   ISBN 9781440872419 (ebook) | ISBN 9781440872402 (hardback)
Subjects: LCSH: Liberalism—Moral and ethical aspects. | Democracy—Moral and
   ethical aspects. | Political ethics.
Classification: LCC JC574 (ebook) | LCC JC574 .B74 2019 (print) | DDC 320.51/3—dc23
LC record available at https://lccn.loc.gov/2019013678

ISBN: 978-1-4408-7240-2 (print)
       978-1-4408-7241-9 (ebook)

23 22 21 20 19   1 2 3 4 5

This book is also available as an eBook.

Praeger
An Imprint of ABC-CLIO, LLC

ABC-CLIO, LLC
147 Castilian Drive
Santa Barbara, California 93117
www.abc-clio.com

This book is printed on acid-free paper ∞

Manufactured in the United States of America

Contents

Preface

... The world, which seems
To lie before us like a land of dreams,
So various, so beautiful, so new,
Hath really neither joy, nor love, nor light,
Nor certitude, nor peace, nor help for pain;
And we are here as on a darkling plain
Swept with confused alarms of struggle and flight,
Where ignorant armies clash by night.

—Matthew Arnold, *Dover Beach*

Writing in early 2018 about the opioid crisis killing a rapidly mounting number of Americans, Andrew Sullivan called it a story of how people are trying to "numb the agonies of the world's most highly evolved liberal democracy."[1] The crisis, he said, is

> a sign of a civilization . . . overwhelmed by a warp-speed, postindustrial world, a culture . . . trying . . . to end the psychological, emotional, even existential pain [that our way of life inflicts on us. We have created] an overly atomized society, where everyone has to create his or her own meaning, and everyone feels alone. [We are suffering from the] waning of all [the] traditional . . . supports for a meaningful, collective life and their replacement with various forms of cheap distraction. . . . Americans are trying to cope with an inhuman new world where . . . core elements of human happiness—faith, family, community—seem to elude so many.

What can we do about our "overly atomized society, where everyone has to create his or her own meaning, and everyone feels alone"? A good place to start is by making an effort to understand how it came to be. Kierkegaard was surely correct when he observed that, although life has to be lived "forwards," it can be understood only "backwards." Because the best predictor of the future is the past, we ought to understand it as well as we can. If it's true (as Aquinas remarked, paraphrasing Aristotle), that "a little error in the beginning leads to a great one in the end," recognizing an error in the past might help us avert hardship or even disaster ahead.[2]

I believe much of what we find disagreeable and worrisome about contemporary life owes to just such an undiscerned error. Some three hundred years ago, the body of beliefs, principles, and institutions known as the "Enlightenment" ushered in the modern ideas and practices of science, secularism, and individualism. But the transformation that began with the advent of modernity has never been completed. Early on, a seemingly unbridgeable rift opened, not only between science and religion, but between the natural world and the human world, between the objective and the subjective, the rational and the intuitive, the absolute and the relative, society and the individual, "is" and "ought," duty and self-interest. That gap has not closed, or even narrowed substantially. Humanity remains a dispirited occupant of what Weber called our "disenchanted world," and Mumford termed our "disqualified universe"—a world with no quality or meaning beyond what we can derive from our personal satisfactions in life.

Visiting America some twenty years before Arnold wrote *Dover Beach*, Tocqueville worried (as did Weber a half-century later) that, as the modern world develops,

> skepticism emerges to reinforce sensualism, man no longer cares what will happen in the afterlife, and hence they succumb to the "natural instability" of changing desires in a joyless quest for momentary happiness. The "mad impetuosity" of materialism has arrived.[3]

A society whose members devote their energies to satisfying their personal desires—for money, power, sex, status, prestige—is a society that no longer helps them to live on through the fruits of their mortal endeavors. In such a society, nothing endures. Everything is impermanent: the things we desire, the goals we work for, the successes we achieve. We lose our ability to pass on anything of lasting value to the future.

Along with science, the Enlightenment gave us liberalism—the system of moral, political, and economic beliefs and principles that inspired its proponents to challenge traditional authority with reason and to replace hierarchical governance with democracy. Liberalism was, and always will be, one of the most valuable achievements of humankind.[4] But it has reached the limits of its ability, without further modification and supplementation, to continue meeting our most important needs in the face of unprecedented change and complexity. In its name we have permitted inequality to grow, conflict to persist, alienation and hopelessness to take root, and public life to become vexing, abrasive, and discouraging. This is not at all to say that we can or should dispense with it entirely. But we do need to breathe new life into it.

Human beings need a persuasive and animating vision of their place and purpose in the great scheme of things. Such a vision supplies an answer to the fundamental questions of ethics: *How should we live?* and *What kind of people should we be?* Liberalism offers no answer to these questions. Because its ideal is a plurality of self-chosen approaches to life, it seeks to remain neutral with respect to different views of the good and the right and leaves the question to the individual to answer for herself. But it does nothing to support her in this. It doesn't even encourage her—out of pure self-interest—to reflect on the desirability and acceptability of the approaches that are open to her. Its subjective, "laissez-faire" approach to ethics—often conflated and confused with pluralism—leaves us to gin up a vision of our place and purpose in life out of our limited personal resources. Not surprisingly, when thus left to our own devices, we end up turning to "personal gain of one sort or another" as a basis for our values. "The end result," writes Jacob Needleman, "is despair."[5]

Because it treats value (goodness) as a function of personal desire and treats freedom (chiefly in the form of individual rights) as the basic principle for resolving conflict, liberalism turns the political arena into a kind of market in which groups and individuals compete with each other to determine "who gets what, when, and how." It offers no objective or even cooperative way of securing agreement concerning the ethical dilemmas underlying many of the political issues that divide us. This deficiency disables and deters us from deliberating together. As a result, power becomes the only political currency that matters, and liberalism ends up sending the message—as witness the current state of partisan politics in the United States—that we may use any means necessary to achieve our self-chosen ends.

The liberal formula for the pursuit of happiness—guarantee everybody certain basic rights, and otherwise leave them free to choose what to do in life and how to do it—has been parroted so mindlessly for so long by so many that it seems as self-evidently and universally true as any proposition about human beings can be. From the beginning, though, it has contained the seeds of its own destruction. On reflection, it's plain that, over time, personal desires and the freedom to pursue their satisfaction erode and ultimately dissolve the practices, principles, and institutions that help human beings meet their need to live together peacefully in conditions of order, justice, and security.

We lack a ready and convincing answer to Tocqueville's question: whether democracy in the United States (or anywhere) can survive if neither religion nor "enlightened self-interest" can imbue politics with integrity, character, and a genuine goodwill toward others. I believe the answer increasingly is clear: neither of them can. If we're going to arrest the accelerating decline of our culture and society, we will have to rid ourselves of the delusion that we can make life worth living through our personal efforts to secure good lives for ourselves *as individuals*.

The most pressing problem facing us—as a nation, as a civilization, as a species—is our failure to recognize the basic human need to live with a sense of purpose and direction. This is a "spiritual" need. It can't be reduced to a mere physical or material or even emotional desideratum. And it can't be met through the pursuit of strictly personal aims. Creating and sustaining the sense that we are part of some great cause, enterprise, or project that stands for something of true and enduring importance is an inherently collective undertaking. We can't achieve it in isolation from each other, as disconnected social "atoms."

Constructing a sense of purpose and direction requires that we talk with each other. Specifically, we need to establish a practice of public ethical discourse, one that informs our democratic political decision making. We must seek knowledge of what is genuinely good and best, both for *any*one and for *every*one. We must strive to act on that knowledge while remaining open to finding it wherever our searching leads us, and while always bearing in mind the lessons painfully learned in the past about our fallibility and our susceptibility to hubris.

This is the way forward, beyond the "disenchanted world" of dispirited liberalism, toward the construction of communities and societies in which people might once again pursue their goals and aspirations through public life, find fulfillment by achieving reputation and influence within them, and gaining a semblance of immortality in their collective memory. We need not—indeed, should not—expect to arrive at full and final answers to these questions. What is good, better, and best will always depend on the (ever-changing) conditions and circumstances in which human beings find themselves, and so must remain provisional and open to revision. But continuous effort is indispensable.

We need to begin thinking ethically—*together*. In the book that follows, I explain why we should and how we can. Whether we can reach agreement on any of the important issues that divide us matters far less than whether we can talk constructively and productively about the connection between ethics and democracy. This book is an invitation to begin.

A NOTE ON READING THE BOOK

I hope everyone will read at least the Introduction and Chapters 1, 11, and 12. For those of you wanting a general overview of the argument that we need to place democratic politics on the foundation of a robust practice of public ethical dialogue and deliberation, read the Introduction and Chapters 1, 2, 4, 7, and 10 through 12. Finally, if you have an interest in the more technical aspects of the argument, you will find the relevant material in Chapters 3 and 5 through 10.

Introduction

Saving Liberal Democracy from Itself

Since the 1960s, political conflict in the Western world has been growing increasingly adversarial and intractable. In the United States, we have now reached the point where political opponents agree on almost nothing, not even the most basic facts. People have sorted themselves into ideological "tribes" whose worldviews are increasingly at odds. Support for democratic ideals and principles, such as tolerance and compromise, are weakening. It's not simply that formal institutions have been shaken—the informal norms that underpin them have become more fragile.[1] Rules concerning transparency, conflict of interest, civil discourse, respect for the opposition and freedom of the press, and equal treatment of citizens are all eroding. Much of the public is angry, resentful, and preoccupied with problems and issues that have no apparent solution. Many people seem to be open to "alternatives" to liberal democracy.[2]

But why? After all, as Steven Pinker points out, the history of the United States (and indeed, of the entire Western world) over the past three centuries is a story of gradual, not always even, but nevertheless continuous progress: expanding freedom, growing tolerance, rising prosperity, improving health and safety, advancing knowledge, and burgeoning technological prowess.[3] Why, then—despite all the achievements of liberal democratic societies in the long struggle to eliminate the perennial woes and ills of human existence—is there so much discontent, misery, and rage? Why aren't we all ecstatic about the immense gains we have made and the promise of even greater achievements to come?[4]

The short answer is that liberalism—the body of beliefs, principles, and institutions that emerged during the cultural revolution known as the Enlightenment—has succeeded *too well*.[5] To its credit, liberalism has sought to free people's minds from ignorance, superstition, and arbitrary authority, especially the power of the State, so that civilization might progress. It emphasizes reliance on reason; individual rights; democratic decision making; secularism; moral, legal, and political equality; and the freedoms (among others) of speech, the press, religion, and economic activity.[6] Its durability and widespread acceptance testify to the many benefits it has bestowed on people fortunate enough to live in liberal societies. Why, then, does our public life evince so much frustration, bitterness, and anger? Why, for example, have right-leaning authoritarian political movements arisen that exhibit antipathy toward the values and principles that are central to liberal democracy?[7]

Andrew Sullivan offers a concise explanation: Despite its merits, liberal democracy "has left a hunger for shared public conceptions about the purpose of life. . . . It is dogged by a nagging question: *'Is this all there is?'*"

> We have lost something that undergirds all of [our progress]: meaning, cohesion, and a different, deeper kind of happiness than the satiation of all our earthly needs. . . . We are a species built on religious ritual to appease our existential angst, and yet we now live in a world where every individual has to create her own meaning from scratch. . . . None of [the progress we have made] solves the existential reality of our mortality; and . . . none of it provides spiritual sustenance or meaning. . . . We have no common concept of human flourishing apart from materialism. . . . We've forgotten the human flourishing that comes from a common idea of virtue. . . .[8]

We lack a common concept of human flourishing and a common idea of virtue because the prevailing liberal ethos insists there can be no single view of either flourishing or virtue to which all might assent. Indeed, it warns that even to entertain the possibility is downright dangerous—we risk tyranny by pursuing that age-old chimera, the common good. Instead, liberalism celebrates a plurality of responses to the fundamental question of ethics: "*How should we live?*" That is its great strength, of course. But it is also a weakness. Meaning-making—the effort to ensure that "this is *not* all there is"—is an inherently collective activity. We can construct meaning and purpose, both for ourselves as individuals and for our society, only within a social and cultural setting that supports and encourages our efforts to do so. Liberalism's highly individualistic, "laissez-faire" approach to ethics, however, provides little support for our efforts to reflect on and pursue a meaningful life. Indeed, it actively discourages that effort. Because it treats value (goodness) as a function of personal desire and sees individual freedom (especially in the guise of rights) as the preferred solution to all political disputes, it rules out of court any suggestion that we try to construct ideals of human flourishing and virtue that might help restore meaning to contemporary life.

Most of liberalism's tenets are unobjectionable, even praiseworthy. The trouble lies, ultimately, with two of its (historically foundational) elements—the way we think about the individual in relation to society, and the way we try to justify our beliefs about what is good and bad, right and wrong—and with the negative reaction they have provoked. Because these two problematic components of liberal doctrine are so deeply rooted, fixing them will require a sustained commitment to a specific type of reengagement between people with conflicting worldviews: a sustained practice of public dialogue and deliberation that, in both its aims and its methods, is determinedly *ethical*. Only ethical discourse will help people meet two of the most basic requirements we have as human beings: the need to form and maintain a secure identity, and the need to ground our beliefs about good and bad, right and wrong, in something sturdier than subjective opinion.

LIBERALISM'S "BAD SEEDS"

1. *"Atomism."* Human beings are social creatures. We depend on communities of our fellows to nurture us, to provide the means by which we can meet our most important needs, and to offer us opportunities for development and expression of our unique aptitudes and interests. But Enlightenment thinkers imagined they could design an ideal form of government by studying societies in the same way that scientists studied nature: by analyzing and understanding their smallest units—"atoms" in the natural world, individual persons in the social world. This new "scientific" view treated communities and societies as abstractions. In contrast, only individual persons are "real," and their motivations originate within them—not in the social environment they inhabit.

Instead of seeing atomism for what it is, though—an artifact of a simplistic conception of scientific thinking misapplied to the human world—we have embraced it. As a result, we've lost sight of the true sources of personal identity and have blinded ourselves to the damage we've done to the connections that once bound us to others. Traditionally, a person's identity was tied to the place where he was born and raised and to the other people with whom he shared a history, religion, values, ways of making a living, an outlook on what life is and how it should be lived. Over time, however, identities have been weakened by the uprooting of people and the breaking of connections to family, place, and history. People now are more likely than previously to think of themselves as discrete, self-sufficient entities who are also self-made. They form their identities around educational achievement, career success, mobility, personal experience, and looking to the future more than to the past. Unfortunately, as research by scholars such as Robert Bellah has shown, our efforts to conceive of ourselves almost exclusively as (atomized) individuals—abstracted from any defining social context—have left us with little to fall back on when we need psychological security most.[9] The result is a widespread "identity crisis."[10]

In *This Land of Strangers*, Robert Hall describes how Americans have devalued relationships in all facets of life: family, friendships, work, politics, and religion.[11] This poses an immense threat to the emotional, social, political, and economic health of our nation. "The simple truth," writes David Brooks, "is that relationships are the most valuable and value-creating resource of any society. They are our lifelines to survive, grow, and thrive." Yet they continue to deteriorate. Loneliness and social isolation

> are the problems that undergird many of our other problems. More and more Americans are socially poor. And yet it is very hard . . . to even see this fact. It is the very nature of loneliness and social isolation to be invisible. We talk as if the lonely don't exist.[12]

People who lack intimate connections in their lives are more likely to try meeting their needs for moral and emotional confirmation by identifying more closely with their political, ethnic, and other "tribes."[13] The "values" we associate with our "in-groups" have thus taken on great importance. We rely on them to tell us not only what's important in life, but also who we are. Because what we care about is tied so closely to our self-conceptions, obtaining confirmation of our values is tantamount to being validated as persons.

2. *"Subjectivism."* The other flawed element of liberalism, though less fundamental than atomism, is more troublesome because it lies closer to the surface of our political disagreements. "Subjectivism" holds that the truth of evaluative propositions—that is, statements asserting that something is good or bad, right or wrong—is individually ("subjectively") determined, whether based on one's personal experience, intuition, or interpretation of purportedly authoritative texts. Because there exists no "objective" standard or criterion of value that anyone—including the individual

herself—can invoke in order to assess what the individual believes or wants, the beliefs, attitudes, and desires of individuals must be taken as given.

But if our values at bottom are nothing more than feelings or desires, our political views can never be mistaken, no matter how poorly supported or wildly implausible they might be. And if we can't be mistaken, then we may discount or dismiss what *others* claim is good or bad, right or wrong as "just their opinion." Because subjectivism recognizes no common currency of good in terms of which the merits of divergent proposals can be compared, weighed, and prioritized, it makes all assertions about the good and the right relative. Subjectivism is thus responsible for much that is wrong with contemporary public discourse.[14] Public debate grows increasingly angry and unproductive. It strains the civic relationships that hold communities and societies together, while keeping our minds closed and deterring us from learning.[15]

THE PROBLEM WITH ETHICS IS THE PROBLEM WITH POLITICS

In combination, atomism and subjectivism have several pernicious consequences, which we will consider in Chapter 3. Here, let us return to Sullivan's observation that the sense of meaninglessness that pervades liberal democracies—the absence of a "deeper kind of happiness than the satiation of all our earthly needs"—owes to our lack of a common concept of human flourishing and a common idea of virtue. Liberalism tells us that such notions are illusions, and dangerous if pursued. But if the project of forming shared ideals of human flourishing and virtue is closed to us, so too is the task of seeking an answer to the fundamental question of ethics: *How should we live?* Liberalism thus renders ethics irrelevant to democratic politics.

That irrelevance deprives democracy of its lifeblood. The direst threat to contemporary democracies—the United States not least of all—is their growing inability to govern effectively and authoritatively; that is, on the basis of sound justifications that are widely understood and accepted.[16] Their inability to do so is rooted in the current condition of democratic thought and practice more generally, which is in a state of confusion and contestation. In turn, the confusion and contestation that marks democratic politics is directly related to the equally confused and contested state of our ethics.

Probably most of us would say that democracy has (or ought to have) a basis in ethics. Yet we *practice* democracy as if ethical considerations were irrelevant. As in business, law, and other practices, in politics the more important question is whether an action is *legal*. "There's no law against it" seems to be everyone's favorite justification for acting self-interestedly, without regard for the impact of their actions on others. Perhaps we imagine that democratic politics supplies its own set of rules, which render ethical principles superfluous. Or maybe we believe ethical discussion is futile, incapable of settling disputes that are rooted in conflicting values and beliefs about how people ought to live. Maybe we believe that's a good thing—because ethics fails to respect diverse views about what's good and bad, right and wrong, we *ought* to banish it from political debate. When different systems of ethical thought yield incompatible conclusions, democracy supposedly provides fair rules and procedures for obtaining the mutual accommodation that lets us live together despite our disagreements.

But it is precisely in this regard that democratic republics are not functioning well. As Alasdair MacIntyre observes,

> most public argumentative debate is sterile. . . . Ask yourself when last the United States Senate assembled with senators ready to have their opinions formed *through* debate, rather than bringing intransigent opinions *to* debate.[17]

In large measure, the sterility of public debate owes to the fact that contemporary ethical theory and practice are "in a state so disastrous that there are no large remedies for it."[18] It is a condition, moreover, that almost nobody recognizes:

> The most striking feature of . . . the debates in which [moral] disagreements are expressed is their interminable character. . . . There is in our society no established way of deciding between these claims that moral argument appears to be necessarily interminable. From our rival conclusions we can argue back to our rival first premises; but when we do arrive at our first premises, argument ceases and the justification of one premise against another becomes a matter of pure assertion and counter-assertion. . . .[19]

Because (we believe) we can't turn to ethical reasoning to settle—or at least to mitigate, constrain, or temper—the virulent disputes that break out again and again in our public life, the partisans in political disagreements turn with impunity to nonrational methods such as fallacious argumentation, disinformation, emotional manipulation, character assassination, equivocation, mendacity, and outright lying. No laws or purely political principles can deliver democracy from the feckless rhetorical brawling that now afflicts it.

Beneath nearly all of the fraught and intractable political disputes that bedevil our public life lies the substantive ethical unwellness that MacIntyre describes with such acuity. The ethical malady brought on by atomism and subjectivism underpins the "mad scramble" that is contemporary life: an ever-accelerating rush to "get more"—more money, more attention, more influence, more authority, more power. It manifests itself in the drive to advance our self-interests with scant regard for the impact of our actions on others.[20] It reinforces the mind-set Robert Fuller calls "rankism"—the apparently incurable compulsion to seek ever-higher positions within the hierarchies that human beings seem forever bent on erecting to protect themselves against the "humiliation" of being regarded as other people's equals.[21] In the end it turns life into a low-grade "war of all against all," corroding everything of enduring value and turning skepticism and nihilism from philosophical bad dreams into self-fulfilling realities.

The twin obsessions of "getting" and "climbing" run directly counter to the core premise of ethics: namely, that every human life has value, that each matters, and that in consequence we owe every person the same basic respect, concern, and goodwill we want for ourselves. Neither a free society nor a just one—including one in which meritocracy is valued—can survive unless the choices we make and the actions we take are shaped and guided by ethical thinking. By submitting ourselves to the requirements of ethical thinking, we accept personal responsibility for safeguarding the value we place on freedom, on democracy, and on the opportunity to live our lives in conditions that promote individual wellness, growth, and flourishing.

If fixing what ails our public life is to be a genuine social and cultural transformation and not just an interlude before the ingrained habit of "getting" and "climbing" resumes, we will need a new practice of public ethical thinking and discourse through which people—with reason and mutual respect—can resolve or at least mitigate their disagreements concerning what is good and bad, right and wrong, obligatory and optional. Unfortunately, public debate of such matters continues to focus narrowly and superficially on the question of the proper role and scope of government in our way of life. Viewing every issue of public policy as, at bottom, a stark choice between being "progovernment" (favoring the interests of society as a whole over those of individuals) and being "antigovernment" (favoring the interests of individuals over those of society as a whole) does not bode well for the cause of democratic renewal and resilience in the face of ceaseless (and often highly disruptive) change. In particular, it complicates the task of redeeming our formal political institutions in the eyes of those many of our fellow citizens who feel alienated from them.

That is worrisome because we need those institutions in order to prepare for and respond to challenges now and in the future. Faced with new as well as old conundrums that remain stubbornly resistant to solution, contemporary democratic societies will find life increasingly unsatisfactory in the continuing absence of a widely accepted practice of ethical dialogue and deliberation. We can construct such a practice, but only if we reconsider and revise some of our most deeply held misconceptions: about freedom and democracy; about ethics; and ultimately about what it means to live life well.

FREEDOM, DEMOCRACY, AND THE PURPOSE OF LIFE

The key premise of democracy—that all persons are of equal political worth—is the political expression of the fundamental premise of ethics in its interpersonal dimension: that all persons are of equal moral worth. From that conviction flows the injunction to show others, and their values and interests, the same respect and concern we show our own. Democracy as a way of life is not sustainable if people don't accept this prescription and allow it to guide their actions. Everything depends on it: not only politics, but also business, education, health care, public safety, civic responsibility, relations with other nations, and much more.

We value freedom because we want to have the choices and control that enable us to achieve the unique configuration of good things that reflects and expresses our individuality. Our idea of freedom is bounded, however, by our judgments of what might be worthwhile doing. There is a necessary connection between a course of action being valuable or desirable and the judgment that my freedom has been unjustifiably restricted. Moreover, like every other principle or value, "freedom" cannot always come out on top—it is not absolute. We have never come to terms with this fact, however, and as a result we have never solved the problem of how to foster acceptance of a principle of social responsibility and obligation to offset our mania for ever-expanding freedom. In the social, cultural, and economic conditions that prevail in our country at present, we need desperately to begin resolving political conflicts that are rooted in divergent worldviews and value systems—especially conflicts between personal freedom and social responsibility. A public process of ethical thinking, dialogue, and deliberation would help us situate freedom within the context of the good for all, and thereby serve as a countervailing principle by which the freedom to act can be weighed and balanced against the interests of all who may be affected by its exercise. It would accomplish this by enabling us collectively to determine, in a case of conflict between values, which should take precedence.

A practice of ethics confined to resolving conflicts between values, however, cannot by itself rescue democracy from the clutches of the "disenchanted world" of modern liberalism, with its atomistic conception of society and its subjectivist theory of good. Something is missing. The contemporary world is one in which human beings' *spiritual* needs are met neither by science, nor by consumerism and materialism, nor by increasingly anachronistic religious traditions. By themselves, secular ideals such as freedom, justice, and democracy do not elicit from us the goodwill toward others that ethics requires, and upon which our well-being, both as individuals and as societies, depends. Nor do they inspire in us a commitment to the flourishing of each person in his or her individuality.

Human beings require a persuasive and animating vision of human place and purpose in the great scheme of things from which standards of good and right can be derived. This liberalism fails to provide. If such a vision doesn't exist, it must be constructed—explicitly or implicitly—through an ongoing practice of public dialogue and deliberation that, directly or indirectly, begins to supply answers to the questions "How should we live?" and "What kind of people do we want to be?"

Without imprudently ignoring liberalism's warning about losing our freedom in the service of some overarching value, we must move beyond it. We shape our society, our communities, and, not least of all, ourselves by making hard choices together about what to "prize and prioritize." We can't make these choices, however, without some sense of *purpose*. "The question," Jacob Needleman has written, "of what America currently is and of what it has become in our day and age leads all of us directly into the question of the purpose and destiny of human life itself."[22] The reason it does so is that it's impossible to decide what is good or bad, right or wrong, fair or unfair, desirable or undesirable, without an idea of purpose to serve as the standard and gauge of value.[23] We must think about what at bottom matters most for human beings.

Moreover, as Ross Douthat points out, civic values we consider essential to sustaining a democratic way of life, such as respect for others and showing restraint in how we use our freedom, are virtues that depend on a deeper consensus:

> They can't . . . sustain themselves in cultures and institutions that are simply going bad. "Classical liberalism" is a superstructure that can easily be pulled apart from below by contending factions, or crumble when its cultural foundation disappears. . . . If you want a healthy culture of debate, you need your own idea of what . . . human life itself [is] *for*.[24]

Lastly, we require commitment to a common purpose to offset the motivational power of our natural egoism, one that possesses the psychological potency of the natural instinct for self-preservation. We need a sense of shared purpose because its absence undermines our ability and readiness to engage each other in ethical thinking, making it harder to resolve conflicts between values and disagreements between persons.

But what *is* that purpose? We need not—indeed, should not—expect to arrive at a full and final answer to this question. The answer will always depend on the (ever-changing) conditions and circumstances in which human beings find themselves, and so must remain provisional and open to revision. We can agree, though, on many principles for living together "without first achieving consensus on the upper reaches of human aspiration."[25] We can agree, for example, that government shouldn't concern itself with many "purely private" choices, choices that have no substantial effect on anyone but the person who makes them for himself or herself. But perhaps we can agree as well that it's a mistake to imagine that what people choose has *no impact whatsoever* on the kind of people they become, and hence no impact on the quality of our collective life.

In this time of accelerating change and mounting complexity we need to maintain "an unreserved opening of the mind to the truth, whatever it may turn out to be."[26] We need less *conviction*—"the insistence that the truth is what one would believe or wish it to be"—and more *faith* in what Abraham Lincoln called "the better angels of our nature."[27] To maintain that unreserved opening of our minds—indeed, to ensure the sheer survival of those minds—we need to rehabilitate and revitalize the ideas and practices of freedom, of ethics, and of democracy. Can we do that?

Let us see.

ONE

Individualism versus Individuality

THE POLITICAL "MARKET" AND THE THREAT TO DEMOCRATIC LEGITIMACY

In theory, there are various ways by which the public in a democratic republic might exercise its authority to influence the policy-making decisions and actions of elected officials.[1] One version holds that governmental institutions and processes can and should be arranged so that the policies government officials adopt maximize the satisfaction of people's private wants or preferences. This is the so-called market model of democracy developed by Joseph Schumpeter[2] and subsequently elaborated formally by Anthony Downs[3] and by James Buchanan and Gordon Tullock.[4]

The market model rejects what Schumpeter called the "the classical model" of democracy, in which the purpose of government is to act as the instrument of the people *as a whole* in effecting the popular (or general) will. In contrast, the market model dismisses as conceptually confused the notion that a *society* can form and articulate a desire or an intention. It views society as an aggregate of individuals, each of whom has his or her own desires and priorities. Because satisfying individual desires is what *economic* markets attempt to do, the market model of *democracy* suggests that elections can be viewed as a quasi-market mechanism for the same purpose.

As in a market economy, in a market democracy participants can be thought of as consisting of consumers and producers. The latter compete for the favor of voters by promoting their "brand" (e.g., Republican or Democrat) and its "product" (the party platform, candidate promises, etc.). They try to sell potential buyers the principles, programs, and policies they're touting. Consumers go to the polls to spend their "democracy dollar" on the party and candidate they believe are most likely to act in a manner that promotes their interests. Each successful candidate is expected to spend her term in office furthering the wishes of the constituents who elected her. If all elected representatives do this, the policies enacted by the legislative body as a whole will, to a greater or lesser degree, reflect the preferences of a majority of voters. As the political scientist, Harold Lasswell, once put it, politics is the process of determining "who gets what, when, and how."[5] The institutional arena of politics—popular elections, votes in legislatures, decisions made in government departments and agencies—is where the question of "who gets what, when, and how" is answered. Government in the political "market" is the sole "manufacturer" of political goods. Those goods are its "products"—laws, policies, regulations, rulings, subsidies, and tax breaks. "Customers" are the constituents, interest groups, and voters who want those products.

The market model of democracy has been subjected to much criticism.[6] For present purposes, though, one criticism deserves special emphasis. As the readiness and frequency with which we describe ourselves as "taxpayers" suggests, we think of ourselves, not as citizens, but as consumers of what government can deliver. Taxpayers are persons whose chief concern is how much money they're spending for the goods and services their tax dollars buy. Taxpayers are consumers, and political consumers expect public officials to *serve* them, to do things for them.[7] They see their own role as confined to alerting officials to their desires and opinions, and advocating actions and policies they believe will benefit them.

Unfortunately, most people aren't getting what they want out of democratic politics. As a result, by a number of measures it's evident that democracy is now facing the greatest threat to its existence in more than half a century. What is especially worrying about the current threat is that it originates not from without but from within. According to political scientist Ronald Inglehart, in the United States "democracy has become appallingly dysfunctional."[8] His assessment is echoed by twenty leading political scientists who gathered at Yale University in 2017 to discuss the question of whether democracy is in decline. The general consensus was that "American democracy is eroding on multiple fronts—socially, culturally, and economically." We are seeing "breakdowns in social cohesion, the rise of tribalism, political polarization, the erosion of democratic norms such as a commitment to rule of law, and a loss of confidence in the electoral system."[9]

In contrast to the market model of democracy, the "republican" (or "civic") tradition of democratic politics, which stretches from the great figures of classical Athens to their counterparts at the founding of the United States, views society's members not as consumers but as politically responsible, politically active, self-governing decision makers. It holds "that [genuine] liberty depends on sharing in self-government, . . . deliberating with fellow citizens about the common good and helping to shape the destiny of the political community."[10] From this perspective, the market conception of democratic politics contains a fundamental flaw: it fails to enable and encourage citizens to deliberate together, as members of a public, for the purpose of reaching a shared judgment and making a genuinely collective decision about what to do. And because it fails to do so, the market conception permits citizens to escape personal responsibility for making the hard choices that inevitably arise in the public life of their communities and society.

Democratic self-governance is a constituent of, and an indispensable means to, human well-being. Deliberating together in order to make hard choices is the process by which we shape our society, our communities, and ourselves. It must be a purpose of democratic politics, therefore, to facilitate the development of worthy desires and the achievement of worthy aims. It must support our efforts to determine not only what we want but what we *ought* to want, individually and collectively. As George Will puts it, politics should share with religion this all-important task: "the steady emancipation of the individual through the education of his passions. . . . If you believe in the better angels of our nature, then the purpose of politics is to summon them."[11]

Why, then, do we continue to think of politics as a type of market? What disposes us to conceive of democracy as an activity in which people compete with each other in order to determine "who gets what, when, and how"? The answer begins to come clear when we recognize that the inadequacies and distortions of the market view of democratic politics stem from the assumptions, values, and ideals that underlie it—ones we associate with the most popular and enduring idea of political liberalism: the deeply ingrained doctrine of *individualism*.

LIBERAL INDIVIDUALISM'S "BAD SEEDS"

From the start, writes Kurt Andersen, "our ultra-individualism was attached to epic dreams, sometimes epic fantasies—every American one of God's chosen people building a custom-made utopia, all of us free to reinvent ourselves by imagination and will."[12] In this assessment we hear echoed the voice of Frederick Jackson Turner, the historian who, at the close of the 19th century, wrote that "at the very heart of the whole American movement" lies the ideal of *individualism*.[13]

The term "individualism" encompasses several related but distinct propositions.[14] *Moral* individualism asserts that the well-being of every person is of paramount moral importance. *Political* individualism makes the wishes of each citizen the ultimate consideration in decisions concerning the use of governmental power.[15] Neither singly nor paired with the other does either of these notions necessarily work to the detriment of democratic practice; quite the contrary—they are indispensable to it.

Two other elements of individualism, though, have decidedly deleterious effects. One, "ontological" individualism (often termed "atomism"), is the belief that human beings are discrete, self-sufficient entities—self-sufficient not in the sense that we do not need others for the material, physical, or emotional support they provide, but rather in the sense that we can become and remain fully human (and uniquely so, as individuals) without enmeshment in a dense weave of relations with other persons, including those to whom we are not connected by virtue of kinship or choice. This understanding of the individual treats the person as if he or she were a "social atom" who is neither defined nor constrained by the unchosen bonds of a common history and future, shared values, or mutual duties and obligations.

The other unhelpful element of individualism, though less fundamental than atomism, is more troublesome because it lies closer to the surface of our political practices. "Axiological" individualism (which from this point forward I will call "subjectivism") holds that the truth of evaluative propositions—that is, statements asserting that something is good or bad, right or wrong—is individually ("subjectively") determined, whether through personal experience, intuition, revelation, or reasoning.

Neither atomism nor subjectivism is tenable. Because they aren't, individualism as a whole must be rejected. The aspiration to *individuality*, in contrast, offers a richer, ethically more defensible, and politically more constructive basis for individual freedom in a democracy.

ATOMISM

The contention that society is nothing but an accumulation of preexisting individuals is as outdated and inaccurate as the belief that the natural world is composed simply of particles of mass called atoms. There are four substantial problems with atomism:

1. The Illusion of Self-Determination

Atomism holds that human beings can achieve full personhood without being shaped and influenced by social practices of the sort that encourage and support that goal.[16] It claims that it's possible, at least in principle, for a human being to acquire—without the assistance of norms established and maintained by social groups such as one's community, culture, and society—all the characteristics that make a person what he or she ("authentically") *is*. In effect, atomism says that, by and large, individuals make themselves.

Atomism fails to acknowledge the extent to which each person is a product of her total social environment. Whether we accept or reject the beliefs, attitudes, values, principles, roles, goals, aspirations, and so forth that our community and society present as "normal," they shape us to the very core of our being. The "atmosphere" they generate is as pervasive as the air we breathe—and as easily taken for granted. We may make choices for ourselves *within* the invariably limited confines of the environment into which we are born and within which we grow to physical and mental maturity. The social practices and rules of that environment determine the number, the variety, and the quality of the choices that are available to us. Through the language and the informal rules and customs (*morés*) we learn as we develop, our environment promotes certain goods or values and discounts, disapproves, denigrates, or denies us others.

Insofar as a person is unable or unwilling actively to question (or, where appropriate, reaffirm) the assumptions, beliefs, attitudes, values, principles, roles, goals, and aspirations of her community and society, to that extent she permits others to determine the choices that are available to her. Only if her community and society encourage and support her efforts to choose her own path can she flourish in the way that is best suited to her unique needs, abilities, dispositions, and so forth. Indeed, as we will see shortly, the (normative) ideals of individuality and autonomy, which are central to the way we think about individual freedom and the grounds on which we justify it, require constructive engagement with members of "out-groups"—groups of people who are not part of the primary groups from which the individual derives her identity ("in-groups"). Understanding and appreciating the differences between a person's in-group and other groups allows her to reflect on the beliefs and values into which she is socialized. If a society discourages or prevents its members from engaging and comprehending difference, it inhibits the development of the ability to choose. Without difference, there is nothing to choose between.

2. The Conceit of Success and the Burden of Failure

Atomism understands people as existing prior to and independently of a social context. As such, they are abstractions with no essential relationship to anyone or anything in their environment. One consequence of this is that the individual bears sole responsibility for the course her life takes. On the one hand, atomism permits her to imagine that her successes owe entirely to her personal efforts. But it also forces her to accept that every failing, frustration, and misfortune is no one's fault but her own. Atomism thus lends support to the "success ethic"—the "belief that material prosperity is the ultimate value in life and that a person's worth can be measured by material or social standards."[17]

This unfortunate expression of individualism pervades American society, our economic and political systems in particular. These systems offer people incentives for performing at a high level and promise them rewards in the form of money, status, and power. One of the (many) problems with individualism expressed as material success is that it leads us to measure our successes and failures by making comparisons. Life is a competition, we believe, and a competition requires keeping score. We succeed or fail, not in relation to our own standards, but relative to what others do—both within our own socioeconomic group and in comparison to the members of other groups: us versus the "one percent," for example, or men versus women, or the college educated versus those with less education, and so on. As Joseph Epstein writes, ". . . not to succeed means to fail. . . . [T]he crux of this distinction is that it enters everyone in the race for success"— whether or not they want to run.[18]

3. Self-Reliance and Its Pernicious Consequences

In the early 19th century, the transcendentalist philosopher Ralph Waldo Emerson espoused a doctrine of individual "self-reliance" that remains deeply embedded in our culture and in ourselves.[19] Emerson's conception of individualism is certainly not without merit. What he calls "the capital virtue of self-trust" leads the individual to rely on himself rather than on others—a habit most of us probably agree is good for people to cultivate.

But self-reliance carries with it a less admirable implication: that the individual should seek to prevent others from becoming dependent on him. For Emerson, permitting others to make claims on the individual's resources—time, money, knowledge, skills, energy, goodwill, even sympathy—is downright dangerous:

> A sympathetic person is placed in the dilemma of a swimmer among drowning men, who all catch at him, and if he give so much as a leg or a finger, they will drown him.[20]

To be sure, coming to the aid of someone who is struggling to keep his head above water is potentially hazardous to a person's own well-being. That's why, as a matter of law, a person has no duty to attempt a rescue of someone who's literally in deep water, floundering, and in danger of drowning. An action can't be required if it compels the individual to disregard her own well-being and sacrifice it in order to benefit someone else. Trying to save another's life is an act of altruism, of self-abnegation. It goes beyond the basic requirement of ethics: that we must treat all persons, *including ourselves*, as bearers of life having equal worth, and that in consequence we must weigh and balance their interests with our own. In the case of a person who literally is drowning, then, Emerson's conclusion is warranted.

The vast preponderance of cases, however, in which ethical questions arise are not ones in which a person must choose whether to risk his own life in order to save someone else's. Precisely because the circumstances are so extreme, the example of a drowning person is a poor guide to ethical action in situations that are much more common and much less demanding.[21]

4. Atomism and Adversarial Politics

Atomism makes it difficult for people to think of civic relationships as connections with others they need to keep in good condition even if occasionally the going gets tough, and even if at times it appears those connections are more trouble than they're worth. It obscures the fact that we are interdependent and that our fates are intertwined. It masks the essential role each of us plays in cultivating and nurturing a democratic way of life. The responsibilities and duties of citizenship appear alien to us when we imagine politics as a collision of political atoms.

By stressing the "separateness of persons," atomism leads us to view politics as the unsavory business of selling, arm-twisting, maligning, manipulating, and "playing hard ball." Politics divides people and brings out the worst in them. It forces us to conclude that the conduct of public affairs is chiefly about groups doing whatever it takes to advance their narrow interests at the expense of others, rather than what it should be about: the indispensable task of building and sustaining our communities and society, without which we have—and are—nothing.

SUBJECTIVISM

Since its emergence, individualism has extolled freedom from the constraints and burdens that others might place on a person. Today, though, many Americans seek not just freedom but what amounts to *escape*: the ability to flee the influence of—indeed, even mere exposure to—any beliefs, values, rules, social norms, duties, obligations, or expectations that are not authentically "theirs." What Robert Bellah calls the "quest for the self" is a search for a freedom so complete that the person's decisions about what to believe, to value, or to do are shaped by nothing that is not an expression of her "authentic" self. It is the only authoritative source of guidance she recognizes. The people Bellah and his colleagues interviewed for their book, *Habits of the Heart*, frequently invoked their "values" as the touchstone of their choices.[22] But it turned out that by "values" they meant simply the choices they would make if the people they "really are" were choosing with complete freedom.

It is impossible, though, for a person to know—through just the act of freely choosing—whether an option is truly, genuinely, authentically valuable for her. When we make genuine choices, we do so for *reasons*—considerations that provide information about the likely consequences of selecting one option rather than another. But choice of the sort that Bellah's interviewees imagined involves no reason-giving; it is "choice" attempted in the absence of any knowledge of what has value. Without standards or criteria for what counts as good, "choosing" becomes an act no more significant or profound than picking a flavor of ice cream or the color of an item of clothing. That's alright if the choice involves nothing more substantial than personal tastes. But if the choice is an important one with implications that extend far beyond the chooser herself or beyond the present moment—for example, the choice of how to live her life—questions of prudence and ethics inevitably arise. For such choices, we need to seek out reasons for assigning one option priority over another.

Suppose, for example, an election is coming up and I need to decide what our society's future policy should be regarding penalties for convicted felons. Here are three options for me to consider:

(a) Our primary goal when incarcerating persons who commit serious crimes should be to prevent them from committing such crimes again.

(b) Our primary goal when incarcerating persons who commit serious crimes should be to help them develop the moral, emotional, and economic ability to become and remain law-abiding citizens.

(c) Our primary goal when incarcerating persons who commit serious crimes should be to punish them for the suffering they have inflicted on their victims.

In this example, each prescription embodies a distinct value. In (a), it is the value of public safety and security. In (b), it is compassion for and belief in the intrinsic worth, potential, and redeemability of all human beings. In (c), it is deterrence, justice (in the "eye for an eye" sense), and the psychological compensation or consolation of victims. If I try to choose between the values these options embody without considering reasons for and against each of them, my choice will be arbitrary. It won't deserve to be taken any more seriously than my choice of a flavor of ice cream. Without reference to criteria for evaluating them and without reasons for preferring one to the others—the choice I make may be a free one, but it won't be sound or wise. It might not be what's best for me. It also won't be responsible.

But there is an even more basic problem with the notion that choosing freely qualifies, by itself, as a genuine choice. If simply choosing without constraint is what makes something valuable, then *anything* I choose will have value. In the case of punishing felons, let's say I like the idea of corporal punishment. For me, then, "choosing" corporal punishment is good—it has value. Equally, however, a thing has no value unless I choose it. So if, for example, I don't want felons to be taught to read, or to learn a skill while incarcerated, I would have to say that these activities aren't good. For me, rehabilitation has no value.

That might sound unproblematic, so consider this: if the fact that I freely choose something is what gives it its value, then whatever I believed yesterday had value (because I chose it yesterday) will not have value tomorrow if, come the day, I do not choose it. If yesterday retribution (e.g., corporal punishment) was valuable (because I chose it) and tomorrow it won't be (because I don't choose it), then either my belief yesterday about the value of retribution was wrong or my belief tomorrow about it will be wrong. I can't be right both yesterday and tomorrow.[23] Hence for me it's impossible to say that retribution is valuable or is not valuable. There is no way to distinguish between what is valuable for me and what I happen, at any given time, to desire or feel. For me, saying "retribution is valuable" is just another way of saying I desire or like it.

The result is to obliterate the idea of *value* altogether. I can say only that I desire a thing (or don't), that I feel positively disposed toward it (or don't). It may be a fact that person "A desires X." In that case, though, we can say nothing about "X" except that it is *desired*, which is not the same thing as saying it is desir*able*. But this conflicts with our sense that, when we say something *has value*, we are stating a fact.[24] The unease that attends the intimation that our beliefs about what holds value are no more than subjective desires or feelings does not, however, keep us from behaving, inconsistently, as if they actually possess the characteristics of "objectivity" that factual propositions are supposed to have. When we subscribe to a particular evaluative belief, it *seems* objectively correct. But when a position or view to which we don't subscribe is being urged on us, we often feel compelled to retort that "values are subjective," or "what's good or bad is a matter of personal choice," or "that's your opinion—I'm entitled to my own."

If the beliefs about good and bad, right and wrong on which we base our ethical and political views ultimately are nothing more than the expression of desire or feeling, this helps explain why ethical and political arguments always seem to break down into mere assertion and counterassertion.[25] Reduced to merely repeating what we feel, we turn up the volume. The shrillness of people's assertions, MacIntyre says, derives not just from frustration with their inability to convince others of the correctness of their views. We speak loudly as much to convince ourselves as to convince them:

> If I lack any good reasons to invoke against you, . . . I lack any good reasons [whatsoever]. . . . Corresponding to the interminability of public argument there is . . . a disquieting private arbitrariness. It is small wonder if we become defensive and therefore shrill.[26]

We are not talking here about *pluralism*, the view that "the good" is constituted of a variety of distinct values that cannot be reduced to a "common denominator." Individual and collective efforts to discriminate among putative values—to order and prioritize them, to reject some and embrace others—are indispensable to adaptation, growth, and progress. Every community and every individual needs to embrace the difficult task of working toward a sound judgment about how to resolve a conflict between competing goods. But value subjectivism is another matter altogether. It is pluralism's *reductio ad absurdam*. Though pluralism conduces to the ability of persons and communities to make genuine choices, subjectivism has the opposite effect: it turns all choices into arbitrary selection. Criterionless choice—choice without reference to goods, ends, purposes, etc.—is not genuine choice; it is a simulacrum thereof.

Directly or indirectly, value subjectivism is responsible for much that is wrong with contemporary public discourse. Public debate about what is good or bad, right or wrong, desirable or undesirable is increasingly bellicose. Such talk strains the civic relationships that hold communities and societies together. Subjectivist discourse does not advance inquiry. It does not encourage us to investigate the (historical, cultural, ideological, psychological, religious, sociological, economic) roots and sources of our disagreements. In short, it does not dispose us to learn.[27]

THE BITTER FRUITS OF INDIVIDUALISM'S BAD SEEDS

In combination, atomism and subjectivism have several pernicious consequences:

First, they lie at the heart of contemporary liberalism, with its "sink or swim," "every man for himself" ethos that leaves us feeling stressed, lonely, and vulnerable. In this raw state of mind, we become hypervigilant and overly sensitive to conflict. We begin to perceive others' beliefs, attitudes, and actions as a challenge to, or even an attack upon, who and what we are. Seeking shelter, we retreat into the safety of partisan "bubbles." Disagreements become intensely personal and exasperatingly difficult to resolve.

Second, atomism and subjectivism make us susceptible to "chronic freedom deficit disorder," the feeling that the freedom we have is never enough. Having to cede an inch of our freedom feels like losing a part of ourselves. We become preoccupied with our personal freedom, imagining it's constantly under siege. In an attempt to relieve the dread of being confined, we try to expand our influence and control over the world outside us. Because others interpret this stance (just as we interpret theirs) as a threat to their own interests, interpersonal relations quickly degenerate into a struggle for power.

Third, atomism and subjectivism undermine our ability to distinguish between what is true and what we happen to believe. Unfortunately, it's a short psychological step from insisting that "*X* is *good* because I believe it is" to "*Y* is *true* because I believe it is." The dissolution of the distinction between publicly accepted facts and personal opinions means "we can believe anything we want; . . . our beliefs are equal or superior to anyone else's . . . Once people commit to that approach, . . . the credible becomes incredible and the incredible, credible."[28]

Fourth, atomism and subjectivism mislead us into believing that, as individuals, we are the ultimate authority in the matter of the values we should aspire to and the character virtues we should cultivate. As David Brooks notes, however,

> the first threat to liberty is actually the tyranny of our own desires. . . .
> Most of us require communal patterns and shared cultural norms and certain enforced guardrails to help us restrain our desires and keep us free . . . It takes a village to do both these things. . . . It's not a do-it-yourself job.[29]

Finally, because atomism and subjectivism reduce the value we discern in the world to the objects of our personal interests and desires, they drain the public world of any inherent goodness of its own. Nothing beyond our narrow interests and desires matters. Life seems to hold no larger purpose or significance. The result is what Weber famously called "the disenchanted world" and Mumford memorably called "the disqualified universe": a world with neither quality nor meaning. This is the world into which all of us alive today were born.

NOT INDIVIDUALISM—INDIVIDUALITY

In his book *On Liberty*, John Stuart Mill sets out an ideal he calls "the free development of individuality."[30] Mill's notion of individuality offers a richer, ethically more defensible, and politically more constructive basis for individual freedom in a democracy than does the crude atomistic subjectivism that underpins contemporary liberal individualism. In the ceaseless quest to liberate ourselves from all constraint whatsoever in order to pursue the satisfaction of any desire whatsoever, we have saddled ourselves with an impoverished conception of the individual, a self-defeating conception of the good, and a simplistic conception of personal freedom that undermines our ability to live together.

For Mill, individuality is the project of developing one's potential to become a human being of unique character. Different persons require different conditions to achieve the fullest expression and flourishing of their unique potential.[31] Hence the value of pluralism: the encouragement of multiple modes of living that assign importance to different values or value priorities.

In Mill's view, it is good—it is valuable and desirable—for human beings to develop their distinctive "endowments" (talents, capabilities, interests, and passions) and "faculties" (observation, interpretation, critical reflection, judgment, deductive and inductive reasoning, creative imagination, technical skills, ethical thinking and action, etc.). In the course of doing so, their uniqueness emerges. Individuality is thus the condition in which a person's unique self is developed fully, to the highest degree compatible with her optimal well-being.[32] The more fully developed the person, the greater is her individuality.[33] It doesn't just contribute to a person's well-being, however; it is an essential component or element thereof.

The conception of optimal well-being, or "flourishing," I invoke here requires that we reflect on our nature as human beings—in particular, on the various *needs* that humans universally and consistently seek to fulfill. Knowing these needs and the good that results from fulfilling them does not by itself allow us to identify the precise form that flourishing will take for each individual. The form of flourishing that is best for you depends importantly on what is unique and distinctive about you: your predispositions, sensitivities, capacities, interests, talents, etc.

Individuality—individual flourishing—thus requires the ability and readiness to make deliberate and considered choices between alternative beliefs and patterns of life. (For this ability and readiness I use the term "autonomy." We will return to it in Chapter 3.) A genuinely free and deliberated choice is what enables the individual to discover the sort of person only she can become, the sort she might wish to become if she were to examine and evaluate the possibility open-mindedly, thoughtfully, and with adequate information. This ideal—the fully developed unique individual—is something every human being should aspire to achieve.

Mill's concept of individuality stands in contrast to the kind of person all of us find it too easy to become and remain: unreflective creatures of habit who conform readily to prevailing social norms, ideals, and expectations, and who too seldom question, or even think very hard about, our beliefs, attitudes, desires, and decisions. In a society like ours, in which the pressure to conform is (paradoxically, given our rhetorical emphasis on the individual person and her freedom) both subtle[34] and substantial,[35] genuine individuality is not easily attained or practiced. Tocqueville's observation from the 1830s is as apt today as it was then: "In the United States, the majority undertakes to supply a multitude of ready-made opinions for the use of individuals, who are thus relieved from the necessity of forming opinions of their own." Observing the country today, Mill might justifiably describe us as living in a state of "mental slavery," unaware of and unconcerned with alternative conceptions of what is true, what is valuable, and how we should live.

Mill thought we ought to be active participants in the construction of our way of life. His argument for individuality is thus an argument as well for a *society* that is open to a variety of influences and ideas and that does not try to control, restrict, or manipulate knowledge. Only in such a society can we discover and create what is truly valuable, truly important, and truly worthy of our energies, our strivings, and our sacrifices. To take the uncritically accepted beliefs, attitudes, and desires we happen to have as the basis for making both personal and public decisions, without regard to the way they are formed, is to "surrender to the tyranny of current orthodoxies."[36]

This is not to say, of course, that a person should be free to act only insofar as her choices are ones she has made thoughtfully, after having obtained and considered all the information relevant to her decision, and after having deliberated carefully in order to ascertain which course of action will optimize her well-being and realize her full potential. A person can be properly described as choosing freely (indeed, generally should be permitted to choose freely) even if what she chooses has little or no value beyond the satisfaction that results from acting without external restraint. Being able to choose and act freely is an important good in its own right. Mill's liberty principle confines justifiable interference with a person's freedom to situations in which exercising that freedom might result in harm to others. Although it can be argued that a person's failure to realize her own individuality has undesirable consequences for others (e.g., by failing to participate in maintaining a society open to multiple influences and instead adding to a climate of intolerance), such failure usually does not warrant interference with her freedom.

Similarly, restricting one person's freedom in order to help others develop their individuality typically will not suffice as a justification for such a restriction. As Mill put it in *On Liberty*, there is no reason that all human existence should be constructed on some one or some small number of patterns. If a person possesses any tolerable amount of common sense and experience, his own mode of laying out his existence is the best, not because it is the best in itself, but because it is his own mode.[37]

For Mill, in short, choosing and acting freely has value in itself, and we must take care to avoid denying people that value by restricting their freedom except in order to prevent substantial negative consequences for others.

But what counts as a negative consequence? How substantial does it have to be to justify restricting one's freedom? How do we make that determination? In order to answer these questions, let's look more closely now at the principle of freedom.

TWO

Interference, Independence, and What's Worth Doing

FREEDOM AND VALUE

In general, we don't expect people to justify their actions to us before they act. We've adopted, in effect, a "principle of noninterference" (PNI)—a rule that says no one may prevent, impede, deter, restrain, or unreasonably encumber a person with regard to an action she wants to perform without having a good and sufficient reason for doing so. The burden falls on those who want to interfere to show why interference is warranted. In other words, the PNI creates a presumption in favor of free action.

But limiting a person's freedom is not necessarily wrong. Doing so might be justified; there might be good reasons for interfering with her action. If those who want to interfere with that action can offer such reasons, the PNI will shift the burden of justification to the person who wants to act freely. If she can provide good reasons for acting without interference, she can overcome the burden of justification and shift it back to those who wish to prevent her from acting. Sometimes, too, we might want to say that interference reduces a person's freedom even if it is justifiable. If she wants to do something contrary to her self-interest (as we normally would view it)— to starve herself to death as a protest, for example—and it's truly important to her that she be allowed to do so, we should concede, even if our intervention is justified, that interfering with her action will reduce her freedom.

There are cases, though, in which the PNI does not apply, and the burden of justification does not shift from the actor to the interfering party. Rather, it remains up to the person wishing to perform an action to justify it. For example,

> there is something paradoxical about saying that a person is either free or not free to starve, to cut off his ears, or die; one would commonly add the ironic qualification: "if he wants to," precisely on account of the standard association between "being free" and experiences or activities *normally regarded as worthwhile. . . .*[1] (emphasis added)

Usually, cutting off one's ears isn't the sort of thing that anyone would reasonably want to do. It's hard to see any value in doing such a thing.

In general, then, when we say a person is (or should be) free to act, we presume that her acting freely won't have consequences that are contrary to her own interest in realizing value for herself. Equally, when we say a person is not (or should not be) free to act, we presume that her acting freely would be contrary to her interest in realizing value. To say correctly that a person is or should be free to act, we must be able to see that there *might be some point* to her action.[2] Our conception of freedom is bounded by our notions of what *might be worthwhile doing.*[3]

As I will argue shortly (and throughout this book), not just *any* sort of satisfaction obtained through acting freely counts as value, and not just *any* activity or state of affairs may be counted a source of value. Although any satisfaction *could* be valuable, in fact not every satisfaction is. This is so because not every satisfaction human beings are capable of experiencing meets the criteria determined by the rules we've established for properly or appropriately using terms like "good," "desirable," "beneficial," "advantageous," "valuable," and so forth.

FREEDOM AND ETHICS: THE "HARM PRINCIPLE"

John Stuart Mill famously wrote that

> the sole end for which mankind are warranted, individually or collectively, in interfering with the liberty of action of any of their number, is self-protection. That the only purpose for which power can be rightfully exercised over any member of a civilized community, against his will, is to prevent harm to others. *His own good*, either physical or moral, *is not sufficient warrant*. He cannot rightfully be

compelled to do or forbear because it will be *better for him* to do so, because it will make him happier, because, *in the opinion of others, to do so would be wise, or even right. . . .*[4] (emphasis added)

Mill's "harm principle" requires qualification, though. His test for determining the extent to which we may justifiably limit a person's freedom—preventing harm to *others*—is too stringent. It makes assumptions about the person whose freedom is at stake that will not stand up to scrutiny, and about whether others have a legitimate interest in that person's well-being.

As it happens, Mill qualifies the principle himself, as we'll see. Here, I want only to reinforce the point that *there is a necessary connection between judgments of unfreedom and judgments of value.* If an action would result in an outcome that is not *in fact* valuable or worthwhile—to at least some extent, in some way, and from the actor's own point of view—it is not appropriate to say that her freedom is significantly diminished when her action is interfered with (except insofar as there is value in being free to act per se, which is a value that may be outweighed by other values).

If the person is a small child, for example, and someone were to argue that his freedom is diminished when his mother takes away from him the fork he's been gleefully waving about at the dinner table, we would find that assertion odd and not worthy of serious consideration. In a narrow sense, the child's range of options for free movement has been reduced. But clearly he does not yet possess the ability to choose for himself whether to pursue the action that realizes the most value for him. Because his judgment is not yet adequately developed, other persons must substitute their own for his. If just *anything* can count as a restriction on a person's freedom, saying a person is "unfree" becomes almost useless as a principle for protecting and promoting everyone's interest in choosing courses of action that will help him or her achieve individuality.

Like all social rules, the principle of noninterference is a response to the inevitability in social life of conflicts between values, actions, and persons. It exists because we care about the impact that restricting one person's action might have on anyone who could be affected, including others who also have an interest in acting without interference to realize value for themselves. "Freedom" is part of our collective effort to sort out who should be permitted to do what, when, and how.

That makes the principle of noninterference a principle of ethics. By sustaining a claim that I'm unfree, I accomplish an ethical purpose: requiring that interference with my acting be justified, and securing acknowledgment from others that I lose something of value even when interference is justified. When we use a term like "unfree" in our ethical and political discourse, we are saying something about what we believe is good or bad, right or wrong—for human beings generally and for some persons in particular. Thus, whenever we concern ourselves with constraints on human action, we are engaged in an *appraisal of value*—both the value of the action a person might freely take *and* the value that might be realized by interfering with that action.

Other things being equal, acting without constraint is valuable—it's satisfying to do so, and it contributes to a person's well-being. For this reason, we frequently invoke "freedom" as a substantive ethical principle—usually by asserting that people have a *right* (i.e., a specially protected freedom) to live or act freely. Unfortunately, when freedom serves as the sole or paramount justification for a person's taking action, appealing to the principle that each person should be free to act as she wishes can mask the harm such action would inflict on others or that she would incur herself. Because of its historical association with individualism (especially atomism and subjectivism), people tend to forget that freedom can have adverse consequences, and so might justifiably be restricted. We have grown accustomed to thinking of freedom as not only *always* good but as the *highest* good—something *so* valuable it must never be limited. We have made "freedom" a principle of near absoluteness; we invoke it as if it were the ultimate ethical principle, capable of trumping all competing claims concerning the protection or promotion of other values.

Treating freedom as the highest value can make it seem that the question of what's right to do when freedom conflicts with some other good or value has already been settled. It's not uncommon for people to think that they don't have to justify an action they're free to perform even if it could prove harmful to others or to themselves. It's easy, moreover, to infer from the fact that I *am* free that I *ought* to be unconstrained in attempting to do what I wish to do. If what I want to do isn't against the law, I might conclude that it isn't *so* wrong that I should refrain from doing it. By not legally proscribing such actions, society can seem to sanction them.[5] That's the downside of relying on freedom as a principle of ethics.

INDEPENDENCE

If it's important for the project of developing one's individuality that we be free to form our own purposes, identify our values, establish our own priorities, set our own goals, and act in pursuit of them, then each of us must be concerned with the conditions that enable us to perform these tasks successfully. If we aspire to the full expression of our uniqueness as human beings, we must possess the ability to shape and to some substantial degree effectively control the conditions in which we pursue them. A person cannot be fully free unless she is also to some substantial degree *independent* of others, that is, not reliant on them for resources (e.g., for food, shelter, knowledge, skills) without which she cannot act *effectively* in pursuit of her individuality. She must be free of indirect and unintended constraint as well as direct and deliberate constraint, provided someone can and should be held responsible, at least in principle, for imposing or removing that (unjustified) constraint.

It might be objected that, although a person perhaps shouldn't lack for the ability or power to make use of her freedom, this doesn't mean she's not free. Greater resources, for example, may enable a person to act, but not in the same way that removal of coercive pressures imposed by others does. But we need to be careful here. The word "ability" (or more precisely the infinitive "to be able") is ambiguous, and it's often employed in the sense that conveys the meaning of "unconstrained." Confusion over which sense of "able" is being used produces related confusion in understanding what it means to be "free."

For example, if someone were to ask whether I'm free to walk across the Atlantic Ocean, the response might be, yes—if I'm able. This sense of "able" refers to something like physical wherewithal, competence, or "power to"—that is, "ability" in the sense of having the potential to execute an action if unconstrained. Accordingly, it's reasonable to keep this view of "ability" distinct from uses of "free" and "unfree." Freedom, it might be argued, *presupposes* ability but is not identical to it. *If* freedom presupposes ability but is not identical to it, augmenting the resources a person can draw on in utilizing her freedom can be said to increase her freedom only if previously she was "unfree," that is, "able" but "constrained." Otherwise, it increases her ability only.

Conversely, someone might ask whether a person will be "able" to reenter an office building after regular business hours. Here, "able" means something very close to "free," that is, unconstrained. Examples of this use of "able" abound: Am I able (free) to sleep late on Saturday mornings? Will I be able to (may I freely) go in to the event without a ticket? J. P. Day says the necessary and sufficient condition of unfreedom is a person's being made "retrievably unable."[6] He uses "unable" in the sense that implies "constrained"; hence his use of the qualifier, "retrievably." To be "retrievably unable" is to be impermanently unable—in other words, subject to some constraint that is not irrevocable but remediable. No doubt there are many cases in which we wish to preserve the kind of distinction Day wants to maintain between "able" in the sense of competence or power and "able" in the sense of unconstrained. For example, it might be better to say that a person who was rendered quadriplegic in the course of participating in a military operation has been deprived of his ability to walk, not his freedom.

But is it only his ability to work as, say, a firefighter or a police officer that has been impaired? Why not say he has been denied his freedom to be employed thusly? After all, the *opportunity* open to others having full use of all four limbs is closed to him. Imagine an act of enslavement effected and made irremediable through some destruction of the enslaved person's abilities—say, through partial lobotomy, or brainwashing, or some other manipulation. Can we still say unambiguously that it is only his power or ability that has been curtailed, and not his freedom? As in the example of a person who has lost use of his arms and legs, he has been deprived of his freedom by being deprived of some ability through an (unjustifiable) act for which another human being might be held responsible. An enslaved person might be constrained by being mentally controlled, thereby obviating the need to keep him in chains. The important point is that, if talk of inability is not admissible in connection with freedom, too many cases are ruled out of court. In some cases, if we lack ability, then we lack opportunity. And if this is so, are we not unfree?

There are other important instances in which "ability" figures so substantially in our estimation of what constitutes freedom that we are inclined to believe that inability is tantamount to unfreedom. Ability can be so crucial to the notion of freedom that we can't talk about the latter without implying the former. For example, if you own the rights to all drinkable water where we live, and you will sell it to me only at a price I can't afford, don't you restrict my freedom when you withhold it? There's very little I can do without water. If I weren't dependent on you for water, wouldn't I be much freer?

Or consider the matter of sexual relations, an area of human action in which nonparticipants usually have little, if any, justifiable interest. Would we say that the availability of effective contraception makes people freer to engage in such behavior, or better able? If we say the beneficiaries of contraception are merely better able to take advantage of the freedom they enjoy, this is to employ "able" in the sense that really means "unconstrained," rather than "having the power or ability." What concerns us here are the constraints imposed on people wishing to engage in sexual relations. Having better access to contraceptive methods means greater *freedom* to do so.

A different sort of example is provided by the guarantee of counsel in criminal proceedings. Because we consider the possibility of conviction and the attendant liability to deprivation of freedom by the state to be a profoundly important matter, we do not simply equate the procedural safeguards and guarantees with the right (in this instance to a fair trial) itself. This basic "freedom" must be made *effective* by providing counsel to the indigent defendant, without which he would be unable to take advantage of the opportunity his right affords him. Again, the constraint involved here is a type of inability and clearly a remediable one.

In his discussion of the concept of "can" and its relation to the question of free will, P.H. Nowell-Smith argues that ability and opportunity are conceptually related, that we could not have either of these concepts unless we had both.[7] In fact, he says, we have a single complex concept—the "all-in" sense of "can"—not simply two related ones. To say someone has an opportunity is to say that the conditions for exercising a particular ability obtain. An opportunity is a chance for someone who *has* an ability to exercise that ability. If a person lacks the ability, it cannot be said that she has an opportunity. We can't say categorically that a person can do something unless she has both the ability and the opportunity. Clearly, if she is able to do X but is denied the opportunity, she cannot do it. But just as clearly, if she lacks the ability, then even if no obstacle exists that would deny an able person the opportunity, she still cannot do it.

In sum, independence is a condition in which a person is *able* to act because she possesses sufficient resources—physical, mental, material, informational, etc.—that any person requires in order to act. If achieving and expressing our individuality is important to us, then each of us must be concerned with the conditions that enable us to do so. If remediable and unwarranted, adverse conditions that keep us dependent on others constitute constraints that limit our freedom. Independence makes a crucial contribution, just as liberty does, to each person's efforts to achieve and express her individuality.

Let's turn now to another indispensable resource for achieving and expressing one's individuality: personal *autonomy*.

THREE

Autonomy

FREEDOM AND CHOICE

Abstracting the individual from her social context and treating her as a separate, disconnected "atom" has misled us into thinking that freedom, conceived in its "negative" form—as the absence of constraint—suffices for the purpose of regulating our actions when these could have adverse consequences for others. If we think of the individual as existing prior to and independently of social practices, norms, and social institutions, it's easy to imagine that our responsibility for the consequences of our actions extends only as far as refraining from preventing, impeding, deterring, restraining, or unreasonably encumbering the actions that others might want to take.

Freedom from external constraints, though, is not a *sufficient* condition for the achievement of individuality. As we saw in Chapter 1, Mill argued that achieving individuality requires us to develop the ability and readiness to make deliberate and considered choices between alternative beliefs and modes of life. A person who possesses this ability and readiness is "autonomous." Autonomy is indispensable for individuality because lacking it opens a person's choice-making up to influences that, were she aware of them and able to recognize them as inimical to her effort to develop her individuality, she might want to resist. The type of adverse influence in question here stems from ideas, perceptions, habits of mind, dispositions, values, and priorities that a person absorbs through social inculcation and reinforcement.

A normal, rational person can be constrained by "internal" and "internalized" factors to such an extent that they adversely affect her ability to assess and weigh reasons for pursuing the courses of action that are open to her. There are times, therefore, when we need to be able to say that a person who decides to do X when there is a stronger reason (which she would recognize if she fulfilled the conditions for autonomous choice) for doing Y has been or will be rendered effectively unfree by the constraining effect of internal or internalized factors that others should be held responsible for remedying. To see why this is so, let's examine the idea of acting for reasons.

ACTING FOR REASONS

Every genuine instance of action—that is, every conscious, voluntary doing of something—is performed by a person because she desires some good—something having value—that she believes she can obtain or achieve through the action she takes.[1] To say this is to say that action is connected psychologically to desire—no desire, no action. Motivationally speaking, desire is a necessary condition of action.

A person won't act on a desire, though, unless she also holds a belief that she will gain something of benefit by performing the action. Beliefs of this sort are "reasons." Reasons tell us "there is value in doing X." All actions are done *for* a reason, as seen from the actor's point of view. Even an act that person A performs from simple inclination ("I felt like it") is done for a reason. In this instance, her reason is that she believes satisfying her inclination is a good or valuable thing in itself.

The amount of thought required in advance for a person to do X for a reason is minimal, and it doesn't have to take place in the instant before the action occurs. A person can act out of habit, for example. But she would never even scratch her nose unless at some time she had considered, however superficially and fleetingly, whether satisfying her urge to relieve itching is good, valuable, or satisfying.

This isn't to say that all desires *originate* with beliefs about value. Desires can arise from biological urges, emotional reactions, behavioral dispositions, and so forth. But when we're talking about genuine cases of *action*, an element of belief is always involved. All actions are done *for* a reason—that is, because of a belief that performing the action will lead to value being realized. This is important, because the element of belief involved opens up the possibility that we can modify our emotions by changing what we believe.

Note that it's the belief *content* behind a person's action—that is, the proposition that "X is valuable"—that constitutes her reason for acting. When we *explain* a person's action, we're not concerned with the *truth* of this proposition. What matters is whether she accepts it. Thus, a person can act for a reason she doesn't in fact have. The sort of reason that actually motivates a person (the reason *for* which she acts) is her belief that the action will produce something of value for her. The sort of reason a person *has*, in contrast, is connected to the world of facts to which her beliefs may or may not accurately correspond. The former type of reasons we can call motivating or explanatory reasons, and the latter type warranting or justifying reasons. The two types can coincide, of course. If somebody leaves a building because she believes it's on fire and it's in fact on fire, then the reasons that explain and warrant her action are identical. But they aren't necessarily so.

A person can be motivated by a reason and yet can act on the basis of a false belief. That is, she can be mistaken in her belief that the reason for which she acts is in fact warranted. If a person leaves the building where she works for the reason that "it was on fire," but it actually wasn't on fire, then "the building was on fire" was not a reason to evacuate, and she did not have a reason for evacuating the building. Of course, the fact that smoke was coming in from under her door may have been a reason for believing that the building was on fire, which would make her action reasonable. But the building's being on fire could not be a reason for leaving if it's not true that the building was on fire. No reason in fact existed for her to leave the building.

A reason to act can exist, then, without a person acknowledging it or even being aware of it. As long as she would in fact gain something of value by acting—so long as she herself, were she able to experience the result of the action, would recognize it as valuable for her—then there exists a reason for doing it whether or not she presently desires to do it. Of course, if she doesn't accept the proposition that acting on it will yield value for her, she won't develop the desire to act. To count as a reason for acting, therefore, a belief has to be linked to a potential desire of the person. It doesn't have to be tied to an existing desire.

Put another way, a person has a reason to do something that she only "hypothetically" would desire to do. For example, a child has a reason to eat peas (or learn to play the piano, or read, or whatever) if he would discover that eating peas is valuable, even though he doesn't currently believe this and consequently doesn't desire it. If he can discover that eating peas is valuable, he will want (when conditions are favorable) to do it. The experience of value generates a desire by creating the belief that the action is valuable, thereby providing him with a reason, and hence the motivation, to perform the action. A reason for doing something can thus exist independently of a person's current desires.

This is important, because it's a widely held view that what's good—what has value—is whatever satisfies our desires. People tend to think a reason exists for doing something if—indeed, that it exists only if—it would satisfy a desire a person happens to have. Desiring something, however, is neither a necessary nor a sufficient condition of something's having value. It's not desiring that bestows value on a thing, but rather the thing's potential for generating satisfaction that a person would experience on realizing or obtaining it, whether or not she can envision or even imagine it.

The value of an end or activity—be it eating peas or (say) paying taxes—may reveal itself if a person thinks about it in a way that's open-minded, well informed, and carefully reasoned. Equally, thinking of this sort can reveal that there's less value (or even none at all) in an end or activity (e.g., buying something that will soon lose its appeal) she presently believes she has a reason for pursuing. An action is warranted if it has the potential to lead to value being realized, whether or not a person has discovered this. And, as we will see shortly, that can't be discovered unless it already exists.

One key feature of autonomy, then, is the ability to discern—to see, to recognize, to identify—the potential value that would be realized by taking a given action. Closely related to discernment is a second indispensable element of autonomy: the ability to deliberate—to assess and weigh reasons that support (or that count against) pursuing each option that is actually open to the chooser. I can't realize the full value of the freedom I enjoy from external constraints unless I'm able to evaluate considerations that indicate the existence of value (or lack thereof) that would be realized by pursuing the courses of action I am free to pursue. By relying on reasons to guide me, I gain a measure of control over the influence exerted on me by strong emotions, ingrained attitudes, insistent desires, and mistaken or inadequately supported beliefs.[2] The more successful I am in achieving this control—the more autonomous I become—the more likely my decisions and subsequent actions will produce the best consequences for myself—and, as we will see, for others as well.

REASONS AND THE SOCIAL ENVIRONMENT

There is a potential for coercion by society, Mill observed, that can be as restrictive of individual freedom as coercion by government. An important element of autonomy, therefore, is the ability to question, critique, and challenge the reasons that inhere in the practices of one's community, society, or civilization and in the rules that constitute those practices. Social practices generate and reinforce beliefs, ideas, values, customs, habits, aspirations, expectations, and so forth that we take for granted. Socialization is powerful because deviation from prevailing conventions usually is punished or otherwise discouraged, and because when we are born we are to a substantial degree tabulae rasae—most of what we can know we have to learn. Social practices teach the explicit and implicit "lessons" we learn growing up. They shape the inclinations, needs, sensitivities, and interpretations of the experiences we have as children and adolescents, and even as adults.

Social practices both provide and shape the reasons we draw on in explaining and justifying our actions. That is, they affect the public store of beliefs about what has value and about whether value will be realized if one performs (or doesn't perform) a given action. The reasons we accept, either as an explanation of a person's action or as a warrant for it, are a product of and are governed by rules that our society (or culture, community, etc.) has created to guide people in their thinking and acting. If a reason is not grounded in rules that we accept for what a normal, rational person thinks and does, typically we'll reject it as having no validity. It won't "count." What we believe about the world and about ourselves depends on rules that tell us—within relatively broad limits—what to do, how to live, what experiences to have, what to expect, what things to value, and so on. They don't "micromanage" what we believe and feel. But they do establish boundaries and create proclivities.

Indeed, most of what we believe to be true about the world and other human beings—including what they do and why, and whether they are justified in doing so—we believe just because our beliefs are built into the very concepts we use in our language. We take them as self-evidently true because they're the only concepts we have access to.[3] As Simon Blackburn puts it, "a system of thought is something we live in, just as much as a house is. . . ."[4] Until we experience—either directly or vicariously (i.e., through education, broadly defined)—another way of thinking, living, and acting, we can think and believe only what the ideas in our own language, and the rules that govern our use of them, allow us to think and believe.[5]

REASONS AND REFLECTION

Most of the reasons we take into consideration when determining what is good or best for us as individual persons are the product of experiences that *others* have had in the types of situations we encounter most frequently in ordinary life. They become available to us through the norms and conventions embedded in our language and in the social practices of the way of life we are born into; they suffice as guides to action. We take them into account and arrive at a judgment about which reasons carry the most weight in the circumstances. When we need to explain or justify our conclusions (to others or even to ourselves), we cite these reasons. They play an important role in our motivation, indicating as they do the prospect that we will realize value by acting on them. In this way they contribute to the formation of desires. (They also help us "rationalize" desires that arise spontaneously from unmet needs.) At any given time, we have a large store of such reasons and associated desires.

Occasionally, though, our supply of reasons for acting or not acting, or for doing one thing rather than another, doesn't indicate a clear and straightforward conclusion. Someone might give us reasons we hadn't considered before, so that now there are reasons pointing to other courses of action. Sometimes our reasons just don't seem to apply to the situation we're in, which might be one we've never encountered before. Or maybe they appear too rigid or too severe, and making an exception might be in order. New experiences or new information may create uncertainty. Or perhaps we just aren't getting the good outcomes from believing X or doing Y that we used to. In short, occasions can arise in which our continuing to believe X or do Y just doesn't seem as unproblematically good (or bad) as it used to be. When this happens, we need to stop and *reflect*.

Open-minded, well-informed, soundly reasoned thinking is the essence of autonomous choice, and reflection is essential to it. Reflection is the process of reexamining the reasons with which we explain and justify our convictions. It involves questioning and reassessing our established and habitual patterns of expectation; the frames of reference we rely on to make sense out of the world, others, and ourselves; and the most fundamental propositions we have employed to define (frame) problems we need to solve. It's the task of determining whether what we've learned previously remains well founded in present circumstances.

Reflection doesn't come easily, however. Research from the fields of psychology, neuropsychology, and the cognitive sciences generally shows how difficult—almost how "unnatural"—it is for human beings to reflect critically about their assumptions and other beliefs. We resist altering our beliefs, attitudes, and habits. We don't let facts determine what we should believe, but rather look for facts to confirm what we already believe. We even fail to notice events happening right in front of us because we see what we're predisposed to see.[6] Another impediment to reflection is our tendency to look for explanations for our failures and frustrations in the actions of other people, rather than in the beliefs, attitudes, and so forth that we carry with us and bring to every situation we encounter.[7] Too often, we blame everything and everyone but ourselves. We're strongly inclined to reject the possibility that we might be mistaken. We'd rather defend our opinions than learn and revise them.[8]

"Deep-level" beliefs and attitudes can prevent us from adapting our actions to the actual world we live in.[9] Even if they're poorly grounded, incomplete, out of date, naïve, or distorted, they can be extremely difficult to modify or eliminate. Because they occupy such a central place in our psychology, they're hard to identify and even harder to alter. Just becoming *aware* that certain basic beliefs underlie our thoughts, feelings, attitudes, and dispositions is enormously difficult. The more fundamental a belief is in our frame of reference, the more we take it for granted—treat it as an assumption—and forget that it can, and perhaps should, be reexamined.

The centrality of such beliefs to our psychology means they typically are supported by multiple connections in a vast network of such beliefs. Breaking one connection doesn't necessarily affect the others that support the belief. We've so deeply internalized our assumptions that, when we become aware of them at all, they seem "obvious" or "just common sense." In many cases, it's almost impossible to conceive that they could be false. That's not a problem when we assume, for example, that yesterday is gone forever (time doesn't flow backward) and that what goes up will always come down (gravity's a permanent condition). But there are some basic beliefs, especially those concerning human nature and motivation, that we really need to take a fresh, hard look at from time to time.[10]

Our basic belief systems, or frames of reference, include not only *what* we believe but *how we go about* ascertaining what to believe—that is, how we learn.[11] For example, we don't like difficult decisions, and we go out of our way to avoid them. We want the choices we face to be clear and easy. Once we make a decision, moreover, our minds unconsciously reinforce it, protecting it from internal review and external challenge. This "thirst for certainty" is in many ways the primary driving force for other dispositions that distort our thinking. For example, we are predisposed to accept simplistic "good versus evil narratives." Specific stories help us organize facts and opinions, but we edit them to fit a preexisting metanarrative, or story line. We are quick to label as "wrong," "not credible," or "evil" those that are at odds with our metanarrative. This makes the arguments others offer easier to dismiss—especially because, generalizing from our own psychological egoism, we assume others have ulterior motives for misrepresenting facts and the conclusions they draw from them. Because we assume our goals and intentions are good and our judgments are right, we infer incorrectly that people who contradict us or oppose us are wrong and even perverse.

As Jonathan Haidt observes, we are not selfish, but tribal, or "groupish."[12] We define ourselves in large measure negatively, as "*not* them." We grow up among people who are like us, especially in the way we think. Throughout life, we find it more comfortable being around such people and seek them out. The like-mindedness we share reinforces our dichotomous same-versus-different, good-versus-bad, righteous-versus-evil metanarrative. On top of that, we filter evidence to support our views. We expose ourselves selectively to different sources of information, readily accepting some sources while trying to insulate ourselves from others. We "let in" only information we can interpret in a manner that's compatible with our existing beliefs, attitudes, and inclinations. We apply tougher rules of evidence for information that runs counter to our existing perspective ("confirmation bias"). We add anecdotes from our own experience, further weighting the evidence in favor of the conclusion we're predisposed to reach. If that weren't enough, our minds unconsciously shape and revise the information we retain, turning our memories into distorted copies of the original.

Our thinking is subject to other errors as well. "Epistemic" distortions include, for example, the false assumption that people are naturally rational, that they make choices based on a clear understanding of the advantages and disadvantages of each option that is open to them, and that therefore they are fully responsible for their decisions and actions. "Sociocultural" distortions include taking for granted beliefs that reflect and lend authority to the existing distribution of social, political, or economic power and the social relationships, practices, and institutions that maintain them, simply because these exist. "Psychic" distortions stem from unexamined assumptions that support emotional, cognitive, or conative states that induce people to take action they would not otherwise take, or that keep them from acting. Beliefs, attitudes, and desires shaped by advertising and propaganda (including "spin," "alternative facts," and "fake news") fall under this heading.[13]

We are most likely to resist critical reflection when our psychological needs—such as the need for an acceptable self-image—are strong and reexamining our basic beliefs feels threatening to the coping strategies we've developed in order to meet our needs. Frequently, such strategies prove inadequate or less than ideal; they're substitutes for the optimal ways in which human beings can meet their needs. Because the strategies we adopt for dealing with strongly felt needs are essential to helping us function, we cling tightly to them, even if those strategies prove counterproductive. We often fiercely resist reexamining our beliefs no matter how much changed circumstances or new information might warrant reconsideration. Precisely because we sense that reflection and reconsideration might lead us to alter, modify, or transform the beliefs and assumptions that constitute our worldviews, we avoid or reject these essential elements of learning. Even when reconsideration might actually reinforce our beliefs by helping us find stronger reasons for holding them, we refuse to put them at risk of change. We refuse to learn.

In short, we look for, highlight, alter, and misremember the facts and examples that fit our preexisting perspective and avoid, dismiss, distort, and forget those that don't. As a result, we seldom change our own minds and hence hardly ever change anybody else's. Indeed, the stronger the evidence and arguments we're presented with, the harder our minds work to weaken them. We do whatever we can to avoid recognizing dilemmas that would require a difficult choice.

OPENNESS

Facts of human psychology such as the foregoing underline the importance of cultivating certain intellectual virtues and habits of mind. Foremost among these is *open-mindedness*.[14] The achievement of autonomy, and through its exercise the realization of our potential and the full expression of our individuality, is impossible without the readiness to take account of all relevant information and, if needed, to reconsider our beliefs, attitudes, predispositions, and priorities. When familiar values, principles, or priorities conflict, or when they do not apply clearly and straightforwardly to a new situation, our ability and willingness to think and act in a way that yields the best outcome depend on being open to the possibility that the "right answer" of the past will prove inadequate to the present.

What a person should believe, desire, or do depends on the circumstances in which she chooses. Her deliberation must be sufficiently exhaustive for her to have a defensible confidence that she need not regret in the future deciding as she does now. What is sufficient is difficult to specify. But being alert to contradictions and weaknesses in the complex web of beliefs she has internalized is certainly part of it. So is recognizing that the information available to her might be insufficient, out of date, or unreliable. That doesn't mean she must continuously reevaluate her beliefs. Reevaluation isn't necessary before *every* decision to act, because the reasons she has for pursuing X or for choosing Y instead don't suddenly and completely gain or lose validity. Most of her decisions will be appropriate but undeliberated responses to situations falling into fairly standard, recognizable categories.[15] Acting on one's existing beliefs and desires is not unreasonable. They may deserve periodic reexamination, but they need to be reconsidered only if countervailing considerations appear that suggest they are not as strong or important as they have been previously believed to be. Autonomy is not hyperrationality but rather the ability to think critically and open-mindedly when the need arises.

We seldom have all the information, time, experience, and skill we need to make the best possible decision. In such circumstances, there really is only one source we can turn to for assistance: other people. By considering their views, we can gain perspective, thereby prompting us—if we're willing—to reflect on our existing beliefs, attitudes, needs, feelings, and desires. By drawing on others' knowledge and experience, we can better weigh alternatives, including ones we might not even know exist. If instead we choose, decide, and act solely on the basis of our existing stock of knowledge, experience, and predispositions, we may end up realizing less value than we would otherwise. Our development as autonomous persons having an interest in fully realizing our individuality depends on our success in taking into account the information that only others can provide.

What are the optimal conditions, then, for making a genuine choice? Let's begin with the notion of a rational "ideal observer" like that proposed by Richard Brandt, R. M. Hare, and others.[16] Such an observer is fully informed, impartial, and in a physical and mental state healthy enough that it will not adversely affect her ability to think. Building on this definition, we might say that a person chooses autonomously to the extent that she chooses in the conditions that are optimal for making a sound choice, namely, she

1. is free from external constraint or coercion;
2. is not dependent on others for essential resources (food, shelter, health, etc.);
3. possesses all the information that's relevant to her decision, does her best to verify its accuracy, and evaluates it thoroughly;
4. resists the adverse effects of limitations on and distortions in her thinking[17] and reasons skillfully about the circumstances in which she is

choosing, the nature of the issue before her, and the options that are open to her;[18]

5. deliberates carefully;[19] and

6. seeks to arrive at a judgment that indicates which course of action open to her is likely, on balance and all things considered, to yield the best possible consequences in terms of her well-being.

Insofar as she deliberates and chooses in these conditions, to that extent her choices will be made autonomously, and her desires will be authentically her own. They will be the desires she *should* have, because they are the ones she *would* have if she made her choice in the foregoing conditions.

AUTONOMY AND INDIVIDUALITY

Autonomy is important in human life for the same reason freedom is: because human beings possess the ability to form their own conceptions of how to live life, and because it enables the person to develop and express her individuality by choosing her own mode of life. This is the conclusion Mill reached. Unthinking submission to the customs and traditions of a person's society is at odds with Mill's belief in the value of individuality— what he calls "character." An autonomous person's desires, feelings, and attitudes arise from beliefs she has subjected to conscious reflection and are not uncritically adopted from external sources.

Mill's belief in the importance of "character" stems from his view of the process by which people form their desires. For him, the *way* in which a person's beliefs and attitudes are formed is important. The free and deliberate choice of a mode of life is only one component of Mill's ideal of individuality. He valued *self-development* as well. A person's choices, he believed, should help her develop her potential. The "right" choice for each individual, of course, depends on the characteristics, factors, and circumstances that make a person the unique human being she is, and thus varies from person to person. But Mill sees a connection between individuality and what he calls the "higher pleasures" (or "enhancement values," as I prefer to call them), which cannot be attained except through the pursuit of self-development and the exercise of autonomous choice.[20]

There *is* such a thing as a person's authentic self. It is not identical with her current self (or, we might say, with the present stage of the process of becoming the person she is). She is not *just* the person who has the beliefs, intuitions, feelings, and desires she happens to have at a given time. She is also the person she can become, the person who can have the beliefs, intuitions, feelings, and desires she *would* have if she allowed them to form in the course of making autonomous choices. To achieve her aspiration to realize her authentic individual self, she must work to transcend those elements of the world that have shaped her, rejecting, reaffirming, or modifying them as she believes warranted. Although she shouldn't cast them aside cavalierly, they are likely to prove inadequate to the long-term project of knowing and realizing her uniqueness. The self that develops through autonomous choice is the self whose unique potential has been fully realized, and who in consequence thereof is able to experience and express what I, following Mill, have characterized as his or her individuality.

FOUR

Freedom, Rights, and Conflicts between Values

THE PLURALITY OF VALUES AND "NEGATIVE" FREEDOM

The most persuasive defender of freedom since Mill was Isaiah Berlin. Berlin argued that, when we have to decide what to do, often we'll be faced with the necessity of choosing between multiple values—things that are good, desirable, worthy of the effort required to obtain them. Each of these is unique, qualitatively distinct from the others. Faced with a choice, we may discover it's not possible to realize or obtain one without giving up something in terms of the others. It's not possible to assign one priority without foregoing at least some of the value we would realize if we were to give a different one priority. Candor, for example, often conflicts with sparing another person hurt feelings and preserving her dignity. Impartiality or even-handedness may conflict with special responsibilities or obligations we have to promote someone's well-being. Justice or equity might conflict with mercy, compassion, and forgiveness. Prudence and adventure might prove incompatible. Long-term gain usually means making do with less in the short term. Freedom often must be sacrificed in order to protect others from harm.

Nor is there any single correct method for deciding which good things to assign priority over others. *We have no overarching, general concept of the good*, Berlin argues, that puts all good things in rational, fixed relationship—a single order of relative priority—that everyone must agree with. Our conceptual store of purposes, ends, goods, and values contains a plurality of such items that ultimately are incommensurable[1] with each other, and—even more significant—irreducible to a common measure of goodness or value. That is, they can't be compared with each other in such a way that one can be translated into the other, or into some "common currency," like happiness or pleasure, that would enable us to rank them.

Yet Berlin wasn't a relativist. As Richard Wollheim has written, his argument concerns only the *internal* nature of an individual's system of values.[2] It says nothing about the rules for resolving disagreement between persons who have different value priorities. Berlin specifically does *not* say there must or even can be a multiplicity of (ethical or moral) rules for resolving disagreement. A plurality of values for individuals is perfectly compatible with the belief in a single set or system of interpersonal rules to which the different value rankings of different individuals ought to conform. In short, he allowed that different individual rankings of values might be reconciled by ethical moral rules or principles that apply to everyone.

Moreover, Berlin did not contend that all values are *equal*, that each is *never* more important or less important than any other one, or that we can't with good and sufficient reason decide to accord one value priority over others in either particular cases or over a range of cases. Nor did he suggest that values are the equivalent of desires, feelings, opinions, or tastes. In fact, Berlin conceded the possibility that there may be an objective order of values independent of our personal preferences.

What he did insist on was his claim that it's impossible even to conceive of a rule or principle of logic, rationality, or theoretical necessity for choosing between two or more different values that would require us invariably to assign priority to one of those values. If you find X more important than Y, I can't challenge your preference for X by arguing that Y or Z is logically or necessarily more important than X. I can't successfully challenge your preference for X on *that* ground because there just is no rule or principle that requires X invariably to be subordinated to (say) Y (or some other value). It might be that, on a particular occasion or in a particular set of conditions or circumstances, Y (or some other value) is more important (more desirable, more valuable, etc.) than X. But the priority of Y over X can't be established by invoking some rule or principle of logic, rationality, or theoretical necessity that Y *always* must be ranked higher.

Berlin was concerned that allowing ourselves to imagine that there's a rule or principle of logic, rationality, or theoretical necessity for choosing between two or more different values that would require us invariably to assign priority to one of those values would have two adverse consequences.

First, it would obscure the fact that, whenever we must make a hard choice between two or more goods, we lose or forego the value of the good thing that is not chosen. Berlin wanted us to recognize and acknowledge that every choice between X and Y involves a sacrifice. We shouldn't imagine that we can gain the value associated with X without incurring a cost in terms of the value we would realize if we were to select Y instead.

Second, failing to recognize and acknowledge the value we forgo when we choose one good rather than another could open the way for a government, a group, a ruler, a dominant class, or a society to impose their beliefs about what is good or bad, right or wrong, more important or less important, on others who disagree with them. He was afraid such thinking would make it possible to justify compelling people to sacrifice what holds value for them to what holds value for others. He worried that failing to recognize and acknowledge that something of value will be sacrificed when a choice between goods must be made would enable those on the side of the "winning" good to justify labeling those on the "losing" side as misguided, perverse, illogical, or irrational.

These concerns led Berlin to make another argument that, on its face, seems inconsistent with his insistence that there is a plurality of incommensurable values. He argued that the *fact* of value pluralism implies that there *is* one value that rationally, even objectively, should always be given priority: *freedom*. On Berlin's view, if assigning one value priority over another always involves the sacrifice of the value not chosen; if there's no way to compare values and translate them into "higher," more "basic," or more general values; and *if what has value is simply what people believe has value*, then the most important value—the absolutely indispensable value—is freedom of choice.

He went further: he argued that freedom must be equated with what he called its "negative" form, that is, as the absence of externally imposed constraint. Freedom, in his view, must be understood as freedom *from interference by others* with the individual's choice. This is the basic and most widely understood conception of freedom we discussed earlier: the freedom protected by the principle of noninterference. Berlin insisted that conceptions of freedom that emphasize a person's "freedom *to do*" something—such as independence and autonomy—should not be confused with freedom in its most important sense: freedom from active interference with our choices and actions.

We can grant the importance of Berlin's insight and the wisdom of heeding his warnings without succumbing, however, to the temptation to treat freedom as a value and principle that is absolute and always must defeat other values and principles with which it conflicts. We can grant that freedom from interference is a distinct, distinctive, and extremely important—even central or foundational—value. But we can't avoid the task of forming judgments about what people—both ourselves and others—*should* be free to choose. If we don't even attempt to make these judgments, we can't choose in a way that's not arbitrary. We can't make choices that are sound. We can't make decisions that are justified. We can't evaluate options and identify the one among those available to us that, on balance and all things considered, will have the best consequences—that will achieve the greatest net good for everyone affected.

Moreover, if we don't determine which goods are relatively more important than others, some might gradually diminish in importance or even disappear without anyone realizing or caring. If we focus solely on our freedom to fulfill our existing desires indiscriminately, we might fail to notice that we have lost the opportunity to fulfill desires we have not yet formed, or even imagined. In particular, we may need to reach a judgment about a person's ability to recognize and choose values that she does not actually or currently desire, especially if we have reason to believe that lacking that ability would diminish her independence or her autonomy. As we have seen, interference can result not just from coercion, intimidation, or other kinds of actions that prevent or deter a person from choosing, but also from the influence of things like internalized role expectations, socially inculcated norms, ignorance, lack of self-knowledge, distorted perceptions, self-satisfaction, aversion to risk-taking, overwhelming needs, and so forth.

Even Mill, along with Berlin the most persuasive and eloquent defender in our political tradition of the value of freedom, recognized that his own seemingly absolute version of the principle of noninterference did not account adequately for the constraints imposed on us by what appear to be our personal beliefs, attitudes, perceptions, desires, habits, and dispositions:

> Society . . . practices a social tyranny more formidable than many kinds of political oppression, since, though not usually upheld by such extreme penalties, it leaves fewer means of escape, penetrating much more deeply into the details of life, and enslaving the soul itself. Protection, therefore, against the tyranny of [government] is not enough; there needs [to exist] protection also against the tyranny of the prevailing opinion and feeling, against the tendency of society to . . . fetter the development and . . . prevent the formation of any individuality not in harmony with its ways.[3]

THE NONSOLUTION OF RIGHTS

The principle of noninterference says no one may prevent, impede, restrain, or unreasonably encumber a person's acting without adequate justification. But if someone says he has a *right* not to be interfered with, he is asserting that no such justification exists, or perhaps even that no justification *could* exist. It is important to understand that, in either case, he may be mistaken.

The notion of a "right" raises certain questions. One of these is the problem of conflict between rights. It's not unusual to encounter a situation in which person A has a right to do (or receive) X and person B also has a right to do (or receive) X. Or it might be that A has a right to do (or receive) X and B has a right to do (or receive) Y. For example, person A might claim a right to dump waste in a stream, and person B might claim a right to draw clean water from that stream.

Because rights can conflict, *no right can be absolute*. To be absolute, a right would *always* win in a conflict with another value. Like other rights, the right to freedom is not an absolute right. For example, we have no right to infringe another person's rights. We have no right to break the law. We have no right to cause others harm. We have no right to do wrong. We have no right to behave unethically. As we will see further on, values other than those protected by an alleged right, X, can take precedence over the value X protects or supports.

Not surprisingly, people disagree over what rights there are. They also tend to expand the number and types of rights they believe exist. (This phenomenon has been called "rights inflation.") Expanding the number of rights has a paradoxical result, however: the more rights people have, the less freedom they have, because rights have the effect of preventing people other than the right holder from acting freely. Each right constitutes an area within which people who hold the right are protected from interference by others. But every right that assures its holders that they may act freely diminishes the unprotected freedom that other people enjoy. Because every right entails a duty on the part of others not to interfere, growth in the number of rights reduces the total amount of unprotected freedom in the system.

There are some rights, of course—particularly "negative" ones—that we do regard as absolute, or nearly so: for example, the right to not be tortured (although since September 11, 2001, some people seem to think that right doesn't exist). But most rights allow for exceptions. Even the right to free speech doesn't cover everything a person might say—for example, racist or pornographic speech; revealing information during a time of war that might aid an enemy; shouting "fire" in a theater when it's not actually on fire; intentionally or negligently making false statements that harm another person's reputation, and so forth.

Even widely recognized rights can be used by the right holder to inflict harm on others. If person A believes he has a certain right, this may encourage him to invoke it without regard for the well-being or interests of person B. As noted above, person A's exercise of his right to do (or receive) X always causes some harm—if nothing else, by reducing the freedom of person B, who (if A's right is recognized as such) has a duty not to infringe it. Whenever a right is invoked, value is at stake on both sides of the conflict. Not surprisingly, claiming a right often makes it harder to resolve ethical and political issues. In claiming a right, a person seeks to prevent further discussion—he puts forward his ostensible right as a trump card that he hopes will force discussion to stop.

Finally, and most important, there is the problem of identifying a basis or foundation for rights. Rights can be created by consensus or by acts of legitimate political or legal authority. But so-called "human" and "natural" rights for the most part remain only *claims*—they are expressions of the belief that such rights *ought* to exist. What brings a right into existence is being recognized broadly and enforced consistently and assiduously. If a community or society cannot provide or chooses not to provide that recognition, at least within that community or society the right-claim remains just that: a claim. (Of course, other communities or societies that do recognize the claim as a right may extend their recognition to members of a community or society that does not, as in the case of universal human rights.)

Because of the problems just identified, disagreement exists over which rights people have and how important they are relative to each other. How do we decide what rights people should have, who should have them, and what relative priority they should have? And how do we justify the existence of these rights? A leading legal theorist of rights, the late Ronald Dworkin, argued that people have moral rights that derive from a primary or fundamental (moral or human) right to "equal concern and respect."[4] That is, every human person is entitled to be treated *well*. Not to treat some persons as well as they are entitled to be treated violates this primary right. The primary right to equal concern and respect is based in turn on our belief that the *value* of enjoying the concern and respect of others is fundamentally important. As we will see further on, Dworkin's conclusion is essentially correct as a fundamental premise of ethics. But he doesn't demonstrate convincingly that people have a *right* to equal concern and respect. He argues only that we *should* treat people with concern and respect. But why should we? Simply asserting the existence of such a right does not, by itself, establish that it is a right in fact.

So where does this leave us? It leaves us with the task of proposing and evaluating rights-claims in specific areas of activity in which we believe the principle of noninterference should apply. We must be able to justify the principle *with reference to the type of activity* under consideration, and we must justify it well enough that our community or society reaches a working consensus that everyone has a duty to recognize that type of activity as valuable enough to warrant the protection that a right would afford it. In order to make this determination, we must engage in public ethical dialogue and deliberation concerning it.

THE ETHICAL INADEQUACY OF THE FREEDOM PRINCIPLE

When we use terms like "free" and "unfree" in our political discourse, we are saying something about what we believe is good or bad, right or wrong, desirable and undesirable, for human beings. There is a necessary connection between judgments about "freedom" and our beliefs about which actions, situations, and states of affairs qualify as good or valuable. Only the recognition that something has value for a person entitles us to conclude that someone else could be held responsible for unjustifiably preventing, impeding, or unreasonably encumbering her actions.

The connection between the term "freedom" and the inescapability of rendering judgments about the value of actions that people should (or should not) be free to perform makes "freedom" an *ethical* term. Ethics has to do with values, virtues, and principles for living a good life: rules for what we should and shouldn't do, the duties and obligations we have, the kind of people we ought to be, the good things we should aspire to and the bad things we should avoid. "Freedom" is an ethical term because the "purpose, point, or need"[5] (PPN) it was formed to serve in our language and way of life is an ethical one: to recognize, protect, and support the interest every person has in acting to realize value—to experience what is good—without being unjustifiably prevented, constrained, interfered with, or unreasonably encumbered.

By arguing that she is unfree, a person seeks to accomplish the *ethical* aim of requiring that interference with her acting be justified. But negative freedom—"freedom from"—*by itself* is inadequate to the task of serving fully the concept's PPN. When the freedom of one person conflicts with that of another person, or when freedom conflicts with a different value that also is important (such as the ability to take advantage of her freedom, to use it to meet her needs and to realize her ends), we must choose which to assign priority. In turn, this requires us to *weigh the goods in conflict and to choose between them*. This is the essence of ethical decision making.

The principle of noninterference does not help us with the task of weighing values (i.e., deliberating) and prioritizing them. It tells us interference must be justified, but it does not tell us how to determine what is justifiable. Justifiability is the product of the effort to resolve conflicts between goods. Is there a principled way to resolve such conflicts? In order to evaluate and compare the goods in tension, we need a procedure, a way of thinking that helps us weigh and balance them. In a word, we need *ethics*.

FIVE

Ethics and Rules

WHAT IS ETHICS?

Ethics is a social practice. Its content consists of the rules, principles, and values that constitute the (always provisional) conclusions we have arrived at over time, as communities and societies, in our efforts to determine what is good and bad, right and wrong. It is also the continuing *process* by which we arrive at judgments about good and bad, right and wrong, for ourselves or for others.

The process of ethics helps us make two kinds of decisions. We face one type when our action might affect someone else—especially if it might cause them harm. Typically, we call these quandaries "moral" issues. (They might also be called decisions concerning one's duties or obligations. Philosophers often call this type of decision "deontological" or "other-regarding.") In contrast, when our decision about what to do is likely to affect chiefly ourselves and is unlikely to affect others substantially, it's better thought of as a "values" decision. (Philosophers often call this type of decision "prudential" or "self-regarding.") In practice, these two types of decisions are closely related: every action has consequences, and consequences can be beneficial or harmful—for ourselves, for others, or for both.

The practice of ethics probably emerged in human societies because it proved beneficial to the small groups that adopted and enforced certain rules for what their members were allowed or required to do or were prohibited from doing. Ethics as we know it didn't spring into existence fully formed, of course; it began simply and changed over time. It seems likely that it was preceded by the practice of *reciprocity*, a form of cooperation that continues to influence our decisions and actions today. (The classic example from American history is rural barn-raising.) Reciprocity says, "If you help *me* do something I can't do by myself, then when you need help, you can expect me to help *you*." Conversely, "If I help *you* do something you can't do by yourself, then when I need help, I expect you to help *me*." Reciprocity creates a kind of social contract consisting of mutual obligations. When people in general recognize that it's good for them if everyone abides by this principle, it builds trust within the group, creates stability and predictability, and keeps interpersonal relationships resilient.

Notice that the reciprocity rule rests on the unstated assumption that it's *good* for people to give and receive help. Why is it good to do so? Because that way people can meet their individual *needs*: for safety, food, shelter, care, learning, work, and other requirements for living. Unless people can meet their needs, they can't thrive or flourish—and might not even survive. Even in the contemporary world there are things we simply cannot obtain and secure by ourselves alone: public safety, material prosperity, freedom, knowledge, and justice, among others. Because none of us has any choice or control over the circumstances or the kind of life we're born into, there's no guarantee that any of us will be able to fulfill his or her needs. The reciprocity principle helps people meet not only their own needs and those of their children and other family members, but the needs of everyone in the group—their tribe, clan, village, community, society, and so on.

Humans are interdependent social creatures. Everyone depends on others—totally, early in life, and to some degree throughout. Moreover, every person contributes something of value to the shared life we live, to our life in common. Slowly and gradually, we have realized that each of us deserves a certain measure of consideration for his or her well-being. It seems plausible that at some point this realization combined with the reciprocity principle to produce the first and most basic ethical rule: that each of us should treat every other person with respect and goodwill—in short, the way any of us would want others to treat us. In the sense that each person deserves the respect and goodwill of others, ethics presupposes that the importance any of us attaches to her own well-being is "equal" to that of anyone else. You and I are equal in this most fundamental respect: that each of us looks out onto the world around us from the perspective of an aware, sensing, feeling human being who is impelled by nature to seek and obtain the good things that, in turn, enable us to meet our personal needs, to achieve well-being, and if possible even to thrive or flourish.[1] The ethical practice of treating everyone with respect and goodwill helps *all* of us pursue this universal goal.

The purpose of ethics, then—its "point," the need we have for it in our way of life—is to protect and promote the well-being of all persons, to support each of us as we try to identify and realize those goods (values) that will enable us to live well, to thrive, to flourish. It exists to help us live in relative harmony with each other and to ensure that that no individual's well-being is compromised, sacrificed, or diminished by the actions (or inactions) of others without compelling justification. In order to fulfill the purpose of protecting and promoting the well-being of all, ethics seeks to address and answer questions not only of what is right and wrong, but also of what is good and bad. Over time, the answers we settle on take the form of rules (principles, norms, expectations) that shape, influence, and constrain what people do.

Those rules support, protect, or promote goods we believe are important. They are embedded in examples, analogies, metaphors, parables, adages, maxims, proverbs, aphorisms, recollections of our own or others' experiences, and the opinions of "authorities" in various traditions of thought (e.g., scientific, social, religious, humanistic). Ethical rules include directives such as "Keep your promises" (which reflects the value we find in responsibility and reliability); "Honesty is the best policy" (which reflects the value we attach to truthfulness, candor, and transparency); and "Don't take what isn't yours" (which reflects the value we place on our ability to make, acquire, and use things that in turn contribute to our well-being). Other rules—such as "Tell the truth," "Obey the law," "Respect people's rights," "Do no harm," "Practice what you preach," and "Play fair"— support, protect, or promote additional goods or values.

RULES, DILEMMAS, AND ISSUES

Most of our ethical rules are the product of experiences people in our community or society have had in situations that occurred in the past. Our forebears confronted situations both similar to and different from those we encounter today, and found a way to deal with them satisfactorily (at least for the era, the place, and for the people who benefited most from establishing them). In time, those solutions were generalized and formalized as ethical rules, principles, "values," and the like. As generalizations, ethical rules resemble legal principles that have developed over time through the accumulation of court decisions in a large number of individual cases. (A judgment in a particular case can establish a new principle that becomes "precedent" for making decisions in similar cases, but the principle itself develops and solidifies only as it is applied in individual cases that are decided subsequently.) Similarly, ethical rules begin as particular judgments about what is right or obligatory in specific situations that require us to make a decision about what to do.

Much of the time, we can arrive at a clear answer to the question of what we ought to do, of what's right to do, by identifying and choosing the ethical rule that is most appropriate for the situation in which we find ourselves. But this isn't always a straightforward matter. For example, consider the rule, "Never tell a lie." If we reflect for a moment, we realize that there are situations in which telling "the truth, the whole truth, and nothing but the truth" would be imprudent, unsafe, unhelpful, unfair, or unwise—and hence difficult to accept as the right thing to do. This kind of conflict between different goods we find important is an ethical *dilemma*. Should we tell the truth in this situation, or should we apply some other rule that will help realize a different value that's arguably even more important? Ethical dilemmas arise whenever we're uncertain about which of our existing stock of rules should apply in a situation where we want an unambiguous, compelling, and readily recognizable instruction to tell us what to do.

When an ethical dilemma becomes a matter of public concern, an ethical *issue* arises. An ethical issue is the expression of a disagreement between groups of people who hold divergent beliefs about how an ethical dilemma should be resolved. Unfortunately, the fact that an ethical dilemma exists is often obscured by the muddled, emotional way people respond to it. Instead of focusing on the values or principles in conflict, they may quarrel about whether a problem exists; what kind of problem it is; about how serious or pressing it is; about what's at stake; whether a response is required; how much or what kind of response is appropriate; who is responsible for solving it; or any number of such questions. As long as these questions deflect attention from the conflict at the heart of the matter, the real source of their disagreement—the ethical dilemma—likely will go unrecognized and unresolved, and the issue will persist, frequently and perennially reemerging in a variety of guises.

An important reason why ethical dilemmas are so difficult to bring to the surface and describe clearly is that they almost always exist *within* each of us as well as *between* us—a fact we're slow to recognize and concede. The interpersonal disagreements that mark ethical issues typically have their roots in dilemmas of choice between distinct and competing goods. For example, if I (and people who share my view) value novelty and you (and people who share your view) value routine, the issue between us will appear to be whether I should be able to enjoy the novelty I want or you should be able to enjoy the routine you want. The issue, however, is seldom whether N(ovelty) is good and R(outine) isn't, or vice versa. Rather, it's whether in the circumstances N is *relatively* more important to support than R is, or vice versa. That is, the conflict that poses a dilemma of choice for us is between competing views of which should take priority. Both novelty and routine are good (valuable, desirable); each of us values both. It's just that I believe novelty, in the circumstances, is better than routine and should be preferred, while you believe that routine is better than novelty and should be preferred. The *dilemma*, to which we offer different strategies for resolving it, is which to give priority. The *conflict*, however—that is, the incommensurability—is between two goods that both of us value: novelty and routine.

Ethical dilemmas and the hard choices they create almost always involve conflicts between two or more things we *all* consider good, valuable, or desirable. Telling the truth can conflict with keeping a promise. Being fair can conflict with being compassionate. Health and safety can conflict with adventure and risk-taking. Impartiality can conflict with being loyal, which can conflict with truthfulness. Conflicts arise either because the goods are inherently incompatible (e.g., material values versus spiritual ones), or because the circumstances are such that they cannot be given equal emphasis or support (e.g., when the supply of drinkable water in the ground is limited and none of us can take as much as we would like). The important point is that we can't obtain the full measure of one good without accepting a lesser measure of the good with which it conflicts. There is always a *trade-off*: more of one means less of the other.[2] That is what makes a choice hard. It's what turns a conflict between goods into an ethical dilemma.[3]

In order to resolve a dilemma between conflicting goods, and thereby settle (or at least mitigate, temper, or manage[4]) the issue it leads to, we must turn to ethical thinking understood not just as a *set of rules* for indicating what we should seek and do, but as a *process* for reaching a sound judgment concerning how best to make the hard choice we can't avoid.

ETHICAL RIGHTNESS AND DUTY

Ethical rules exist to support (protect, promote, etc.) different goods—objects, experiences, actions, activities, states of affairs, and so on—that are generally considered desirable or valuable. Such rules tell us how we should act—what we ought to do in a given type of situation—in order to protect or promote the goods embodied or embedded in those rules. Put another way, ethical rules tell us what's *right* to do. But how do we determine what's right? In particular, how do we determine what's right when ethical rules conflict?

To answer this question, let's look at three views of ethical duty. "Rightness" theories of ethical duty emphasize the importance of following rules.[5] Theorists who support the rightness approach to determining ethical duties argue that rules are valid independently of whether they promote the good— that is, it doesn't matter whether or not they produce good results, have good outcomes, or yield good consequences. It's the nature of the rule itself—like "keep promises," or "tell the truth," or "don't torture sentient creatures"—that makes it right, not the fact that keeping a promise or telling the truth or refraining from torturing produces good consequences. Supporters of this view contend that ethical rules are fundamental; are rooted deeply in human experience (or even human nature); and can be recognized either intuitively or with a bit of careful reflection. They are "self-justifying." Why should we always follow the rule "Tell the truth"? Because we "know" telling the truth is the right thing to do. Telling the truth *just is* our duty.

The rightness approach says that our decisions about what to do in particular ethical choice situations *always* must be determined by these fundamental rules. Ethical conclusions (e.g., the contention that person A has a right to do X) are *categorical*. That means the requirement to act as the rule dictates holds regardless of the situation, regardless of who's involved, and regardless of the consequences. Categorical requirements are both *universal*—that is, they apply to all relevantly similar persons—and *absolute*—that is, they override all other considerations and must be followed in every relevant situation without exception.

In contrast to rightness theories of ethical duty, "goodness" theories make ethical judgments conditional, not categorical. They say, "*If* action X will produce more good (better consequences) than action Y, then X is the right thing to do." Goodness theories hold that the ultimate standard or criterion of what is ethically right or obligatory is the amount of good that results from taking a particular action. In other words, what is ethically required of us in our relations with others depends on, or is a function of, the (net) *value* that is realized by our judgments and subsequent actions. An action is ethically right or obligatory if and only if it will produce the most good and the least bad (or at least more good than bad) of all the courses of action a person could pursue. (Notice that goodness theories of ethical duty require that we make judgments about what is good or bad, desirable or undesirable, valuable or not valuable. Such theories require that we think about the *axiological* dimension of ethics—the aspect of ethics that has to do with making judgments of this sort.)

A third view of ethics takes an indirect approach to the question of what's right. The *characterological* (or "aretaic") view emphasizes the importance to the person facing an ethical dilemma of having the right disposition, attitude, or habit of mind (e.g., sound judgment, wisdom, integrity, compassion, empathy, goodwill). Throughout history, both philosophers and ordinary people have believed it's important to cultivate certain dispositions or character traits or habits: honesty, kindness, trustworthiness, loyalty, considerateness, generosity, magnanimity, sympathy, and so forth. Such character virtues involve a readiness or inclination to act in certain ways in certain kinds of situations. On this view, what is fundamental is not actions but rather intentions, motives, and personal qualities. The purpose of cultivating and acquiring virtues is not so much to guide or instruct people in *what* to do, but rather to make it more likely that they will do willingly and readily what virtuous persons do.

For example, it might be argued that caring or compassion is more important than knowing rules or calculating the net amount of good that can be generated by each option for acting, because a person who possesses these character virtues is more likely to do what's right, especially in situations where it isn't clear what rules apply or what consequences are likely to result from her actions. "Care"—which we might think of as a stronger and more proactive form of benevolence (goodwill)—consists of recognizing the needs that all human beings have and of taking responsibility for supporting their well-being, especially those with whom one has a relationship established by shared social norms.[6] On this view, an ethical person is a caring person, and a caring person will, without having to be reminded or persuaded, demonstrate the required care. "Care ethics" is an ethics of virtue. In particular, care might be construed as the virtue of adopting and acting from the ethical point of view. People are more likely to arrive at a sound ethical judgment and to act ethically if they so thoroughly "put themselves in the shoes of others" that they will *care* about those others.

The important point about aretaic ethics, though, is that it directs our attention to the task of developing our own "excellence of character"—to acquiring and improving those qualities traditionally called "virtues." In many ways, shaping our habits and dispositions to meet the highest standards of human thought, feeling, and action both resembles and complements our efforts to become persons who are autonomous in the sense we discussed in Chapter 3. Focusing on our personal beliefs, attitudes, aspirations, and the like helps strengthen our ability to take responsibility for both our person well-being and the well-being of others. As we will see in Chapter 12, this focus on characterological excellence is indispensable to meeting the challenge of building a world in which all people can thrive and flourish.

Which approach to steering our choices and actions in the direction of ethical rightness—of our ethical duty—should we adopt? Should we follow the approach that emphasizes rules (about what is right or wrong); the approach in which we determine what to do by assessing and weighing the consequences in terms of good and bad, benefit and harm, costs and benefits; or the approach that asks us to develop certain attitudinal and behavioral virtues and allow these to guide our judgments of right and wrong?

Or must we choose at all?

THE PROBLEM WITH RULES

Before we try to answer the question of which approach to determining what's right we should take, let's look more closely at the nature of ethical rules. After several centuries in which the concept of rights has been central to Western ethical and political discourse, we might be inclined to believe that there are some rules, principles, or values that *always* should take precedence, that may never be subordinated to other considerations. But examples abound of ostensibly "hard and fast" rules that admit of exceptions. For example, consider the right of free speech. There is no absolute right to speak freely because there are situations in which giving that right priority would have unacceptable adverse consequences. No one has the right to yell "fire!" in a crowded theater if there's no reason to think a fire exists. A ban on false advertising is a legitimate limitation on speech, as are libel, slander, and perjury.

Our beliefs about what is good and bad, right and wrong are generalizations. Every one of my beliefs about what's good or bad, right or wrong, is based on a large but nonetheless limited number of experiences that I or other human beings have already had, not ones I might or will have. No matter how firmly we believe something, no matter how many times a belief has been reinforced, no matter how obviously and absolutely without exception it might seem, it remains a generalization. It does not cover—it cannot and will not ever cover—every situation that could or will arise. I may be as convinced that I have a right to use deadly force in self-defense as I am that the sun will come up tomorrow. But like my conviction that tomorrow will come, my belief in the right to shoot dead someone who threatens me could be mistaken. Some situation or circumstance, not yet encountered by me or anyone else, may show that my "right" is more qualified than I had thought.

If our beliefs about what is good and bad, right and wrong are generalizations based on previous human experience (in particular, the previous experience of persons who have been members of the community of our first language), they are also, at least implicitly, *predictions* about what will prove right and wrong for others in relevantly similar current and future circumstances. As I will argue at length further on, evaluative statements are *factual* in nature, albeit *hypothetical* in form. They are propositions that predict what factually *will* be the case *if* one acts in the prescribed (or proscribed) manner. So, for example, a factual hypothetical statement might be something like, "If for most of your life you follow a healthy diet, get enough exercise, sleep enough, and avoid behavior that's harmful to your body, then other things being equal you probably will live many years safe from the threat of serious illness." (A more basic example: "If you put your hand in a fire, you will burn it, and that will be painful and possibly disfiguring or even disabling.")

Applying a rule categorically in a particular case or set of circumstances may lead to consequences that are sufficiently bad or undesirable (e.g., ineffective, disadvantageous, harmful) as to render application of the rule unjustifiable. Based as they are on previous experience, rules are prima facie indications of what actions will lead to the best consequences. General rules—even the ones we hold to most unshakably—give us only a starting point for our deliberations; they serve as "precedent." Our beliefs about what is good and bad, right and wrong, are really *presumptions*. We may treat them as if they are "absolute," provided we realize that situations might arise in which our judgment will recommend that they should be modified. Is lying wrong? "Absolutely." But it might be better to lie than to hurt someone. Is it wrong to kill another human being? "Absolutely." But sometimes it's justifiable (e.g., when defending one's own life or that of another person) or excusable (e.g., in war). Is there an absolute right to use deadly force to preserve your own life? Not in situations in which one person's right conflicts with another person's equal right (assuming neither is more culpable than the other). Is there an absolute right to not to be tortured? Yes—but only because the unjustifiability of torture, like that of murder, is built into its definition.[7]

Because questions concerning what is good and bad, right and wrong may have no determinate (correct) answers, no party to an ethical or political disagreement is ever warranted in declaring, *in advance* of thorough examination and discussion, that his or her position with respect to that issue is in fact *the* right or correct solution. To be sure, it might turn out, upon reflection and due consideration, that his solution is in fact the *best* answer we can give to the matter in question in present circumstances; it might be the one all of us should accept. But neither he nor we can know this *before* all affected parties have engaged in ethical thinking that is (as we will see below) inclusive, dialogical, deliberative, rigorously and thoroughly examined, and provisional (i.e., open-ended, subject to revision or elaboration, etc.).

Rules are necessary, though. If every time we were confronted with an ethical dilemma we had to reflect on and calculate the consequences of our actions, we wouldn't be able to act swiftly and decisively. And even if we did stop to think, we still might come up with the wrong answer. Because rules are generalizations from previous experience, they usually are a reliable guide to the best way to proceed. It's good, then—even necessary— for us to have rules to follow and to follow them. Our best response to an ethical dilemma usually will be the one that our rules tell us is the right one. Having clear, firm rules like "never deliberately harm someone" tends to produce a higher overall level of well-being in our community, society, and world, even if on occasion sticking to them arguably would result in a lower net good being realized.

We should acknowledge, however, that at least part of the appeal of clear, firm rules is that they seem "natural." They just "make sense." Ethical thinking about right and wrong at what I call the rules level involves requirements that are so well established and so firmly rooted in human experience that we usually don't question them, or need to. Rules about right and wrong are so deeply embedded in our way of life, and we learn them unconsciously so early in life, that they seem a part of who we are. They can even seem to be a feature of the natural universe, as reliable and undeniable as gravity. We internalize these rules, and we "intuitively" apply them when we encounter circumstances to which they seem to apply. That's why we sometimes call them "intuitions." Intuitions are learned rules operating unconsciously.

"LEVELS" OF ETHICAL THINKING

For most of the situations we encounter in our normal, everyday lives, solutions are ready to hand. They consist of rules such as "Keep promises,"

"Tell the truth," "Obey the law," "Respect people's rights," "Play fair." To make an ethical decision, we identify the relevant rules; determine which of them fits the circumstances best; and then follow it. When we do this, we are engaged in ethical thinking at the "rules level."

Although ethical thinking at the rules level serves us well in the great majority of cases, we may find that no single rule emerges as clearly more suitable than others.[8] There is always the possibility that it might be better, all things considered, not to follow *any* of the rules that are available to us. Sometimes none of the rules we can identify seem to apply to the situation we're in, which might be one we've never encountered before or haven't faced frequently. Or maybe the most applicable rule appears too rigid or too severe, and making an exception seems justified. Often, two rules are equally compelling, and we can't choose between them. In short, occasions can arise in which the right action just isn't clear and straightforward.

When two or more rules give us conflicting instructions about what to do—if they seem equally important and we can't decide which to assign priority—we must try to determine whether one of the rules ought to take precedence over the other(s). Should I tell the truth, or should I protect my child from harm? In the circumstances, both rules seem clearly right— indeed, they seem to be required. But I can't follow both simultaneously—I have to choose. I want to be able to justify my conclusions (to myself and to others) by saying something along these lines: "I didn't tell the truth because, although we should always tell the truth, we also should protect our children from harm. I believe that, in the circumstances, protecting my child is more important than telling the truth."

But if I can't choose between two rules that give me conflicting instructions about what to do, I have to try something else. What can I do? How should I proceed? To answer this question, let's look at Richard Hare's theory of ethical thinking.[9] Hare's analysis suggests that we combine the rule-focused approach to determining our ethical duties (the "rightness" view) with the good consequences-emphasizing approach (the "goodness" view) in a single whole of which these two approaches constitute different aspects.[10] He argues that there are two levels to our ethical thinking. (Shortly, I will explain why I believe there are actually three levels, or stages.) The first is the "ordinary" level, which is essentially the same as the "rules" level I am describing here. At this level we try to determine what is right (i.e., what our duty is, what we ought to do) by identifying and applying the rule that best fits the circumstances in which the need to make that determination has arisen.

If, however, after trying to apply a rule to a situation we find it doesn't yield a clear, broadly acceptable, and essentially unproblematic answer, we should stop trying to fit it to the case at hand and proceed directly to the next level of ethical thinking. Hare calls this level the "critical" level, but I prefer to think of it as the "exploration" level. This is the topic of the next chapter.

SIX

Exploring Consequences

BEYOND RULES

When the good things that ethical rules exist to protect, support, or sustain conflict with each other; when we are unable to resolve the dilemma by giving priority to one of the rules in conflict; and when each of the rules is advocated by proponents who believe sincerely that following the rule they favor is the right solution to the issue, what can we do to resolve the disagreement? Posing this question leads us to a more fundamental question: what must a proposed resolution accomplish that would make it *right*?

Like other consequentialists, I contend that rules represent prior conclusions about the course of action that we believe will produce the most *good* (value) in the ethical situations in which they are applied.[1] That is, the action that a rule directs us to take—because it is the *right* action to take—is the action that will likely produce the best consequences, on balance and all things considered, for everyone affected by the ethical issue and how it is resolved. At the rules level of ethical thinking and discourse, this prediction is not explicit—it is implicit.[2] For example, the value we find in responsibility and reliability is implicit in the rule "Keep your promises." The value we attach to truthfulness, candor, and transparency is implicit in the rule "Tell the truth." At this level, rules make no explicit reference to the good they can be expected to produce because their purpose is to guide action by telling us what the *right* action is.

But when no rule provides us with a clear direction for action, further talk of what's right becomes unproductive. When this occurs, the question that arises is, "Given that we can't agree on what the *right* action is, what would be the *best* way to resolve the issue?" This question redirects us from the futile effort to determine what's right to the more promising task of ascertaining what's best. It directs us to identify and choose the outcome that will yield the most good—the one that will produce the best consequences.[3] If we believe it's important to continue trying to resolve the issue that divides us, we have no alternative but to work toward a shared judgment about what's best to do. Beyond the rules level (where it is deontological—i.e., concerned with what is right), ethical thinking at the exploration level is *consequentialist*—that is, concerned with what is best.

In order to identify the action that will yield the best consequences, we need to agree on the criteria for calling an outcome "best." But we can't agree about that without agreeing on the criteria for calling an outcome "good. What counts as a good (better, best) consequence? How do we make that determination?

Being unable at the exploration level to rely on rules to tell us what to do creates an additional problem. All our principles, standards, and criteria of goodness (value) are embedded in those rules. Because those rules are no longer unavailable to us, so too are our principles, standards, and criteria of goodness. According to consequentialists like Richard Hare, the only source of guidance that remains available to us is our noncognitive response to the outcomes that different courses of action can be expected to generate. When reflected on in *circumstances that are optimal for identifying them*, these responses—our feelings, desires, sensitivities, intuitions, and so forth—express our deepest sense of what is good, better, and best. They constitute the only information we can bring to bear in determining the relative value and importance of the goods we must reconcile in order to resolve the issue before us. Because the intuitive appeal, or "pull," of good things is all we have to work with, only their relative intensities matter.

At first blush, perhaps, this makes it sound as if we have to abandon rational thought in favor of a purely emotional response to an ethical dilemma. Weighing the intensities of our feelings calls to mind the image of a crowd of people "voting" wordlessly—shouting, cheering, applauding, or in some other way nonverbally indicating the depth of their approval or disapproval. But this won't do. We know people can have intense feelings that are out of proportion or otherwise inappropriate, considering what's at stake. Some folks, for example, feel intensely about saving a few thousand dollars more (to add to their existing millions or billions) when paying their annual taxes. Other folks feel intensely about eating, having a roof over their head, and seeing a doctor when they need to. The former group's desires can be (incredibly, but apparently actually) just as intense as those of the latter group.

In his claim that intensity of feeling is the only evaluative criterion we may consider at the critical (exploration) level, Hare invites an objection that has plagued ethical theories since the day of Jeremy Bentham and that prompted John Stuart Mill to amend his own theory considerably: why should we regard the feelings people happen to have—in particular, their immediate reactions and preexisting desires—as authoritative (definitive, conclusive) information concerning what is good, better, and best?

Hare recognizes we should reject the proposition that all desires are equal, whatever their content, if they are desired with equal intensity. He blunts this criticism by arguing that we need consider only people's "authentic" desires. These are the desires people *would* feel intensely if they were, in effect, autonomous decision makers, in the sense we have discussed in Chapter 3. Hare's critical-level ethical thinking is thus formulated, not in terms of people's existing desires, but in terms of *hypothetical* ones, that is, desires each person *would* have were she to choose in an *ideal choice situation* characterized by impartiality, full information, and sound reasoning. This argument, I believe, is persuasive. But we can elaborate on the formation of hypothetical desires in a way that makes the appeal to feelings and desires less worrisome—and as a practical matter, more workable. (We will address this matter in the next section.)

For the moment, let's be clear that, in determining what to do, a person should be *open to the possibility* that she will want to pursue an alternative to what she currently wants to do. She ought to be open to this possibility because—as a presumably rational decision-maker—she wishes to act in the manner that will yield the best consequences of all the options that are open to her. (See the section "Openness" in Chapter 3.) Although it may turn out that her existing ("de facto") desires are the ones she prefers to act on, at least she will have the opportunity to consider the desires she would have if she considered all the relevant information, examined the issue open-mindedly, and reasoned about it soundly. This conclusion implies that she is not just the person who has the intuitions, feelings, and desires she happens to have at a given time. She can also have other intuitions, feelings, and desires than she currently has—namely, the intuitions, feelings, and desires she would have if she allowed them to form in the conditions required for autonomous choice.

In other words, each of us has a "potential self" that can be realized more fully or less fully, depending on the effort we expend to make our choices autonomously. This self—part of the process that I am, extending backward and forward into time—remains to be realized. I can decide to become *this* self rather than the one I will become if I do not choose autonomously. It is my "prefer-able" self in that I would in fact prefer it, were I able to experience the contrast between it and my present self. The self that develops through autonomous choice is the self whose unique potential has been fully realized, and who in consequence thereof is able to experience and express his or her *individuality* (see Chapters 1 and 3).

THE ROLE OF AUTONOMOUS CHOICE IN EXPLORATION-LEVEL ETHICAL THINKING

As discussed in Chapter 4, when a person is faced with the challenge of making a genuine choice for herself alone (what I called earlier a "values" decision, i.e., a purely "self-regarding choice"—one that is not likely to have a substantial adverse impact on other persons), she should ask herself what she *would* choose in the conditions most conducive to autonomous choice. Thus, a person chooses *autonomously* if, in addition to being at liberty and not dependent on others for any essential resources (food, water, shelter, medical care, etc.), she

1. possesses all the information that's relevant to her decision, verifies its accuracy, and evaluates it thoroughly;
2. reasons properly about the circumstances in which she is choosing, the nature of the issue before her, and the options that are open to her;[4]
3. deliberates carefully;[5] and
4. is able and willing to think and act without being constrained or adversely influenced by limitations on and distortions in her thinking.[6]

These are requirements for choosing in ideal circumstances, of course, and as such represent aspirations rather than preconditions. But insofar as a person deliberates and chooses in these conditions, to that extent her choices will be made autonomously. These are the desires she *should* have, because they are the ones she *would* have if she made her choice in the foregoing conditions. Thus, if she prefers X now, based on what she currently believes and given her current ability to judge the consequences of her pursuing and realizing it, but she *would* prefer Y if she had greater knowledge of those consequences and were better able to assess the information at her disposal, then (assuming she prefers to realize more value rather than less[7]), she should make her choice on the basis of what she *would* desire, not on the basis of what she happens to desire.

Suppose, now, that everyone participating in ethical thinking at the exploration level is also thinking autonomously—as they should be, since each wishes to have his or her desires and other feelings considered in the course of resolving the ethical issue before them. As Hare argues, the desires to be considered by the participants in ethical thinking at this level are their hypothetical desires: the desires they *would* have if they were able to form them in the conditions required for autonomous choice-making. If all participants at the exploration level, in addition to thinking autonomously, "adopt the ethical point of view" (to be discussed in Chapter 7), they will form desires for actions that have *both* self-regarding *and* other-regarding good consequences. They will form desires for the latter because they will desire an ethical resolution to the issue confronting them, one that produces the best consequences for all, themselves included.[8] To achieve an *ethical* outcome, they must not give preference or priority to the well-being of one person over that of any other person. The purpose, point, or need (PPN) we have in our way of life for a word-concept like "ethical" (and related word-concepts such as "right," "fair," "equitable," etc.) is to ensure that we treat *all* persons with the respect and concern that will enable them not only to survive, but to live contentedly or happily and even, if possible, thrive and flourish.[9] This entails being "impartial" between the well-being of one person and that of another.[10]

Ethical choice-making, it thus turns out, has the same form and consists of the same tasks as autonomous choice-making, the important difference being that the former requires that we envision the well-being of *every* person who might be affected by our choice, not just ourselves. The two are identical, save for the difference that ethical thinking specifies one additional, albeit crucial, requirement: *adopt the ethical point of view.*

REAL (NOT IDEAL) DECISION MAKERS

At the exploration level of ethical thinking we try to determine what we *should* do by asking what we *would* choose (desire) to do if we could make our decision in the optimal conditions for thinking autonomously. In practice, of course, we can only aspire to deliberate as an "ideal decision maker," an imaginary person who meets all the criteria for making an ethical choice. (Hare calls her an "archangel.") The point is to strive to attain that aspiration to the greatest degree possible. The closer we can come to meeting each criterion, the sounder our judgment will be. In order to make a sound judgment about what is best for all who might be affected by the decision we arrive at, we must have access to the information contained in each person's perspective on the issue and how it might be resolved: her concerns, needs, intuitions, desires, sensitivities, dispositions, and aspirations, both actual and hypothetical. We obtain that information by *adopting the ethical point of view*. Doing so enables us to achieve the "impartiality"—equal concern and respect for all, ourselves included—that ethics requires.

The ethical point of view, however, is better understood as having as its goal "*pan*-partiality" rather than *im*partiality. To see what I mean by pan-partiality, recall the fable of the blind men and the elephant. The elephant's nature can't be comprehended fully by any of the blind men individually because the perspective of each is limited. Knowledge of the elephant has to be *constructed* from their combined viewpoints. Once each blind man, through dialogue with the others, has comprehended as fully as possible their various perspectives, he shares the information with the others, who have different perspectives. Although each of them retains what made his perspective unique, he adds to the common pool of information and in the process *transforms* it—altering it by placing it *in the context* of the others' unique perspectives. His thus expanded, enriched perspective now closely resembles their (similarly expanded and enriched) perspectives. As a result, each comprehends an emerging, enlarged perspective that they hold in common.

Adopting the ethical point of view requires this sort of melding or integrating of perspectives, in which none is assigned more importance than the others (at least not initially and not unilaterally). The chief step in that task is the effort to understand others' perspectives and to help them understand one's own. When this is accomplished, the participants will have achieved *mutual comprehension*. In the conception of process ethics I am proposing here—that is, a process of ethical dialogue and deliberation— mutual comprehension takes the place occupied in most theories of ethics by the requirement of impartiality. Strictly speaking, "impartiality" means regarding and responding to all individual perspectives equally, including one's own. But some perspectives might be "better" than others in the sense of containing more information or information that is more accurate, more reliable, more useful, more illuminating, and so forth. The point is to ensure that we give each perspective a sympathetic hearing and a genuine opportunity to influence us. Adopting the ethical point of view requires being as sympathetic as possible to those perspectives. "Pan-partiality," achieved through "mutual comprehension," better captures what ethics requires than does "impartiality."

It is difficult, if not impossible, to comprehend another person except through *dialogue*, a form (ideally) of face-to-face communication the aim of which is learning and understanding rather than arguing and persuading, and in which, accordingly, listening takes priority over speaking. In order to reach a sound ethical judgment, I must learn from you (or someone who can speak skillfully and faithfully for you). I must be able to ask you for clarification and explanation. Without you to help me understand, I risk projecting my own perceptions, interpretations, needs, or other feelings onto you.

By focusing on integrating (and subsequently deliberating) the perspectives of the persons who are likely to be affected by how the issue is resolved, we turn Hare's ideal decision maker from an imaginary omniscient individual (the "archangel") into a *group* whose members adopt the ethical point of view; obtain and consider all the relevant information and verify its accuracy; examine the issue open-mindedly; deliberate carefully; and endeavor to be maximally free from the influence of limitations and distortions in their thinking. By doing this, we improve on the idea of the ideal decision maker in two important ways. First, we move from a "monological" conception of ethical thinking to a "polylogical" conception. In the next chapter we will consider why this is crucial. Second, and equally important, we create the possibility of an actual, "real-world" stand-in for the imaginary ideal decision maker, who could never exist in reality. In *practice*, we can make the decision maker a group that, like the blind men in the fable, can know more and think better together than can any of its individual members acting as individuals.[11]

When people try to think ethically without the benefit of dialogue with others, they more closely resemble predialogue blind men than they do a single ideal decision maker. Although even as a group they can never achieve the omniscience of such a decision maker, they can approximate it by striving together to forge a shared perspective that, because all group members have adopted the ethical point of view and have committed themselves to the indispensable ethical requirement of inclusion,[12] contains the maximum amount of information and affords the best possible decision making based on it. The *right* thing to do is what this group concludes is *best*.

SEVEN

The Ethical Point of View

EQUAL CONSIDERATION AND MUTUAL COMPREHENSION

When good things conflict, ethical thinking requires that we adopt the ethical point of view. Often characterized as the ability and willingness to be impartial,[1] the ethical point of view is better thought of as the disposition to treat all persons as deserving of equal concern and respect for their well-being, and hence for what they need, value, and desire. Adopting the ethical point of view is a requirement of ethical thinking because we are bound by the PPN—the purpose, point, or need—of the word-concept "ethical" and its cognates to apply our ethical judgments in a way that treats all persons as deserving of equal concern and respect. If we wish to call our judgments, decisions, and action *ethical*, they must emerge from a process of thinking that fulfills the PPN of the concept.

Treating all persons as deserving of equal concern and respect requires giving "subjectively equal"[2] consideration to their needs, values, and desires. Genuinely equal consideration involves more than simply identifying or recognizing others' affective and conative states: what they need, value, desire, fear, and so forth. It means "comprehending" them in the context of the choice they face—understanding their situation as *they* experience it from *their* point of view. The term "comprehend" has the useful connotation of "encompassing" or "taking in," of "getting our arms around" a thing. To comprehend is to understand and appreciate how some other person, in *her* circumstances, with *her* experiences, needs, sensitivities, dispositions, and priorities, could be motivated as she is.

Why must I comprehend others' motivations? Because only then am I in a position to give them equal consideration as I weigh them against my own. Recall that, in order to be motivated to act, even in my self-interest, I must "appreciate" the potential an action holds for producing a certain quality and quantity of satisfaction. A purely intellectual conviction that a course of action or state of affairs holds value for me will not and could not—by itself, in the absence of a nonintellectual appreciation of the thing I believe holds value—motivate me to act. In order to reach a personal (self-regarding) decision about how to resolve a conflict between competing values, I must feel the pull that each exerts on me (i.e., the desire it stimulates in me).

In an ethical disagreement, however, I must feel the pull of an additional set of desires: my *as-if* desires—that is, others' desires, which I now comprehend. Comprehension—understanding and appreciation achieved through empathy—transforms my choice from an *inter*personal one into a quasi-*intra*personal one, so that when I choose between competing goods (to be precise, between the feelings associated with those goods), I give priority to the option indicated by the strongest desire: my personal (autonomously formed) desire, or my *as-if* desires (i.e., others' autonomously formed desires). Acting on the strongest desire is the *right* thing to do because it promises to yield the *best* consequences—the most good, the most value—for all concerned.

Unlike internal conflicts between goods experienced by an individual person facing a choice, disagreements between persons typically are marked by the inability or unwillingness of one person or both fully to appreciate the goods that motivate the other. For example, you and I shouldn't expect to resolve a disagreement over whether honesty requires complete and unreserved disclosure if we fail to understand and appreciate the deep-level motivations that underlie the other's position on the matter. Because each party to an ethical conflict must comprehend these motivations, a sound ethical judgment requires the *mutual* comprehension of each person by every other person. Mutual comprehension makes it possible to recast an ethical issue as a question of how *jointly* to prioritize goods that all affected by the issue can acknowledge as a justifiable source of motivation. It creates a "we" out of many "I"s.

Mutual comprehension does *not* require that I give up, suppress, or even subordinate the motivations that are the basis for my autonomously chosen priorities. It does require that I *expand my* point of view to include your motivations (that are the basis for your autonomously chosen priorities) so that they become quasi-real for me. Suppose you give priority to motivation M1 (which happens to be third in my ranking of goods), and I assign priority to M3 (which happens to be third in yours). The different orderings, or priorities, we give our respective motivations—specifically, the conflict between M1 and M3—stand in the way of a shared judgment about which to choose. If, however, I comprehend your motivations as if they were my own, and you comprehend my motivations as if they were your own, we can both experience, albeit vicariously, the dilemma that would confront each of us if we were making a purely personal choice between them. Mutual comprehension thus permits us to reconcile our conflicting motivations without giving up or subordinating our own. At the exploration level, equal consideration of our own motivations is built into the process of ethical thinking

Because the ultimate sources of human motivation are emotional in character—need, fear, pain, sensitivity, pleasure, revulsion, longing, and so forth (mediated, of course, by cognitive and quasi-cognitive word-concepts, beliefs, perceptions, interpretations, and so forth)—I can't comprehend with my intellect alone. For Maurice Friedman, writing about Martin Buber, the comprehension required is "a bold swinging into the other that demands the most intense action of one's being in order to make the other present in his whole uniqueness."[3] Only by imagining what it's like to *feel* the way you do can I understand and appreciate why you are moved as you are.[4] I may continue to disagree with you (indeed, I might become even more convinced that you're mistaken), but at least I'll see that you're motivated by considerations that *could* motivate me (or anyone else). At the same time, my own motivations lose none of their validity or force. Indeed, they will always be more real and more powerful, more immediate and potent for me than yours can be, no matter how sympathetic I am.

Comprehension thus requires me, not to put *myself* in your position, but to feel what it's like to be *you* in your position.[5] I must try to avoid projecting my own motivations onto you. If I put *myself* in your position, then what I understand is what *I* would feel in that situation, not what you feel. To comprehend, therefore, I have to use my imagination. Obviously, I don't have *precisely the same* experiences, perceptions, concerns, sensitivities, and dispositions that you have. To comprehend you, I must be able to relate what you feel to a motivation (rooted, as we will see, in a universal human need) that *could* produce such a feeling in *any* human being, myself included. This means that the greater the difference between us, the deeper I must probe in order to locate the motivational level at which we are "the same."

If I fail to locate this level, our differences may overwhelm us, and we'll be unable to understand and appreciate each other's motivation.

For example, consider the debate in the United States about stricter limits on the selling and purchasing of firearms. The ethical issue is whether it is right to restrict access to firearms further in order to reduce the number of fatalities and injuries caused by persons who might reasonably be considered at high risk for using them to commit serious crimes (or to commit suicide, accidentally injure themselves or others, etc.). Donald Braman and Dan Kahan note that the policy issue seems to turn on a narrow factual question: does ease of access to firearms in fact diminish public safety to such a degree that society can no longer tolerate it?[6] Supporters of measures to achieve greater public control over the sale and purchase of firearms argue that we have indeed reached a point at which we can no longer accept the current level of availability. Opponents of such measures do not disagree with the contention that society has reached a level of gun-related violence that is unacceptable. They counter, however, that the current availability of firearms is essential to public safety because it enables potential victims to retaliate or, ideally, to preempt violent acts. (Indeed, some go further and argue that access to firearms should be made easier, not more difficult.)

Braman and Kahan observe that efforts to resolve or mitigate issues that turn, ostensibly, on factual questions and that seem amenable to "objective" or "impartial" solutions concerning what's best for everyone (or for society or the public as a whole) often fail. The reason is that such efforts "ignore what really motivates individuals . . . namely, their cultural worldviews"—that is, their beliefs about what the world is like; what it *should* be like; the purpose of life (as it is viewed from their perspective); the roles people play, and should play, in that life, and so forth.

Supporters of more extensive or more effective regulation of firearms view the desire to possess firearms as evidence of a worldview that accepts resorting to physical force and violence in order to resolve disputes; subordinates values such as rationality, morality, civility, and equality to the value of physical power; tolerates indifference to the well-being of persons other than family, friends, and close associates; and promotes wariness of and hostility toward strangers, especially those who are "different." By calling for greater gun regulation, therefore, supporters implicitly reject the beliefs and attitudes they attribute to their opponents. In turn, they advocate an alternative vision of society characterized (in their view) by values such as rationality, morality, civility, equality, social solidarity, nonaggression, and nonviolence.

To opponents of more extensive or more stringent gun control, in contrast, guns express a worldview that emphasizes values traditionally associated with the frontier: human mastery over nature; individual reliance and self-sufficiency; personal honor and integrity; skepticism about the efficiency, effectiveness, and authority of collective action; the defense of the weak and innocent from social predators and wrongdoers; and ultimate moral equality in a world marked by social inequality. By resisting more extensive regulation of firearms, opponents implicitly reject the beliefs and attitudes *they* attribute to those who advocate a society characterized by values such as civility, social solidarity, nonaggression, and nonviolence, and who minimize or disregard the values that opponents consider important.

Comprehension does not require that we value the specific *objects* of each other's motivations. If you and I both value feeling energetic and physically robust, for example, we don't have to agree that running five miles a day is superior to yoga for this purpose. To comprehend your preference for high-intensity aerobic exercise, I don't have to go in for it myself. I only have to appreciate how, given similar circumstances and experience, you could find such exercise a satisfying way to achieve fitness and health. We'll comprehend each other if we realize that your preference for reenacting the days when we had to chase down our food and mine for relaxed contortion are both expressions of the underlying need for, and hence value of, physical vigor.

Of course, we might still disagree vehemently about the relative merits of these different ways of achieving it. People can remain locked in a disagreement despite having the same ultimate needs and values. But realizing that we have *something* in common, being able to recognize *something* of ourselves in each other, is crucial to achieving the mutual comprehension upon which ethical thinking depends. If we can connect each other's experiences, perceptions, concerns, sensitivities, and dispositions with the human needs we share, we might grasp how *any* human being, ourselves included, could hold the perspective that heretofore those with whom we disagree have considered alien and baffling, or even perverse. The greater the difference between ourselves and others, the deeper we must look in order to locate the motivational level at which we are "the same."

MUTUAL RESPECT

If we were incapable of comprehending each other at all, it would be impossible to form a genuinely shared (common) perspective. And if that were impossible, we would have no hope of participating in ethical thinking that, because it authorizes actions consistent with a shared judgment about how to reconcile conflicting goods, moves us beyond the paralysis that prevails in our rules-level ethical debates. Reluctance to concede that, despite our uniqueness, at some level we are "all the same" causes many persons to balk at the suggestion that we need to comprehend each other's perspective. They argue that we need only show each other mutual respect—as persons equal before the law, for example, or as holders of the same human or constitutional rights. On this view, we mustn't presume that "we're all the same," but rather that we're all thoroughly different. Accepting this fact reminds us that we cannot expect simply to declare our values "correct" or "proper," that instead we must redouble our commitment to the values of free thought and action, tolerance, and compromise. The only commonality we must acknowledge is the fact that we have to live together despite our differences.

Clearly, in many instances of ethical disagreement people possess enough respect for each other to work together despite their differences. Unfortunately, many people today not only presume dissimilarity, they can't see anything but dissimilarity. Difference comes to seem so great that people lose sight of each other's humanity. In extreme cases, people dehumanize others to the point where they are no longer fully persons, but mere objects to be acted on without consideration for what they feel. We should not presume, therefore, that dissimilar people recognize enough commonality even to grant each other a hearing.

Respect of the sort we prescribe for a person's status as a bearer of rights or as a citizen entitled to constitutional protection is too thin a principle to sustain heterogeneous communities and societies. Respect doesn't develop and can't be sustained in the absence of a measure of trust. Trust, in turn, requires acceptance of the "not-unreasonableness" of each other's motivations. How can you trust me without believing that my interests are rooted in needs that themselves are not unreasonable? How can you trust me without recognizing that I am moved by considerations that in the right circumstances might motivate anyone, yourself included? If you can't trust me, it will be hard for you to accord me the respect you owe me—unless it's the sort of pseudo-respect that's based ultimately on fear or shame.

Respect asks me to recognize that what motivates you can be valued by—that is, is "value-*able*" for—any human being, myself included. If I don't understand and appreciate your motivation, I won't see how *you* can value the object of your desire. I will regard *you* as incomprehensible, and hence at best I am likely to remain indifferent to you. Worse, I may attribute to you motivations I find threatening. Unnerved or discomfited, I might project my worst fears onto you. In either case, I won't develop the kind of respect for you that I require in order to work with you. If people who are deeply divided and estranged are to respond effectively to the ethical issues that confront our communities and society today, they must comprehend the emotional hunger, fear, anger, and other manifestations of unmet need that lead them to "objectify" others rather than work with them out of equal concern and goodwill.

Respect isn't automatic, and it doesn't arise in response solely to the recognition of different interests. For this reason, it can't be assumed. As Amy Gutmann and Dennis Thompson have written, genuine respect requires "a favorable attitude toward . . . the person with whom one disagrees."[7] A favorable attitude is what we mean by benevolence or goodwill. But goodwill depends on seeing that others are motivated by considerations that are comprehensible and that therefore might influence any human being. In some disputes, our awareness of commonality is overwhelmed, and we must try to interact in the absence of the respect we need in order to deliberate, judge, choose, and act together. But this is precisely why the effort to achieve mutual comprehension is imperative. If we can't assume that people are able and willing to comprehend each other, then ethics must enable and encourage them to do so.

Achieving mutual comprehension is the product of successfully adopting the ethical point of view. It joins our individual perspectives in such a way that we lose nothing of the distinctiveness and worth of each individual perspective, while at the same time we enhance each through exposing it to the others. Integration of perspectives does not entail the dilution or dissolution of our unique responses to the world. In the story of the blind men and the elephant, the men's individual perspectives are neither true nor untrue. The point has to do, rather, with completeness. No matter how substantial or significant it is, a single view remains incomplete—it captures only part of knowable reality.

On the other hand, the fact that each individual's perspective is limited and incomplete doesn't mean that any view is as good as any other. A given view may contain more information, or information that is more accurate, more relevant, more useful, or more important, than that of other views. Some views *are* better than others. Nevertheless, as George Watson has written, "the best view of the Taj Mahal is only one view among many. . . . The best [reading] of *Hamlet* still leaves things out."[8] Every person's perspective has something important to contribute to our understanding. Ignoring it, failing to give it its due, merely deprives us of potentially crucial information. The challenge is to preserve the unique contribution of each perspective while complementing it with the (partial) reality or truth of every other perspective.

When we comprehend others' motivations, it's important to acknowledge them. Explicitly acknowledging that we comprehend others helps achieve what Friedman, following Buber, calls "confirmation."[9] In general, to confirm a thing is to approve it, chiefly in the sense of attesting to its truth or vouching for its genuineness. In the context of ethical discourse, confirmation means that we attest to the validity, to the truth, of the needs, the beliefs about value, and the desires that motivate us. Confirmation serves what is perhaps the most important need we have when we're engaged in an ethical disagreement with others: our need for reassurance that we are individual human beings who have needs, beliefs about value, and feelings that are essential to our unique identities. Confirmation helps break down the isolation and anxiety we feel when we find ourselves in disagreement. It thereby opens the door to mutually supportive, and hence productive, working relationships.

Note in this connection that, because what we seek is confirmation as individuals, we need to be comprehended and confirmed by people who are similar enough to understand us, but who also differ from us. Our sense of uniqueness depends on being comprehended and confirmed by those whose dispositions, sensitivities, longings, experiences, beliefs, values, aspirations, and priorities contrast with our own. Such confirmation is more powerful than confirmation by people who are like us. Of course, because seeking confirmation from those who differ from us carries with it the risk that we will fail to obtain it, seeking confirmation from them is also more frightening.

IDENTITY NEEDS

Comprehension is especially important if people's identities are threatened by conflict. As Milton Rokeach observed, there is a class of beliefs that are even more important for a human being than what he or she values: the beliefs that collectively form her conception of herself, that tell her who she is.[10] These include conscious and unconscious physical, moral, and intellectual images; national, regional, ethnic, racial, and religious identities; and sexual, gender, generational, occupational, marital, and parental roles. "Identity cleavages" are political divisions that result from our differing identity-supporting beliefs.

"Identity" and the need for recognition (confirmation) of one's identity have grown in importance in recent times because the connections that once tied us to family, community, religion, ethnic origins, and other traditional sources of identity have weakened to the point where we've become unsure exactly who we are. Research by scholars such as Robert Bellah and his colleagues reveals a society populated by persons whose tendency to conceive of themselves almost exclusively as (atomized) individuals—abstracted from any defining social context—has left them with little to fall back on in the effort to define themselves.[11] For this reason, our values have taken on huge importance. We rely on them to tell us not only what is important in life but also who we are. Because what we care about is tied so closely to our self-conceptions, obtaining confirmation of our values is tantamount to being validated as persons. Hence we become anxious that what we care about will be challenged, undermined, or ignored.

Of course, this is just what occurs when ethical issues, and political issues that turn on them, arise. Involving as they do conflicts between things we value, such issues are likely to implicate our self-conceptions.[12] Because we crave the agreement and approval of others, we become defensive, intolerant, or hostile when what we care about isn't confirmed. How can I feel good about myself if I can't get others to confirm the feelings that are the touchstones of my worth as a person? Of all a person's psychological needs, the need to maintain an acceptable self-conception is the most important. Hence any belief or action that threatens a person's self-conception likely will be rejected. As a matter of psychological necessity, if what I care about conflicts with what you care about, I will resolve the conflict in favor of the self-conception I am most familiar and comfortable with.

The more dissimilar you and I are, the deeper will be the level at which comprehension must occur in order for us to recognize our common humanity. The more dissimilar we are, the less we share experiences, perceptions, circumstances, priorities, sensitivities, dispositions, and so forth. Only at the most basic levels of human motivation—at the level of universal human *needs*—can we reliably find the commonality that enables us to comprehend each other. Conversely, the more similar you and I are, the easier it is (other things being equal) for us to comprehend one another. The more we share or hold in common—values, beliefs, experiences, cultural background, personality characteristics, habits, personal circumstances, and so on—the less we have to struggle to understand and appreciate each other's motivations. Within a friendship, a relationship, a family, or even a community, mutual comprehension might be more or less automatic. But as difference grows—across personality types; value systems; cultures; socioeconomic classes; generations; religions; ideologies; perceptions and experiences—the more difficult it becomes to comprehend, and the more it becomes imperative to do so.

DIALOGUE

Fortunately, the uncertainty we experience concerning what we value, and the psychological insecurity that accompanies it, naturally incline us to care what others think. If those others stand ready to comprehend us, then ethical engagement can provide us with the recognition—the confirmation—we need. We might not get the agreement that initially we want and think we must have. But we can get something that, when it comes, we realize is even better: understanding, appreciation, and acknowledgment from persons who differ from us, and who differ with us.

Mutual comprehension depends on *dialogue*. As I use the term here, dialogue is an interpersonal process of listening, clarifying, and explaining undertaken for the purpose of comprehending peoples' concerns, experiences, needs, emotions (fear, anger, frustration, revulsion), sensitivities, values, priorities, and so forth. Dialogue is the communicative vehicle through which comprehension is achieved. It is thus an essential prerequisite for or concomitant of deliberation that moves toward a sound and broadly accepted collective conclusion, judgment, or decision.

Burkhalter et al. acknowledge that dialogue enables participants in ethical discussion to "jointly forge a shared way of speaking." They argue, however, that dialogue does *not* make it possible for participants to "see the world through one another's eyes" or "stand in each other's shoes."[13] Achieving this, they contend, would require participants to free themselves from their own cultural and historical experiences and in effect become the other.

This claim can be misinterpreted, however. The point the authors are warranted in making is that we should take great care to ensure that we see the world through the *other* person's eyes—not the world as *we* would see it were we in her circumstances. The danger is that we may put *ourselves* into the other's position, when what is needed is to understand how the other experiences things from her subjective point of view. It is correct to contend that this aspiration can never be realized fully, because it is impossible actually to be the other person. It is thus impossible for people to "shed their own cultural and historical experiences" fully.[14]

We must reject the conclusion, though, that we can know *nothing* of another person's subjective experience. Both logically and psychologically, it *is* possible to "see the world through another's eyes," to "stand in another's shoes," and to do so without "shedding" one's own point of view.[15] The self is more porous, its borders more permeable and flexible, than many identity theorists like to admit. Comprehension achieved through imaginative analogy to one's own experiences and perceptions is both feasible and essential. As Terentius said, "I am a human being. Nothing human is alien to me." Empathizing in no way diminishes the reality or importance of those aspects of one's own point of view that are constants in one's life. This, at least on one interpretation, is the moral of the blind men and the elephant.

Like ethics itself, mutual comprehension is an ideal to be pursued. No doubt we can never completely comprehend another person. But we shouldn't underestimate our capacity for comprehension. If it doesn't take much probing on my part to understand and appreciate your perspective, so much the better. Yet even when I do have to get well beneath the surface to comprehend your motivations, that undertaking requires only that I be able to relate imaginatively to motivations that any human being could have.

AGAINST EMPATHY

Reviewing Steven Pinker's book, *The Better Angels of Our Nature*, David Brooks writes that

> people who are empathetic are more sensitive to the perspectives and sufferings of others. They are more likely to make compassionate moral judgments. . . . [B]ut it's not clear [that empathy] actually motivates you to take moral action or prevents you from taking immoral action. . . . [I]t doesn't seem to help much when that action comes at a personal cost.[16]

Brooks cites the work of Jesse Prinz, who concludes that "empathy is not a major player when it comes to moral motivation. Its contribution is . . . nonexistent when costs are significant." Empathy is easily crushed by self-concern. Moreover, according to Prinz, empathy subverts justice; juries give lighter sentences to defendants that show remorse.

The point, Brooks says, is that empathy isn't enough, by itself, to ensure that people do the right thing. Indeed, empathy may not actually lead to choosing the ethically right course of action, especially if by doing what's right we incur a cost to our own interests. People who actually perform prosocial action don't only feel for those who are suffering—they feel compelled to act by a *sense of duty*. This is true. But it is true because most of us most of the time confine our ethical thinking to the rules level, where conventional principles and reasons usually suffice to guide our action. Like most of us, though, Brooks equates ethical thinking with the rules level and neglects the exploration level. At the former, acting ethically can, and frequently does, conflict with self-interested action. Conflict occurs because, at the rules level, ethical values and principles have been formulated without factoring in to the ethical decision-making process each actual person's interests, desires, needs, aspirations, values, principles, and so forth. At the exploration level, self-interest is factored in to the calculation. Exploratory ethical thinking asks me to give equal consideration to the interests, desires, needs, aspirations, and values of the other parties affected by the ethical issue, *and to my own*. It does not require me to ignore the question of what is good or best for me, but rather asks me only to weigh others' interests against my own and to work with them toward a judgment that will achieve the best consequences for all of us.

Moreover, I don't contend that empathy is a *sufficient* condition for *acting* ethically. Acting also requires desire, discipline, fortitude, determination, stamina, and persistence (and, at the rules level, good reasons). In a word, it requires character. Nor is empathy a sufficient condition for all that ethical thinking involves. Mutual comprehension is a necessary condition for thinking ethically at the exploration level, and hence for identifying the best (right) course of action. If ethical thinking depends solely on empathy to motivate people, it will prove beyond the reach of many, whose ability to empathize is limited, whether by nature or by nurture. We must look elsewhere for sources of motivation to adopt the ethical point of view. (We will return to this matter in Chapters 11 and 12.)

Brooks gives further evidence of conceiving rules-level ethical thinking as the whole of such thinking when he remarks that "empathy . . . subverts justice."[17] More precisely, certain *products* of empathizing—for example, compassion, benevolence, forgiveness, and even understanding—may conflict with and even outweigh "justice." At the rules level, such value conflicts are common. Precisely because such conflicts often occur, however, we have to move to exploratory ethical thinking to resolve them. Thus, for example, exploration-level ethical thinking enables us to weigh the good produced by practicing compassion (or "mercy") against the good achieved by pursuing "justice" and arriving at a sound judgment about how to balance the two.[18] If after weighing "compassion" and "justice" people conclude that compassion is relatively more important, then that is the right decision. In that case, compassion *serves* justice by balancing it, and both serve ethical rightness. If Brooks understood the structure of ethical thinking, he would see that exploration-level judgments cannot be critiqued by invoking rules-level principles.

It is reasonable to recommend, as Brooks does, that we "help people debate, understand, reform, revere, and enact their [ethical] codes." That is what exploration-level ethical thinking in large measure is: illuminating, clarifying, testing, critiquing, refining, reaffirming, and so forth—in a word, *reflecting.* Exploration-level ethical thinking is indispensable for sustaining the relevance and robustness of the norms, values, and principles that constitute rules-level ethical thought. But if we fail to go beyond the rules level to reflect on the values and principles that conflict at that level, we will be unable not only to "recover the ability to take satisfaction in doing the right thing," we will be unable to recover our ability to distinguish between good and bad, right and wrong—and hence to reestablish and sustain the social authority of our collective judgments. We will continue to languish in the confused, dispirited world MacIntyre describes, in which Hobbes's aphorism, "Whatsoever a man desireth, that for his own part he calleth good," is widely accepted as true, and Vladimir Bartol's dictum, "Nothing is true, everything is permitted," is widely acted upon.

We can do better than this. Practicing mutual comprehension is the key to adopting the ethical point of view, upon which our future increasingly depends.

EIGHT

Objective Ethics

The Good

"What is good?" How do we know something is good? What gives a good thing its value? How do we know something is more valuable or less valuable than something else? Let's begin with the observation that good is intangible—we can't see it, touch it, hold it. So how do we know what it is? As Hare observes, "good" means, roughly, "having the characteristic qualities (whatever they are) that are commendable in the kind of thing described as good." To say something is good is to commend it, with the implication that we are commending it on certain grounds, because of certain features it exhibits. More precisely, to say something is good is to say that, by having those features, the thing meets certain requirements that are not explicitly mentioned: those associated with the purpose, point, or need (PPN) we have in our way of life for the word-concept "good." Whenever we use "good" to describe something, those requirements must be met in order for our characterization to qualify as a correct application of "good."

The purpose, point, or need for "good" in our way of life, I have suggested, is to enable us to identify, approve, and recommend those things—objects, conditions, experiences, aspirations, ways of living, attitudes, actions, and so on—that contribute to the ability of human beings to live life well: to survive, to thrive, to flourish in their individuality. Things that are good contribute to serving or fulfilling this PPN. For example, consider the concept "chair." Being able to sit on something other than the floor is good because it serves requirements that we human beings have. We have this concept because we want to be able to think about, talk about, and make things that enable us to remain in an upright, comfortable position for long periods of time without having to lie down or stand up. A *good* chair is one we commend for serving this point or need particularly well.

On a consequentialist ethical view (like Hare's or John Stuart Mill's), our fundamental ethical duty is to follow the "greatest happiness" principle: always act so as to produce the greatest total happiness for all persons who will be affected by the consequences of our actions. Good things are things that contribute to this purpose. As we've seen, though, good things frequently conflict. In turn, conflict creates dilemmas of choice: if we can't obtain as much of both goods as we want, how do we choose between them? This question is especially difficult to answer when the conflict gives rise to interpersonal disagreements. If person A values X highly and person B values Y just as highly, how do we weigh and balance these values so that we maximize A and B's happiness?

If X and Y (and the other diverse goods human beings seek to achieve or obtain through their actions) could be translated into different *quantities* of a single measure like "goodness" (or "pleasure" or "utility"), we could compare and rank them. In other words, if we could find some "common denominator" for X and Y, we might be able to calculate a solution like this: "X generates nine units of goodness (for A), and Y generates seven points of goodness (for B), so maximizing their (combined) happiness requires that we make Y a somewhat higher priority than X." Mill's predecessors, Jeremy Bentham and James Mill (his father), attempted to do just that. They claimed that everything we do is motivated, ultimately, by the desire to experience pleasure and to avoid pain. In their view, the goods we seek differ only in terms of the quantity of pleasure or pain they produce. If this were true, we could balance conflicting goods like X and Y by favoring Y slightly over X to ensure than person B gets as close to seven point's worth of pleasure as possible, even if person A gets a little less than the nine point's worth she would like.

Philosophers have had a great deal of difficulty, though, figuring out how to translate conflicting goods into different quantities of a single measure. The chief difficulty is that most goods seem to differ *qualitatively* from each other, making them hard to compare, and hence to rank. John Stuart Mill was one of those philosophers who was dissatisfied with the idea of undifferentiated notions like pleasure and utility. He agreed that some kinds of satisfaction are more desirable and more valuable than others. He found it difficult to reduce distinctive goods like health, freedom, virtue, autonomy, creativity, and so forth to pleasure or utility because these and other goods produce qualitatively distinct satisfactions.

When Mill writes that our ethical duty is to act in a way that maximizes the happiness of all, he has in mind a conception of happiness that is perhaps better understood as human well-being or flourishing, with its implication of diversity, complexity, and structure.[1] He says explicitly that "utility" should be understood "in a larger sense," as "grounded in the permanent interests of man *as a progressive being*" (emphasis added). Mill placed his theory of utilitarian ethics in the larger context of human nature, which is developmental or progressive. That is to say, human nature is not what a human being *is* at a given point in time, but rather a developmental *range* she can pass through.[2] The individual self is a *process*—it can and does change.[3] A person's well-being at a given point in time depends on her developmental stage and on her circumstances.[4] Hence what is good and best for her also depends on these two variables. His theory of ethics, therefore, must be understood in the larger context of a conception of human nature and potential that is developmental or progressive and has as its goal the realization of each person's individuality.

Mill's approach to ethical thinking presupposes, therefore, that we will reflect on what is good and will reach a sound conclusion about which course of action will yield the most benefit for everyone concerned.[5] Reflection is essential because people who have experienced both "higher" and "lower" pleasures tend to prefer the former (the "Aristotelian principle"[6]). Accordingly, a person engaged in ethical thinking must take fully into account— for both herself and for others—the "higher pleasures" that lead to and constitute full human development.[7] If people might achieve a well-being of higher quality by developing their potential, we must weigh that against the loss to them in terms of present satisfaction, happiness, and so forth. This is precisely what we do, of course, when we insist that children acquire an education and that they learn to defer immediate gratification in the interest of a greater or better gratification later on.[8]

Mill's view that ethical thinking requires people to form their own personal conceptions of the good dovetails squarely with Hare's contention that the motivations (desires and related feelings) we must weigh at the exploration level of ethical thinking are the ones people *would* choose to be motivated by and to act on if they were thinking autonomously. If what is best for an individual person is the fulfillment of her potential and the realization of her individuality, then what is best for all people is the fulfillment of everyone's potential and the realization of everyone's individuality. We promote the ethical goal of achieving the "greatest happiness of the greatest number" by seeking the best consequences for all persons in terms of the fulfillment of each person's potential, the realization of his or her individuality. Accordingly, the "greatest happiness" will be diversely constituted—made up of many distinct types of satisfaction, some of which are (depending on the circumstances) better or more important than others.

THE REALITY OF VALUE

At the exploration level of ethical thinking, we reflect together in an effort to identify the desires we would form in conditions conducive to autonomous choice. Those desires and our reflections on them are subjective in the sense that they are experienced by individual human subjects. But this doesn't mean that the ethical judgments we reach are purely personal. Indeed, we may justifiably claim that our ethically deliberated judgments are *objective*.

Here we can benefit from a distinction offered by John Searle.[9] According to Searle, physical things like energy, gravity, and bipedal carbon-based life forms are "ontologically objective"—they have a real existence that's independent of any person's perceptions, beliefs, feelings, attitudes, desires, aversions, and so forth. Brains, for example, are ontologically objective. Minds, in contrast, are ontologically *sub*jective: they don't exist apart from brains and brain-based electrochemical processes. They can be directly apprehended only subjectively, from within the first-person perspective of a sensing, perceiving, interpreting human being. The experiences of pain, pleasure, fear, anger, desire, satisfaction, or revulsion are ontologically subjective as well. So are all products of minds, including perceptions, thoughts, ideas, beliefs, judgments, choices, decisions, rules, aspirations, ideals, and social norms.

What about good (value)? Many good things are ontologically *ob*jective: clean air, for example, or food, or a person we love. But "goodness"—the quality that makes good things good—is ontologically *sub*jective. It can be *epistemically* objective, however. When we engage in ethical thinking at the exploration level—that is, when all of us are striving to choose autonomously and have adopted the ethical point of view—the judgment we reach together will be independent of our personal views, and hence epistemically objective. The (always provisional) conclusions that emerge from our (continuing) dialogue and deliberation at the exploration level thus constitute *knowledge* of what is good and bad, right and wrong. Although we construct that knowledge, we do so by taking an empirical approach that's not so different from the one we take to establish epistemically objective facts about the world.

Is it possible, though, to go beyond epistemic objectivity and move closer to a view of value or goodness that is *ontologically* objective? In *Reason, Truth, and History*,[10] Hilary Putnam explains that the dichotomy of fact and value is overdrawn. It has persisted because of confusion between the *meaning* of a concept and the *properties* (features, characteristics) of things that count as "instantiations" (examples, instances) of the concept. Philosophers long maintained that "good," for example, couldn't be defined as "pleasurable," "satisfying," or other terms, because a thing might be described using any of those terms, and yet the question could still be asked, "But is it *good*?" For example, although someone might assert that taking a narcotic is pleasurable, we could still ask, "But is it good?" Clearly, it might not be. If "goodness" is a property, it can't be the property "productive of pleasure." So "good" must be some "nonnatural" (nonphysical) property that all good things have. But if a property isn't physical—that is, detectable, observable, or measurable the way the real-world objects and phenomena studied by science are—then its existence can't be "confirmed" (verified or not falsified) by scientific methods. If science can't detect, observe, and measure it, it's not real. And if it's not real, we can't learn or know anything about it—there's nothing to know. At most, it's just something human beings feel and express.

But concepts (like "good") and properties (like "productive of pleasure") aren't the same thing. Different concepts can imply or specify different properties. It's easier to see this if we understand that every concept— "chair," "table," "good," "truth," "fact," "knowledge"—consists of what Julius Kovesi calls a *formal element* and a *material element*.[11] The formal element is where meaning resides. Meaning, as Wittgenstein showed, is determined by the *use* we have for the concept in our way of life. In the terminology of this book, the formal element contains the "purpose, point, or need" (PPN)—the "use"—we have for creating and continuing to use the concept. A concept's meaning is governed by that PPN. The PPN tells us what *criteria* a thing must meet if it's to be considered an example of the concept.

The material element, in contrast, is the set of all things that, because they meet the criteria specified by the PPN, may be considered examples of the concept. The PPN of "good," I've suggested, is to help us identify, approve, recommend, protect, and promote things that are conducive to well-being, that contribute to our ability to survive, thrive, flourish, live contentedly or happily, and so forth. Things that *are* good contribute to serving or fulfilling this PPN. If they do, the statement that they are good is a *factual claim* that can be settled, at least in principle, through observation, experiment, and measurement. But "good" (or "goodness") is not a *property* of the examples that make up a concept's material element. "Good" *means* that the examples fulfill or contribute to its PPN. The meaning of an evaluative concept like "good" is distinct from the question of what examples actually fulfill its PPN, and that question is an empirical one: a question we can answer only through careful, systematic observation or experimentation.

Putnam illustrates the relationship between meaning and facts with an example drawn from Saul Kripke's discussion of "epistemically contingent necessary truths," which are "metaphysically necessary truths that have to be learned empirically."[12] These are facts that are determined by the actual world we live in. They can't be known in advance; they have to be discovered—learned empirically. In the case of "good" and related terms indicating value, we can't know what qualifies as an instance or example of it until we find out what meets its PPN.

Putnam asks us to suppose that someone asserts that it's logically possible for "temperature" to be something other than "mean molecular kinetic energy" (its technical definition). According to Putnam, Kripke says that once we've created the term "temperature" to talk about the amount of *heat* in an object; and once we've discovered that, in our actual world where we have a PPN for such a concept, the amount of heat in an object (measured by its temperature) *empirically turns out to be* its mean molecular kinetic energy, it is *not* logically possible for temperature to be anything *but* mean molecular kinetic energy.

Thus, if someone were to imagine a logically possible world in which there are objects that feel hot or cold, and the sensations they produce in a sentient being are explained by a *different* mechanism than mean molecular kinetic energy, then in *that* world temperature is *not* mean molecular kinetic energy. In that world, something other than mean molecular kinetic energy is responsible for how much heat objects contain, and hence for how hot or cold those objects would feel to us. In the actual world we inhabit, however, temperature *is* mean molecular kinetic energy. Anything that indicates temperature—anything that feels hot or cold—is exhibiting mean molecular kinetic energy, and vice versa. Temperature is a feature of our own, actually existing world.

The concept "temperature," then, is tethered by an inelastic leash to the conditions of the actual world in which it has been formed to serve or fulfill that concept's PPN.[13] It's a *necessary* truth, though one *we cannot know in advance*, that temperature *is* mean molecular kinetic energy. Put another way, mean molecular kinetic energy is an essential property of "temperature," though it took empirical investigation to discover this fact. The fact that too much or too little heat can be painful or even dangerous to human beings (or other living creatures) is relevant to how we regard it and how we act in response to it. But it's no less a fact for that—it's not just somebody's subjective belief, opinion, interpretation, preference, or personal definition.

The example of temperature helps explain the relationship between the meaning of "good," which derives from that concept's PPN, and the properties we ascribe to things that qualify as instances or examples of "good." If, first, the term "good" exists in our language for the purpose of (among other things) identifying the quality and quantity of benefit that any human being will find in an object, experience, phenomenon, activity, condition, etc.; and if, second, we've discovered that, in our actual world where we have a PPN for such a concept, good (goodness, value, etc.) is a function of the contribution an object, experience, or condition makes to a person's well-being; then it is *not* logically possible for something to be good unless it has the potential to benefit a person or contribute to his or her well-being. From the beginning, we have had to evaluate objects, experiences, phenomena, conditions, activities, and so on in order to predict whether an experience is one we can safely and usefully desire and seek—whether it will *in fact* support, sustain, or advance the ability of human beings to survive, thrive, flourish, and so forth. All evaluative concepts, from the most general ("good") to the most specific ("bold," "downy," "invigorating"), enable us to identify, approve, know, recommend, recall, and predict whether an experience, situation, object, or other aim of our choice will benefit us.

Propositions about what is good, then—at least insofar as we are concerned with what benefits humans, and perhaps other sentient creatures—are "epistemically contingent necessary truths." They are, at least in part, *ontologically objective*. More precisely, they are *as* objective as are statements about something like temperature. The *concept* of good is ontologically subjective. But the features, qualities, attributes, or characteristics that make good things good *are* independent of our minds. Food, freedom, and fairness, for example, are good because their features, qualities, attributes, etc. cause human beings to have an experience or elicit from them a response that contributes to a person's well-being. To assert that having food, or enjoying freedom, or being treated fairly is good is to make a prediction of the form: if you seek and experience this thing, you will find it is beneficial—it contributes to your well-being. Goodness (value) thus exists in the *relationship* between the features, qualities, etc. of things and the "natural" (typical, statistically normal) human experience of them. In the actual world human beings inhabit, some things do *in fact* support, sustain, or advance the ability of human beings to live life well, and some things *in fact* do not.

VALUE AND NEEDS

Writing about freedom, William Connolly has argued that the evaluative importance we attach to that condition stems from "its identification of factors pertinent to human well-being in situations where something is absent. . . . [Any theory about human beings must make] the assumption that there are specifically or uniquely human capacities. . . ."[14] For this reason, our conception of freedom is bounded by our notions of *what might be worthwhile doing*. There is a necessary connection between judgments about *freedom* and judgments of *valuable* action.

Connolly's observation applies a fortiori to the idea of human good. Whether we are thinking autonomously to determine what is best for ourselves alone or are thinking ethically at the exploration level about what is best for all persons who might be affected by a given way of resolving an issue, we must take account of factual information having a bearing on the evaluative dispositions and desires we are trying to assess, rank, and choose between.

One type of information we must take into account consists of "epistemically contingent but empirically necessary" truths about human nature. An account of human needs, like that first proposed by Abraham Maslow[15] and revised subsequently by others, might give us a starting point for deliberation concerning which actions, experiences, conditions, purposes, goals, states of affairs, ideals, aspirations, ways of living, etc. are in fact good.[16] A theory supported by empirical evidence concerning what has value for human beings would be especially helpful for deliberation at the exploration level of ethical thinking. There, we must decide what things hold value and how much value they hold relative to each other, and we must ask whether the desires we happen to have are the ones we *would* have if we were to think autonomously.

Although it is far from the last word on what human beings require or seek, Maslow's theory of human needs possesses enough empirical and intuitive strength to support the beginning of a dialogue concerning "the good" for human beings.[17] Needs are a fundamental feature of human existence. They are the ultimate source or well-spring of all motivation. Hence they profoundly influence our value beliefs: the reasons we invoke to explain and justify what we believe, feel, want, and do; our attitudes and dispositions; and our desires.

To be sure, cultural and social norms shape and influence both what qualifies as value and how we attempt to realize it. But Maslow showed that all human beings are motivated by needs that are genetic in origin, that are apparently unchanging, and that are common to all human beings. When human ends, goals, and aspirations are studied cross-culturally, he argued, they prove to be far more universal than the various methods taken in different cultures to achieve them.[18] That is, while methods for promoting human good or realizing value vary greatly among human cultures, societies, and epochs, people's ultimate ends seem to be identical. Because human needs are universal, ultimately what is good, valuable, and desirable for human beings is universal as well.[19]

According to Maslow, needs emerge in a rough hierarchy reflecting their relative importance to a person's well-being. He believed that the overall progressive fulfillment of needs from the bottom of the hierarchy to the top is both natural and necessary—natural in the sense that it's possible empirically to observe the spontaneous emergence of needs in the rough order he identified, necessary in the sense that, in general, lower needs (i.e., relatively more fundamental or essential needs, those that assert themselves most strongly and persistently) must be fulfilled to a substantial degree before a person is motivated to seek fulfillment of other needs. Although the idea of a hierarchy can give the impression that needs emerge in a fixed and invariable sequence, this is not the case. Depending on the person's internal conditions and external circumstances, any particular need may take priority over any other, waxing and waning over time. Lower needs never go away; they recede and remain quiescent as long as they are being adequately met, but remain a source of potential motivation.

One way, then, to understand what good or value *is*—in contrast to what "good" or "value" *means*—is to view it as the ability of an object, phenomenon, condition, feature, activity, or experience to generate the satisfaction that comes with fulfilling a human need. This conclusion is noteworthy because it suggests we can construct a theory of ethics in which it is possible to appeal to a concept of the good for human beings that is epistemically objective—and ontologically semiobjective—and hence independent of the beliefs and desires people happen to have, which rest on habit, socialization, tradition, familiarity, predisposition, or arbitrary decree. Evidence like that adduced by Maslow and others supports the proposition that promoting human well-being by enabling people to meet their needs and to realize their full potential as human beings is, as a matter of empirical fact, good. Indeed, he believed the results of his research implied that there are values (including ethical principles) that are common to the human species and that can be supported scientifically by observing the healthiest and happiest among us. Things that contribute to human well-being *are in fact good things.* "Good" doesn't *mean* these things—"good" *is* these things.

Our long experience as an evolving species has revealed (and continues to reveal) what human beings require in order to flourish. In parallel, and as part of our distinctively human cultural evolution, we have sought continuously to clarify the meaning of "good" and to specify its constituent values. *The fulfillment of human needs is a shared purpose that provides us with a universal and constant standard of evaluation.* Having formed the word-concept "good" to serve this purpose, we can proceed to investigate, verify or falsify, and reach sound conclusions (however tentative they may prove to be) about the objects, phenomena, experiences, conditions, and ways of living that, as a matter of empirical fact, constitute this "epistemically contingent necessary truth."

When we undertake that investigation—as Maslow, Max-Neef, and others over the course of human history have done—we find evidence suggesting what, at least prima facie, has value (and what does not). Good (for human beings) isn't something we desire or intuit or have revealed to us—it is something we *discover.* As Putnam notes, our concepts of human nature and human good probably never will settle definitively, because human beings continue to evolve as the world they create and inhabit changes. We revise our theories of both as our experience accumulates and our perspectives change. This process, which Kovesi calls "elucidating the good," in all likelihood has no "ideal terminus." Even so, the question is not one of logic, definition, meaning, or rhetorical bootstrapping, but of discovering the "epistemically contingent necessary truth" about the nature of good (value), *given* its PPN and given the facts about human beings, in particular their most important needs.

THE GOOD AND ETHICS

If one accepts that the PPN of "good" has to do with human well-being (development, thriving, flourishing, etc.), evidence such as that adduced by Maslow, Max-Neef, and others suggests that value—what *is* good—consists in those things that yield the satisfaction that comes with meeting our needs. Thus, when we deliberate at the exploration level of ethical thinking in order to identify and weigh the consequences of different ways of responding to the issue that divides us, we have the material required to construct a *universal standard* to which we can refer as we compare and prioritize the goods in conflict. That standard—human need—is prima facie valid for "anyone" (though not necessarily for everyone).

Maslow believed that the development and self-actualization of people would increase their self-knowledge and self-understanding. As a person comes to know herself, she better understands her own needs and how to satisfy them. But she also comes to understand others as well. Because all members of the human species have the same basic needs, *self*-understanding leads to a better understanding of *other* human beings. The person who recognizes and seeks to fulfill her own higher needs will achieve an "enlightened self-interest" in acting sympathetically, compassionately, and benevolently toward others. As Frank Goble puts it:

> People who have enough basic satisfaction to look for love and respect tend to develop such qualities as loyalty, friendliness, and civic consciousness. In short, the more each person grows and thrives, the greater the total positive effect on society.[20] To accept as intrinsic an antagonism between instincts and society, between individual interests and social interests [is] a terrific begging of the question. Individual and social interests *under healthy social conditions* are synergic and not antagonistic.[21] (emphasis added)

A needs-based theory of human good provides, if not a foundation, at least a point of departure for forming, investigating, and revising hypotheses about what is good. Because promoting the good, or well-being, of "anyone" is encompassed by the PPN of "ethics," we have a jumping-off point from which to begin reconstructing ethics through discussion of both scientific evidence and experience-based traditional wisdom that bears on the nature of human beings, as defined by their needs and potential, and hence on the question of what holds value for them.

"HIGHER" AND "LOWER" GOODS

If Mill's conception of happiness (utility) is diversely constituted—composed of many distinct types of satisfaction—how is the order of priority between these discrete goods to be determined when they conflict?[22] Moreover, how do we ensure that a person's individuality will be developed within "the limits imposed by the rights and interests of others," and that no one, not even "the strong man of genius," will be allowed to develop himself at the cost of the individuality of others?[23] After all, if consequentialism appeals to general happiness (well-being) as the basis for a particular judgment about how to resolve conflicts, then maximizing it might permit, or even require, sacrificing the interests of some persons in developing their individuality in order to promote a net increase in the realization of others.

Richard Wollheim offers a defense of Mill's theory that helps reconcile his avowedly utilitarian (consequentialist) ethics with his contention that there are pleasures or satisfactions that are qualitatively "higher" than others. Wollheim argues that Mill's conception of happiness/well-being is not uniform, but "complex." By proposing that happiness/well-being is diversely constituted, Mill demonstrates that, for purposes of ethical thinking, *happiness properly understood* can indeed be regarded as the highest value. Wollheim supports his claim by comparing Mill's view to Isaiah Berlin's. Berlin is well known for his compelling argument supporting value pluralism: the contention that human values are many, not just one, and that among those many values there is none to which all others invariably must be subordinated.[24] Values tend to appear in groupings in which their role and importance change, both from person to person and even within a given person over time and circumstances. Berlin's pluralism is a pluralism without a settled, unchanging hierarchy.

As Wollheim points out, however, whether we are considering Mill's view of value pluralism or Berlin's, the fact that values are many and distinct is first and foremost an insight applicable to the *individual's* task of prioritizing them for herself. It says nothing about the relationship between one person's ranking of values and another's (except to make it abundantly clear that societies and communities ought to grant their members considerable freedom to make their own choices). Value pluralism does *not* say that there must or even can be a multiplicity of *ethical systems*, that is, different sets of rules for resolving conflicts between values and for settling or managing disagreements between persons. A plurality of values is compatible with a single ethical system that requires that the personal value rankings of different individuals *be reconcilable*.[25] Indeed, this is precisely what both Hare's consequentialist ethical theory (as I have interpreted it) and Mill's utilitarian ethics require. It is the legitimate and indispensable task of people thinking ethically to determine how best to *balance* and *reconcile* values and value rankings when they conflict. The principle of achieving balance and reconciliation must guide our effort to weigh the consequences for all who will be affected by the ethical choice toward which we are working.

Mill accepted that human beings might reasonably choose for themselves among a wide variety of ways of living. But he rejected the view, prevalent today, that virtually any way of living is as valid as any other. Within a certain range, it's difficult to demonstrate that one ideal is better than another. And that's just as well, because people differ in their psychologies, experiences, circumstances, and in the ways these interact. If the freedom to choose a way of life suitable to their individual needs, sensitivities, and dispositions were not available, they would be unable to attain the level of well-being and individuality of which they are capable.

But free and deliberate choice of a way of life is only one element of individuality.[26] A person's choice should also help develop her full potential. What might have been a worthy and reasonable way of living in the (historical, economic, political, social, cultural, personal) circumstances in which it was formed may cease to be so when new circumstances arise. The autonomous person must always be ready to reexamine what she believes and how she lives, and be willing to revise these as new evidence warrants—not just because autonomy is good for her, but because ethics requires autonomous thinkers—especially at the exploration level—to help decide what is best and hence right. As Mill wrote, "there is always need of persons not only to discover new truths, and point out when what were once truths are true no longer, but also to commence new practices, and set the example of more enlightened conduct, and better taste and sense in human life."[27]

NINE

Objective Ethics

The Right

DETERMINING WHAT IS BEST FOR ALL

When the values, purposes, principles, or priorities of two or more persons or groups conflict, *whose* values should be honored first or given priority if not all can be supported equally? If people's values and priorities reflect their needs, then whose needs should be addressed first? And which of one person's needs should be met before other people can expect support in meeting their needs? In other words, at what point in Maslow's hierarchy should we reduce active support for person A's needs in order to increase our support for person B's? Does Hare's consequentialism, like other utilitarian ethical theories, require a nonutilitarian principle of distributive justice to answer these questions?

John Rawls, for example, attempts to predict the substantive principles of justice that rationally self-interested persons would choose if they were to reason together without knowledge of their particular circumstances in life.[1] The liberty principle he postulates says that each person should enjoy the greatest amount of liberty compatible with the same amount for everyone else. The difference principle says that any inequality we permit in the distribution of economic and social advantages must, first, benefit everyone, and second, must benefit the worst off the most. The difference principle ensures that a certain minimum or threshold level of economic and social well-being must be achieved by the worst off before the liberty principle takes effect. Thereafter, the liberty principle takes priority over redistributive goals.

A distributive principle such as Rawls's difference principle is an example of a conclusion that persons *actually participating* in exploration-level ethical thinking might reach. On a consequentialist view like Hare's, however, the only formula available to persons thinking together ethically at the exploration level is: "best consequences for all," interpreted in accordance with the fundamental ethical requirement of equal concern and respect for everyone. It is impossible, though, to predict the details of the judgment that would result from applying this principle, and for two reasons. First, the decision must be made in full knowledge of the actual conditions that prevail in the community or society in which participants are thinking together. Second, participants must know the perspectives and interests of all persons who might be affected by the decision. Because the process of ethical thinking is the only way to obtain this information, a judgment that takes it fully into account will not be formed until the process is complete.

The point is that, no matter how compelling the argument in support of a particular theoretical prediction like Rawls's might be, we cannot know, in advance of people *actually* thinking together ethically, what they will decide. It is therefore unreasonable to expect an answer to the question of distributive justice *before* people engage in exploration-level ethical thinking about it. Whatever distribution they agree to will be the one that ensures the best consequences for all. Moreover, if ethical dialogue and deliberation is, as it ought to be, a social practice that operates continuously, knowledge about what constitutes best consequences will emerge inductively over time as particular judgments accumulate and it becomes possible to generalize across a large number of cases. A widely accepted (rules-level) principle of distributive justice (or any other form of justice) will emerge only *after* we succeed in establishing and sustaining a widely accepted practice of dialogical and deliberative ethical discourse.

Moreover, on the view of ethics I am elaborating here, the ideal decision maker (introduced in Chapter 6) is not an individual, but rather a maximally inclusive group of persons who will be affected, however indirectly, by the exploration-level decision they reach, and who therefore have a stake in how the issue is resolved. In order to fulfill the requirement of the concept "ethics" that all those engaged in ethical thinking adopt the ethical point of view, the group's members must seek to comprehend each other's needs, values, priorities, experiences, prior learning, and other factors that have shaped their perspectives. By achieving mutual comprehension, participants in the process of thinking ethically become better able to reach a judgment *as if* they were an individual decision maker. Their ability to mimic the deliberations of an individual decision maker obviates the need for a distributive principle or formula. Just as a person has no need of a guide for "distributing" her good to herself, so a group of persons who fully comprehend (understand and appreciate) each other's perspective have no need for such a guide. In this way we preserve the pure consequentialism of ethical thinking at the exploration level.

We are now in a position to consider another frequent criticism of consequentialist ethical theories (specifically, utilitarian theories), namely, that seeking the greatest *total* happiness (utility, well-being, etc.) of all who will be affected, no matter how indirectly or slightly, would require us to eliminate all distinctions between people (as Rawls's theory, though not consequentialist, does). For example, utilitarianism arguably would require that any gap in the material prosperity of the wealthiest people and the poorest be closed completely. More fundamentally (and worse, some would say), it would require us to care just as much about people we've never met and never will meet as about the people closest to us: our immediate family and friends. The result, allegedly, would be to abandon the ideas of personal responsibility and justice, which often require that people be treated differently, in favor of a bland and uniform (and possibly harmful) "equality."

But this criticism rests on a profound misunderstanding of what ethics requires. Ethics requires us, after comprehending the perspectives of others, to weigh their interests (needs, values, desires, hopes, aspirations, etc.) against our own. Ethics does *not* demand that gains and losses "zero out" in some arithmetically reductionist sense. The good cannot be reduced to a common denominator that would enable us to add and subtract what one person gains and another loses. People naturally care more about persons closest to them, individuals whose happiness and well-being constitute a substantial component of their own, and for whose happiness and well-being they bear a large measure of responsibility. Seeking to apply some sort of mechanically "equal" or "fair" allocation of good would result in assigning less weight to the well-being of those closest to us than to others who are more distant.

But ethics does not demand this kind of calculation. Instead, it insists that we weigh our own well-being, which may include our desire for the well-being of those we care about, against the well-being of others—but after we have empathized as fully as possible with them *and they* have empathized as fully as possible with us. All parties to a conflict must adopt the ethical point of view and hence must endeavor to achieve mutual comprehension. Moreover, we are bound to compare not the actually exist-ing desires people have, but rather their autonomously chosen ones. If our hypothetical desires are stronger than the hypothetical desires of others, then ours will prevail and the shared decision we reach will reflect that fact.

Thus the criticism fails that consequentialism ignores the claim on us of those dearest to us, of those for whom we bear special responsibility, or of those whom we are actually in a position to help. Such factors must enter into our deliberations. So too must the wise adage that the ideal should not be the enemy of the good, or even the merely better. At the exploration level, intensity of desire shaped by personal autonomy and mutual comprehen-sion helps us determine what is best for everyone affected. "Everyone" will include those closest to us. Human psychology—specifically, our inherited tendency to favor "self-regarding" versus "other-regarding" actions—limits our ability to give equal consideration to people far away, to those quite dif-ferent from us, and to future generations (even to our direct descendants). This is something our partners in ethical thinking will understand and accept.

Critics of consequentialism overlook the question of what our partners in ethical thinking would actually expect from us if they were adopting the ethical point of view and were thinking together with us. Critics conceive of ethics as a solitary practice undertaken by the individual, as a "mono-logical" activity. But if we conceive it correctly as a participatory practice in which people partner with others and engage in dialogue and delibera-tion over issues—that is, if we view it as a "polylogical" activity—the judg-ment indicating the right thing to do will not be "one-sided." Indeed, it seems likely that most of our ethical interlocutors will not seek nearly as much from us as we fear they might. Rawls actually might have made a realistic guess (not recognized as such by his critics) that "the least among us" would not ask for much more than an effective safety net, genuine opportunities to improve their well-being, and a fair set of ground rules that can't be skewed or "gamed" by the more powerful to the latter's advantage.

Even if by natural disposition we can adopt the ethical point of view more readily with regard to persons whom we know and care more about, we nevertheless can aspire to greater empathy, concern, and respect for those not within our narrowly circumscribed sociocultural and temporal circles. The reach of our *collective* empathy can and should exceed the reach of our individual empathy. What we must not do is ignore, minimize, or dis-tort information that reaches us concerning the needs of others. Just as we can develop the virtue of open-mindedness, so we can develop the virtue of empathy for others' needs. Ethics does not require altruism, still less self-abnegation. It does, however, require that we take responsibility for promoting the good wherever it can be most effectively and usefully advanced, whether at home, across town, abroad, or in the next generation.

EXPLORATION-LEVEL THINKING AND CONTEXT

Like the legal principles that have grown out of the common law, the rules we invoke and apply at the rules level of ethical thinking are generalizations that emerged, over time, from a multitude of particular judgments. When they conflict, or when they cannot be applied unproblematically to a novel situation or circumstance, we must turn to ethical thinking at the exploration level. This level is analogous to an appellate court proceeding where judges consider a case that could not be resolved straightforwardly by a lower court. When, as members of a group, organization, tribe, community, culture, or society, we think ethically at the exploration level, we act as a kind of ethical "appellate court" (with the notable exception, of course, that this "court" lacks the socially constructed authority to enforce its judgments; only our acceptance of the procedure and of the judgment reached can influence our actions).

The analogy to the legal system is apt because deliberating values in the abstract—individual freedom versus social harmony, for example—seldom leads to consensus about which to assign priority. In order to determine what weight each should carry, we must place values in the context of a specific instance of conflict. As the venerable legal adage has it, "General rules do not decide specific cases." Although we can imagine situations or circumstances that people have never experienced or (as far as we can know) will ever experience, our ability to predict and evaluate consequences depends heavily on what we have already experienced. The ability to imagine presupposes enough experience to render intelligible what is imagined. If what is imagined or conceived does not bear some relation in some key respects to what people have in fact experienced, they will not make sense of it.

When we think ethically at the exploration level, then, we must know what "our experience" has revealed. To predict and evaluate situations and circumstances that will occur in the future, we must know about the situations and circumstances that have occurred in the past. In short, we must have at our disposal the raw material of examples, instances, and cases. Reaching a deliberative judgment in a *particular* context requires not just weighing the values in conflict, but weighing them in *different* contexts and comparing them. In order to determine whether to assign X or Y priority in situation S, we need first to consider the consequences in instances where each would clearly take precedence.[2]

"Successive approximation," or working "from the ends toward the middle," helps ensure that we take up the most difficult cases—the ones that lie in the "gray area" at the midsection of the continuum—only after having examined less challenging ones that illuminate the quality and quantity of the value that would be realized by choosing X rather than Y, and vice versa. Working toward more difficult examples from less difficult ones affords us the opportunity to consider whether small changes in the facts are substantial enough to alter the way or the extent to which we prioritize X and Y.[3]

TRANSCENDING THE PERSONAL WHILE PRESERVING IT

Like most theories of ethics, Hare's utilitarian consequentialism views ethical thinking as something each individual undertakes independently of others. It asks you and me to think as if we were each an ideal observer (an "archangel") who possesses perfect information and reasons flawlessly and without bias. The implication is that, in principle at least, as individuals we may reach a well-justified ethical judgment of our own. Hare's consequentialism is an example of what Janna Thompson calls "consensus" theories of ethical knowledge.[4] Such theories hold that an ethical conclusion is correct if and only if a person would reach it after reasoning about the issue in an ideal inquiry situation (such as the conditions required to support autonomous choice). This reflects the monological (one "voice" or one perspective) view that agreement can be reached by any person reasoning to a conclusion on her own. Even for Habermas,[5] Thompson argues, dialogue serves the merely pragmatic purpose of making cooperation or a political consensus possible. For most theorists, if we engage in dialogue, we do so not to determine what is ethically true, but only in order to reach a workable agreement.

An objectively correct (true) ethical conclusion, in contrast, would have to be valid from the point of view of everyone affected by an issue and the way it is resolved (and from the point of view of "anyone" who viewed the conclusion from outside the disagreement in the specific situation that occasioned the issue originally[6]). Traditionally, theories of ethics have aspired to the goal of achieving decisions or judgments that are (epistemically) "objective" in the sense of being impartial. The problem is, fulfilling that aspiration typically comes at the cost of eliminating the personal and the subjective entirely from ethical thinking. Rawls's theory is a good example. In the original position, people are permitted to know only the needs and values they have in common with others. They are denied knowledge of their specific identities, personalities, and circumstances. Just for this reason, some philosophers of ethics, such as Iris Marion Young, reject even the possibility of impartiality and insist that ethical reasoning is inescapably "situated." Similarly, Carol Gilligan believes that men and women perceive the world differently, and this affects their ethical reasoning. On her view, the gap between orientations is unbridgeable, at least by any reasoned means.

The answer to this apparent dilemma is polylogicality. Polylogical ethical thinking is ethical thinking that is conducted among persons, not by individuals acting alone. Judgments reached through discussion and conversation (*dia logos*) are collective. Each participant shares in the construction of the judgment. Janna Thompson claims—rightly, I believe—that ethical judgments are necessarily collective, because ethics requires a balancing of competing goods and interests among multiple parties. Those parties must have equally authoritative, equally influential voices in the process. Hence the importance of ethical thinking being practiced polylogically, not monologically.

On a monological view of ethical thinking, then, we individually strive to deliberate as an "ideal decision maker," an imaginary person who adopts the ethical point of view, gathers all the relevant information, examines the issue open-mindedly, and reasons about it soundly. In contrast, on a polylogical view of ethical thinking, the "ideal decision maker" is not an individual, but rather a maximally inclusive group of persons who will be affected, however indirectly, by the decision, and who therefore have a stake in how the issue is resolved.

Following Thompson, I contend that ethical thinking (at the exploration level) should be conceived as an inherently collective—a polylogical—activity in which we engage in dialogue and deliberation with others. As Wittgenstein's argument about the unintelligibility of a private language shows, knowledge is necessarily public. Only a community of inquirers can create (epistemically objective) knowledge through judgments and decisions that are independent of any given individual's partial, limited perspective. We can't accomplish this as individuals because we lack the linguistic authority to create and follow rules that enable us to make and sustain necessary distinctions, such as those between good and bad, right and wrong, desirable and undesirable, beneficial and harmful. We can know what is (objectively) good and right by integrating our epistemically subjective experiences with those of others through the epistemically objective medium of (public) language. Only an actual community can reach a conclusion that will qualify as ethical knowledge (i.e., objectively true ethical belief).

How do we square the "transcendent" nature of polylogical ethical thinking with the personal, partial, subjective character of individual perspectives and judgments without losing what is distinctive and important in each? As Thompson explains, an individual's ethical judgment isn't just affected by personal factors—it is inherently personal. It is rooted in and limited by the perceptions, cognitive processing, experiences, needs, norms, values, desires, and aspirations that make a person who he or she is. Even when it is fully rational and maximally well informed, a person's ethical judgment is incomplete; it is partial.[7] Although individual judgment makes an essential contribution to the construction of a collective judgment—as I have argued autonomous thinking does—only a collective judgment can achieve the impartiality (or better, pan-partiality) necessary to say that an ethical conclusion is valid for everyone (in the immediate case), and for anyone (for those not directly involved in the immediate case), and hence (objectively) correct or true.

But because we don't see how it's possible to achieve a collective (public) perspective while honoring what is valuable in each person's contribution, we have trouble accepting even the possibility of objectivity. In contemporary societies, many of us respond by asserting that a person's ethical beliefs can be called true only for herself. An individual can make authoritative judgments for herself, we assert, but not for others.

Thompson says this contention is no solution. First, the individual can experience ethical conflict within herself and be just as incapable of arriving at an authoritative judgment for herself as she is of reaching one that applies to herself and to others. Second, arguing that, because each person has her own distinctive perspective, she can reach judgments that are correct or right only for her, effectively concedes the point that our individual perspectives and judgments are limited and that others have information, experience, insights, etc. that might have a bearing on any judgment we reach. Third, the notion that our personal judgments can be *inter*personally authoritative runs directly counter to the ethical purpose of resolving conflict between persons having conflicting beliefs about what is good or right. Fourth, as noted throughout this book, Wittgenstein's private language argument shows that no individual can claim her self-generated ethical "rules" are true even for herself.[8]

The answer to this predicament, Thompson argues, is "ethical collectivism"—what I prefer to call polylogical ethical thinking. We can value the contribution of individual judgments, recognize that each is limited, and yet transcend them. At the exploration level of ethical thinking, we treat no individual perspective and judgment as immune from (constructive) criticism. We also have to assume that participants are motivated to reach a conclusion that all can accept as true (i.e., epistemically objective). Again, this is why adopting the ethical point of view is imperative. If each participant accepts that her own view is limited, however well founded it might be, she must accept that it is not ethically true for all, no matter how strongly she is disposed to believe that. Participants join in constructive discourse because they want to work toward the goal of ethical knowledge, which they can reach only by cooperatively thinking together. Whether people can be persuaded to adopt the ethical point of view for this purpose remains to be examined (in Chapter 12).

For Thompson, then, what I call exploration-level ethical dialogue and deliberation gives participants reason to regard their collectively formed conclusion as objectively correct. That said, a conclusion arrived at through exploration-level dialogue and deliberation cannot be regarded as the end point of ethical discourse, for closure is not possible. Rather, it is a continuing process and ongoing practice. The dialectic of ethical thinking does not end when a collective decision is made, because life and the world continue to change. Moreover, even if agreement were possible in principle, in practice participants may fail to reach one and only one conclusion. There is no way to rule out this possibility. Some ethical issues may have no unique solution.

Thompson considers whether ethical collectivism undermines individual responsibility for a person's decisions and actions. She believes it does not. But it *adds* a requirement of *collective* responsibility. Participants in discourse share responsibility for ensuring that their judgment is correct and for acknowledging that the action it prescribes is something they are required to perform. Ethical collectivism shifts some of the burden of ethical judgment from the individual to the collective. Rather than trying to make individuals impartial, it asks us to focus on the community and to regard *it* as the primary source of correct (epistemically objective) ethical decisions.

An individual can strive to live her life in accordance with her values and also strive for consensus about matters of common concern. An ethical collectivist knows the insights she contributes to ethical discourse arise from living her own life, just as others contribute from the experiences of theirs. She doesn't have to subordinate, diminish, or set aside her own concerns and experiences in order to make a contribution to ethical thinking. On the contrary, ethical collectivism encourages respect for individual differences. It inclines us to appreciate people for what they are and to recognize that their uniqueness is itself a reason for valuing and respecting them. An ethical collectivist realizes that her own ethical judgments are not the final word in the matter of what is ethically true. She knows that her ability to be a good ethical judge depends on others. Ethical collectivism encourages the virtues of empathy, tolerance, and humility.

An individual trying to think ethically alone has no means of transcending her limitations. Ethical collectivism enables us to do just that—by approaching the task of generating ethical knowledge as a product of collective determination rather than the determination of any single will. In doing so it gives us another axiological object of aspiration: the collective developmental potential of a community, a society, and ultimately humanity as a whole.

TEN

Negotiating Ethically

At the exploration level of ethical thinking, we attempt to resolve issues arising from conflicts between discrete goods by determining the *best* course of action that is open to us—best in terms of the consequences for everyone who will be affected by the decision we make. To resolve an ethical dilemma and the issue it generates, we must weigh and balance the consequences of different courses of action in terms of the goods in conflict. The measure of their weight is how intensely they are desired. The desires we must weigh and balance, however, are not just the desires we happen to have, but rather our "hypothetical" desires: the desires we *would* have if we formed them in the conditions that are optimal for autonomous choice-making, which we must establish and sustain subsequently as we think ethically at the exploration level.

As we saw in Chapter 3, a person chooses *autonomously* to the extent that she chooses in the conditions that are optimal for making a sound choice. In those conditions, a person

1. is free from external constraint or coercion;

2. is not dependent on others for essential resources (food, shelter, health, etc.);

3. possesses all the information that's relevant to her decision, does her best to verify its accuracy, and evaluates it thoroughly;

4. resists the adverse effects of limitations on and distortions in her thinking[1] and reasons skillfully about the circumstances in which she is

choosing, the nature of the issue before her, and the options that are open to her;[2]

5. deliberates carefully;[3] and

6. seeks to arrive at a judgment that indicates which course of action open to her is likely, on balance and all things considered, to yield the best possible consequences in terms of her personal well-being.

To secure the conditions required for *ethical* choice-making, we add to the foregoing criteria only the requirement that the person thinking autonomously adopt the ethical point of view, which she accomplishes through mutual comprehension of others' experiences, needs, feelings, and aspirations. Adopting the ethical point of view enables each participant in ethical choice-making to construct a shared, composite view of the issue to be resolved. Achieving this perspective mitigates the normal difficulty people encounter in trying to reach interpersonal agreements. By comprehending others, we discover that the ethical conflict facing us is not primarily a problem of the goods others seek being incompatible with those we seek for ourselves. Rather, the conflict is *intra*personal: we face a personal choice between goods that others value but that *we* value as well. Our hypothetical desires expand to include their desires for goods we *both* value. The conflict is not simply between our desires and theirs, but between our desires and our (hypothetical) "as-if" desires—that is, their desires, which we now experience as if they were our own.

Ethical thinking at the exploration level, then, has four chief characteristics: It is

1. *Inclusive.* To the greatest extent feasible, everyone who likely will be affected by the issue and the way it will be resolved participates on full and equal terms with the others. If every individual affected by the issue and the way it is resolved cannot participate personally, the perspective of each must be effectively articulated and advocated by participants who can sincerely and skillfully represent the views of those who are unable or unwilling to speak for themselves.

2. *Egalitarian.* The PPN (purpose, point, or need) of the concept "ethics" directs us to adopt the ethical point of view, usually interpreted to mean we must be impartial in considering both the goods in conflict and the persons whose well-being will be affected by how the conflict is resolved. Impartiality, however, is better understood as the requirement to treat all persons as deserving of equal concern and respect for their well-being. In

turn, showing equal concern and respect requires us as fully as possible to comprehend—to understand and appreciate—the experiences, concerns, values, and aspirations of those whom we owe that concern and respect.[4] Mutual comprehension enables us to make a quasi-intrapersonal choice between our desires and our "as-if" desires. In so doing, it ensures that we give equal weight to the well-being of others and helps prevent us from taking actions that are coercive, manipulative, or otherwise at odds with the best interests of our fellow deliberants.

3. *Deliberative*. In deliberative discourse we work toward our judgment about the best course of action by seeking and considering information that is relevant, accurate, sufficient, and illuminating. At the rules level, we seek to give one another reasons for believing that one rule ought to be assigned priority over another with which it conflicts. At the exploration level, our goal is to determine the *right* course of action to pursue by weighing the consequences of the options open to us and determining which best promotes the well-being of everyone affected.[5] To this end, we give equal consideration to each person's "hypothetical" (autonomously formed) desires.

4. *Objective*. Statements about what is good, better, and best have the same logical form as other statements of fact and can be established as such through empirical investigation of the sort undertaken by Maslow and others concerning human needs, the fulfillment of which yields value of varying qualities and quantities. When substantiated with adequate evidence, they constitute "epistemically contingent necessary truths." Such truths describe a relationship between the ontologically objective properties of objects, conditions, and other observable features of the world and human beings' ontologically subjective experience of and response to them. Statements about that relationship are thus epistemically objective and, at least in part, ontologically objective. Scientific evidence, supplemented by experience-based traditional wisdom that illuminates human needs and potential, provides us with the information we need to begin constructing a standard of value to which we can refer as we weigh and balance the goods in conflict and seek to maximize the well-being of all in terms of each person's interest in achieving and flourishing in his or her individuality.

Carried out with care, goodwill, and persistence, ethical thinking at the exploration level should reduce disagreement to the point where all participants can reach a shared judgment that—in the circumstances, on balance, and all things considered—a particular course of action is *best* among the options that are available to them. Not even epistemically objective collective judgments arrived at through exploration-level dialogue and deliberation are final, however. Like all knowledge, constructed ethical knowledge must be regarded as provisional, always open to revision in light of new evidence and changing circumstances. Because life and the world continue to change, ethical dialogue and deliberation must be a continuing process.

Even in the short term, though, we may reach a point in our discussion at which we can make no further progress. In a pluralist democracy, even exhaustive exploration-level ethical dialogue and deliberation of the highest quality might reach a point of severely diminishing returns without any one view emerging as clearly better supported and better argued than others. Even if agreement is possible in principle, in practice participants might continue to hold well-founded but divergent perspectives that prevent them from agreeing on a solution. There is no way to rule out this possibility. Some ethical issues may have no single, correct solution—there just are multiple objectively right solutions to them.

When further progress toward an objective ethical judgment appears unlikely, but we require a decision in order to move forward as a community or society, how do we proceed in a way that respects the purpose, point, or need we have for "ethical" and related terms in our way of life? How do we continue to think, talk, and act ethically? At what I call the "negotiation" level of ethical thinking, instead of continuing our effort to achieve an objective ethical judgment, we aim to negotiate a modus vivendi that will enable us to move forward despite unresolvable disagreement at the rules and exploration levels. At this third level (or stage) of ethical dialogue and deliberation, we seek "a way forward" that everyone can "live with" or "go along with."[6] Our aim is a broad consensus—not unanimous agreement—about which policy direction likely will produce the best consequences for all.

An important reason for beginning with ethical dialogue and deliberation at the rules level, then continuing our effort at the exploration level, is that participating conscientiously and with goodwill at these two levels (or stages) greatly increases the chances of eventually working out, at the negotiation level, a way forward we can all "live with" or "go along with." Moving through the three levels sequentially improves the prospects for success because it enables us to build a good working relationship with those with whom we disagree. Understanding, appreciating, acknowledging, and assisting others in meeting their needs, fulfilling their desires, honoring their values, and assuaging their concerns goes a long way toward eliciting cooperation from them for the purpose of working out a mutual accommodation.

THE NEGOTIATION LEVEL

The level of ethical thinking we will now consider enables and encourages participants to reach a judgment that all participants (and those who might be affected but cannot participate directly) can accept as the best solution to an issue they cannot fully resolve. That judgment constitutes *practical* ethical knowledge—knowing *how* to act when disagreement can't be eliminated, rather than knowing *that* X is the objectively correct answer. Continuing to observe the requirements of ethical thinking as we deliberate at the negotiation level is essential if we are to figure out the best way to proceed in the circumstances and given our irreconcilable differences.

One way to capture the essence of negotiation-level ethical thinking is to describe it as a principled process of seeking and achieving what Amy Gutmann and Dennis Thompson call *"moral accommodation."*[7] To accommodate another person is to be responsive to his or her needs, interests, desires, and so forth. It is to take them fully into account when deciding what to do—to consider and weigh their needs, interests, desires against one's own in an effort to achieve a fair balance between them.

Accommodation, Gutmann and Thompson argue, implies that

• We should practice "civic magnanimity." We should recognize and acknowledge the ethical standing of other persons and respect any beliefs and desires opposed to our own that are not unreasonable. Accordingly, we should demonstrate our readiness to work out a mutually acceptable resolution of our disagreement with them.

• In order to demonstrate magnanimity, we should practice an "economy of moral disagreement." We should try to find a way to pursue our own interests, values, priorities, etc. that minimizes the necessity of opposing others' efforts to pursue theirs, and that minimizes the adverse impact of our preferences on them. We should look for significant points of convergence between our own goals, objectives, and strategies and those of others we find it difficult to reconcile with our own. An economy of disagreement doesn't require settling for any agreement whatsoever, or pursuing agreement for the sake of agreement. It requires only agreement that is consistent with our own fundamental interests, values, priorities, etc. We should try to accommodate others' interests, values, priorities, etc. to the greatest extent possible without compromising our own. Nor does an economy of disagreement preclude or discourage vigorous challenges to the needs, interests, values, priorities, beliefs, principles, or desires of our fellow citizens when doing so is necessary to make an ethical case for our own position.

PRINCIPLED NEGOTIATION

Because we want to be persons of goodwill who adopt the ethical point of view, and because we must find a way to move forward together as a community or society despite continuing disagreement, at the negotiation level of public ethical thinking we must accommodate as much as possible each other's needs, interests, values, and priorities. It is entirely in keeping with ethical thinking at this level, however, that we ask others to acknowledge and accommodate *our* needs, interests, values, and priorities, just as we try to acknowledge and accommodate theirs.

The idea of accommodating others is consistent with the practical goals and methods of dispute resolution theory and practice. According to Jane Mansbridge,

> [public] deliberation is deeply compatible with several forms of negotiation, which are termed here "deliberative negotiation." . . . These forms are ideally based on mutual justification, mutual respect, and a search for both fair terms of interaction and fair outcomes. Again ideally, they do not involve coercive power. These deliberative forms of negotiation are in some tension with, but in practice can co-exist constructively with . . . negotiation [in which] participants . . . use coercive power . . . to achieve their ends.[8]

Ethical dialogue and deliberation at the negotiation level (stage) is highly desirable for the same reason that negotiation in dispute resolution theory and practice is desirable: because the usual approach of parties to a dispute or disagreement is to state a position or demand, argue for it, and make only such concessions as are necessary to reach agreement. As Roger Fisher and William Ury point out, people tend to see only two ways of interacting with each other: the "tough" way and the "easy" way.[9] A negotiator who takes the easy approach wants to avoid conflict, so she makes concessions to reach agreement. She's easy on both the merits of the issue and on those who disagree with her. The tough negotiator, in contrast, sees conflict as a test of strength and will, in which the tougher fares better. She feels she has to win, because the alternative (she assumes) is losing. She's tough on both the merits and on others. The assumption common to these two views is that there's an inescapable trade-off between getting what is important and getting along with people. The easy approach, though, often leads to painful compromise, while the tough approach often provokes resistance, imposes heavy costs on both parties, and strains their relationship.

Fisher and Ury recommend, therefore, that we practice the mutual accommodation of people's needs, feelings, values, priorities, and desires. They call a process that embodies such accommodation "principled negotiation." Principled negotiation is "tough on the merits of the issue, but easy on other people." It aims to achieve a result that is (1) *wise* (i.e., it meets the legitimate interests of the parties to the greatest extent possible; is durable; and takes into account common interests); (2) *efficient*; and (3) *improves or at least doesn't damage the relationship.*

Like Gutmann and Thompson's notion of moral accommodation, principled negotiation is a close approximation of the negotiation stage of ethical thinking. Adopting the ethical point of view is already implicit in Fisher and Ury's approach and is indicated clearly by their four fundamental principles of negotiation: (1) separate the people from the problem and make the relationship your priority; (2) focus on interests, not positions; (3) invent options for mutual gain; and (4) insist on objective criteria. With only some minor revisions in terminology and emphasis, these principles can serve as a blueprint for ethical thinking at the negotiation level.

1. Separate the relationship from the substance. Fisher and Ury urge us to avoid letting what we think about, suspect, fear, or find disagreeable or objectionable about our counterpart distract us from our goal, which is to reach an agreement. We should build mutual respect, understanding, and trust so that the *relationship* improves as we negotiate. In turn, an improving relationship will help us achieve greater and swifter progress toward an agreement.

Separating the people from the problem means distinguishing relationship issues (or "people problems") from disagreements over solutions and dealing with the two independently. In a subsequent book, Fisher, Ury, and Patton[10] observe that relationship difficulties tend to involve problems of perception, emotion, and communication. They suggest a number of basic strategies for handling problems of perception that are consistent with the rationale for adopting the ethical point of view:

• Respect your negotiating counterparts' interests the way you want them to respect yours. Demonstrate your goodwill. Strive to help them achieve what is best for them so they will reciprocate and help you obtain what is best for you. Your counterparts are your equals and your peers. In terms of negotiating a mutually satisfactory agreement, you are "on the same side." You are partners—you share responsibility for the success of the process and its outcomes. Resolving disagreement requires that people work together. In brief: cooperate, don't compete.

• Don't put *yourself* in their shoes—imagine being *them* in their shoes. You don't have to agree with their perspective. But it's important to understand what they think and feel, and why they think and feel the way they do.

• Discuss each other's perceptions in order to understand each other better and avoid projecting your fears onto one another (i.e., work to achieve "mutual comprehension"). Look for shared perceptions. Acknowledge these and build on them.

• Give your counterpart a stake in negotiating with you by making sure they realize they have no BATENS[11]—*b*etter *a*lternative *t*o an *e*thically *n*egotiated *s*olution—and that negotiating together is the only way to ensure they get the best outcome for themselves. Appeal to their self-interest and express your willingness to help them promote it. Make your proposals consistent with their values, principles, and self-image. Let them save face. Help them come out of the negotiation looking competent, principled, and successful.

2. Negotiate over interests. Concentrate on the things people really want and need, not what they *say* they want or need. Often, these aren't the same. (In the terms of this book, what people "really" want are the objects of their hypothetical desires, those they would identify through autonomous choice-making. Hypothetical desires are usually connected more directly and healthily to people's basic human needs than desires they have formed with little or no reflection.) People tend to take extreme positions that are designed to enable them to appear to be making concessions while gradually arriving at what they really want or need. This just wastes time and risks adding to the other side's distrust. Stating positions and making demands simply shows how little one party respects the other and how unimportant the relationship is.

3. Work toward a fair resolution. Propose, discuss, and agree to criteria that a mutually acceptable resolution must meet (e.g., one that is consistent with everyone's values, principles, and priorities). This is the balance that ethical thinking asks us to work toward. Then propose possible resolutions

that meet these criteria. Look at what others have done in similar situations to achieve good results. Consider adopting their best practices.

TWO EXAMPLES

In Chapter 7 we noted Braman and Kahan's contention that, in the debate over control of firearms in the United States, nearly everyone involved "ignore[s] what really motivates individuals . . . namely, their cultural worldviews."[12] Competing worldviews supply the evaluative and motivational factors that drive the gun control debate, predisposing individuals to accept certain factual assertions and to challenge others. Focusing on facts without first taking steps to comprehend and acknowledge people's worldviews ensures that unmet identity needs will take priority and hence will serve as a kind of emotional "filter" that inhibits their ability to assess factual assertions, both those they are inclined to accept and those they are inclined to reject.

The authors conclude, therefore, that the only kind of policy debate over gun control that might move the stakeholders closer to a shared view is one that intentionally, explicitly, and effectively "confirms" the underlying worldview and cultural vision to which they subscribe and with which their identities are bound up. Accordingly, the best strategy for reducing disagreement rooted in conflicting worldviews is for participants to explore their competing visions in ways that their adherents consider both meaningful and respectful. Put into the terminology of this book, the most effective way to reduce disagreement is for people to participate in dialogue designed to foster mutual comprehension.

Braman and Kahan propose three principles for public discussion of identity-related, emotionally charged political issues like gun control. The first is to place a positive emphasis on the meaning and significance for the stakeholders of their respective worldviews. Doing so implies (in my estimation) encouraging and assisting stakeholders as they undertake two tasks: describing and explaining their worldviews to others; and listening for comprehension as their fellow participants attempt to communicate theirs.

Second, disagreement can be reduced if opinion leaders within the larger communities of those subscribing to different worldviews are recruited (or emerge spontaneously) as supporters of one or more courses of action that the stakeholders might consider acceptable to all. By offering reassurance and political "cover," leaders "whose commitment to [a worldview is] beyond question" can lend their support to possible solutions that would satisfy the most important needs, concerns, and priorities of each community.

Finally, the order in which stakeholders take up matters over which they are divided is crucial. Braman and Kahan observe that the "cultural dispute resolution literature suggests the importance of discourse sequencing." They note that "parties to culturally grounded political conflict often do converge, ultimately, on [a policy or course of action] supported by empirical data and methods." They do so, however, only *after* they have followed the requirements of the first two principles cited above. Once each side's apprehension has diminished that the other(s) might unilaterally "win" the "zero-sum" contest in which they (mistakenly) assume they are engaged, members of all groups will become more receptive to factual assertions and supporting data they otherwise would dismiss as tendentious.

We might restate and elaborate the steps Braman and Kahan recommend as follows. In order to devise a solution to conflict rooted in contending worldviews, the parties to the disagreement should

1. *Engage in dialogue.* They should speak and listen for mutual comprehension in order to understand, appreciate, and acknowledge each other's point of view;
2. *Reframe* (redescribe) *the issue.* They should use language that honors the meaning and significance, and hence the emotional import, that the issue holds for the parties;
3. *Devise and submit policy proposals* that respect the identity needs and value priorities of all who have an interest in how the issue is resolved;
4. (a) *Negotiate mutually acceptable actions* that would help resolve the issue to the satisfaction of all participants, and (b) *invite opinion-leaders* to support (or even contribute to) the reframing and proposed actions being developed.

What kind of resolution might we reasonably expect from a group of stakeholders in the gun control debate if, acting in good faith, they were to participate in a process that meets these criteria? Wisely, Braman and Kahan do not try to predict the outcome: "We [are not] arguing that one can derive or deduce a 'solution' to the American gun controversy from these principles simply by thinking hard about the problem.[13] . . . [Any solution that emerges] will necessarily be shaped *through real-world political activity*" (emphasis added). In other words, every actual attempt to resolve or mitigate conflict is open-ended. It can't be predicted in advance because there simply are too many factors that depend on what a particular group of participants bring to the conversation (e.g., their needs, values, priorities, pressures, personalities, skills); how they frame the issue to be negotiated; and how they respond to each other.

That said, for the purpose of illustration we might speculate about one possible outcome (among a very large number of possibilities). Braman and Kahan, for example, imagine an outcome in which, in exchange for accepting and stating publicly that the Second Amendment creates a genuine individual right to gun ownership, opponents of stricter or more extensive control of firearms would agree to universal registration of all firearms.[14] Additionally, ". . . upon registration [of his or her firearm] . . . an owner would receive a tax rebate" or some other monetary compensation." Further, ". . . any time a citizen registers as a voter, as a juror, or as a keeper or bearer of a firearm, they would be presented with the opportunity to register all three on the same civic registration form."

Braman and Kahan point out that this solution reflects commitment to the principle of fair exchange, or what in this book I have called *reciprocity*, which lies at the heart of ethical thinking and action. It reflects as well the principle that "with rights come responsibilities." No right can be considered absolute because there is always some other good with which it will conflict and that must be weighed against it. Often that good is one that benefits persons other than the right holder, making the conflict an ethical issue. In a democracy, it is everyone's responsibility to think ethically about how to weigh and balance the goods in conflict. For this reason, negotiations over gun control must enable ordinary citizens, not just the most prominent stakeholders, to be involved in a meaningful way.

Braman and Kahan believe that the gun control debate might be resolved as they envision because they detect the same principles at work in the effort to resolve the dispute in France over abortion.[15] As in the United States, the abortion issue in France "had for decades provoked intense controversy between citizens committed to conflicting culturally laden ideals." The chief expression of the "pro-life" view was, of course, the survival and well-being of the fetus. But other concerns and values also were involved: the role played by full-time mothers in the well-being of the family, the community, and the nation; the importance of sustaining the well-being of the nuclear family; the desirability of continuity in families over multiple generations; the value of rootedness and connection to a place and its way of life; the wisdom of revering as mysteries events such as the advent and cessation of life and of accepting the trials and tribulations that befall us at moments throughout. On the "pro-choice" side of the issue, in contrast, proponents emphasized the values of gender equality; freedom (especially control over one's body—in particular, freedom from intrusion by men into decision making concerning the female body); the social and economic independence of women vis-à-vis men; and the importance to both the individual and to society of the full development of every person's human capacities and of equal opportunities to pursue achievements made possible by their development.

To their credit, the French have managed to address the competing concerns and priorities of this issue in a way that is broadly accepted. As a result, the issue has been largely removed as a source of political contention. They accomplished this by enacting a law permitting a woman to obtain an abortion during the first ten weeks of pregnancy (a period of time shorter than the twelve-week window that prevails in the United States). However, she may legally seek an abortion only if she certifies that the procedure is necessitated by an "emergency" or by personal "distress" severe enough to warrant assigning her personal well-being priority over the normal and presumptive right of the fetus to continue its development toward personhood. Significantly, the conditions that constitute "emergency" and "distress" are not defined or enumerated by the law. Moreover, no government official has the authority to second-guess or challenge the woman's certification that such a condition exists. After a woman certifies that she is facing an emergency or is in a state of personal distress, she must wait one week before obtaining an abortion, during which time she must accept counseling about the sources of state support available to her should she decide to forgo the procedure and have her child.

In their analysis, Braman and Kahan point out the ways in which the French law tries to balance the conflicting values that underlie the abortion issue:

> . . . [B]ecause no authority looks behind the individual woman's certification of emergency, those who support abortion rights can see the law as affirming personal autonomy. Yet because the law does require such certification, it also affirms the moral view of those who see fetal life as having intrinsic moral worth, and consequently see "abortion on demand" as a denigration of the sacred value of life. By including in the legislation provisions affirming concern for fetal life, women's liberty, and maternal health, the French legislature made it possible for both opponents and supporters of abortion to find evidence that the state respects their cultural identities.[16]

Braman and Kahan conclude that the success of acknowledging and honoring the meaning and significance that opponents in the French abortion debate attach to their differing worldviews shows that we often overlook a crucial fact about "the political economy of culturally-charged political conflicts." Despite appearances, such controversies are *not* typically "zero-sum"—that is, neither side must necessarily "lose" just because their opponent appears to "win." Granting a benefit to one party does not require that the opposing party accept a sacrifice. Most people in a community or society are satisfied if they believe the law respects their *own* particular worldview—they don't require that it *also* reject, invalidate, disrespect, or diminish the concerns, values, and priorities of people who hold some other worldview.

Much more might be said about how the requirements of ethical dialogue and deliberation at the negotiation level parallel or even restate the principles and methods of dispute resolution.[17] Many books have been written in this field, and the interested reader should consult them. I want to emphasize, however, that negotiating at the negotiation level of ethical dialogue and deliberation in instances of conflict rooted in different worldviews[18] and their associated value priorities is unlikely to prove productive and satisfactory *unless* the people who hold those worldviews and value priorities feel they are comprehended—understood, appreciated, and acknowledged— by others. Mutual comprehension is essential to ascertaining the identity needs of the stakeholders and to confirming their identities. For this reason, the negotiation level (stage) should be preceded by thorough and skillful dialogue and deliberation at the rules level and, especially, at the exploration level of ethical thinking.

ELEVEN

Why Think Ethically?

ETHICAL AND "RATIONAL" THINKING

Thinking ethically is widely considered, by both scholars and nonscholars, to be a personal preference—a free, voluntary choice of values, principles, and priorities for guiding one's own decisions and actions, especially when prevailing social norms offer no ready answer or seem at odds with one's intuitions about what is right, just, or best. As a personal act, thinking ethically may be admired and its absence lamented. But hardly anyone treats it as obligatory, especially when the stakes are high, as they are when an ethical issue has implications for the type of society we should have or the kind of citizens we should be. It's up to the individual, ultimately, to choose for herself. If her thinking leads her to the conclusion that it's in her interest to defer to (say) professional principles, organizational rules and priorities, directives from superiors, social norms, or decisions made by voting or other forms of adding up people's preferences or opinions, she might reasonably allow any of these to take precedence over what participants in a process of collaborative, polylogical ethical thinking would prescribe.

Ethics has long labored in the shadow of the concept of "rational" action and its assumption, rooted in a simplistic model of motivation (psychological egoism), that human beings are always motivated by self-interest, by the benefits that they personally expect to obtain. The worth of the object believed to be good and the desire for it are taken as given; it is assumed that, if a person desires it, then for her, at least, it is desir*able*. The principles and procedures of rational decision making are concerned, not with evaluating the ends of human action, but only with the means by which they may be achieved. Realizing value of the sort that acting ethically can be expected to generate is just one of many ends a rational actor might choose. If a self-interested action would lead to a greater "payoff"—benefit, satisfaction, pleasure, profit, advantage—then choosing that action would be rational, even if everyone else disapproves. Ethical choice and action are fine, but (as someone once quipped) only if a person goes in for that sort of thing.

The challenge for ethics in our era, then, is to show that we have good (and sufficient) reason to think together ethically and to act on the conclusion to which thinking ethically leads us.

BECAUSE IT *IS* IN OUR INTEREST

Generally speaking, the answer to why we should think ethically is "because it's in everyone's interest to do so." Everyone will be better off for participating in a collaborative practice of polylogical ethical dialogue and deliberation. There are a number of ways in which thinking ethically together can serve our interest. Let's consider some of them.

1. *Ethical thinking preserves our freedom.* When too many people use their freedom in ways that are disadvantageous or harmful to others, excessive, or otherwise unacceptable for society as a whole, government steps in. The glut of new laws passed every year by state and federal legislative bodies in the United States is in large measure a response to the fact that people are failing to consider possible adverse consequences of their actions for others and hence are failing to show self-restraint in their actions. That reduces everyone's freedom. If I want to preserve my own freedom, I should want others to join me in thinking ethically so that none of us acts in a way that prompts government to impose restrictions on our freedom.

2. *Thinking ethically helps me clarify what I ought to do and strengthens my resolve to do the right thing.* If an ethical issue arises and I'm unsure what I should do, participating in a public practice of ethical thinking will help me learn or confirm what ethics requires of me. If I've already formed my views, but wonder whether I've taken all relevant considerations into account, thinking ethically with others will help me modify or strengthen my views on the issue in question. It will help me fill gaps in my knowledge and understanding, iron out inconsistencies in my beliefs or intuitions, and develop more persuasive replies to others' arguments.[1]

Moreover, if I understand and accept that everyone's perspective is unavoidably partial and limited, I will realize I can't convince anyone else— and won't even know myself—that my judgment is right, or best, or true until I work through the issue with others, and together we either reach agreement or arrive at the point where no further facts, reasons, or arguments will change the conclusions we've reached. If we can agree, I may feel a satisfaction I haven't experienced previously or haven't been able even to imagine: the satisfaction of *knowing* what is right and sharing in that knowledge with others. Even if resolution proves elusive, by joining in public ethical discourse I can help diminish the frustration many of us feel at our current inability to resolve ethical dilemmas through reasoned discussion.

3. *Because ethical thinking promotes cooperation, it actually protects each person's self-interest.* Ethical thinking can help people generally, and perhaps me personally, resolve our differences without resorting to coercion or manipulation, both of which undermine the trust we need to have in each other and in our society's institutions. Ethical thinking makes it reasonable for us to cooperate. Treating each other with decency and respect helps us resolve, mitigate, or at least manage conflict more effectively, efficiently, and to the greater satisfaction of all. One obvious answer, then, to the question, "Why should I think and act ethically?" is that doing so will help create and sustain a community or society that functions better than one, like ours, in which mutual trust and goodwill are declining. Without trust, we would have to be constantly on guard against people who might take advantage of us or otherwise harm us.[2]

When we aren't sure whether to trust others, we are wary of cooperating with them. As a result, our default strategy is to pursue our self-interest independently of what others want or do. When we don't know whether to trust others, it "makes sense" (on a narrow view of rational self-interested action) for us to pursue our own self-interest independently. But because everyone is reasoning this way, it frequently turns out that we all end up with a less satisfactory result than we would have obtained had we cooperated.

Establishing and maintaining relationships of trust would help us solve one of the most challenging problems in democratic politics: the management of public goods. Examples include clean air and water, roads and bridges, national defense, access to the broadcast spectrum, the electrical power transmission grid, police service, public lands, disaster relief, fire protection, scientific knowledge, the legal system, airports, and the Internet.[3] Scholars have realized that the problem of managing public goods can be understood as a multiperson version of the "prisoner's dilemma" in game theory. In this simplified model of "rational" decision making, individual actors face a choice between pursuing their self-interest independently and pursuing it cooperatively—that is, while taking into account others' interests. As the prisoner's dilemma shows, the strategy of independent pursuit of self-interest typically leads to outcomes that are irrational. In contrast to free market exchanges, where (theoretically) everyone benefits from self-interested action in pursuit of private goods, prisoner's dilemma situations often arise when public goods are involved. For example, it's rational for anyone in the commercial fishing business to fish independently, but competition between commercial fishing interests can lead to depletion of the resource, which harms everybody. It's rational for a person to drive her own vehicle to work, but if everyone does that the highways become clogged with traffic. It's rational for people to disregard the pollution they contribute to the environment, but if everyone does that pollution reaches intolerable levels for everyone. It's rational for people to use as much water as they can afford, but when everyone does so there soon may not be enough for anyone.

Ethics protects against this condition (of rational individual action leading to irrational collective results) by making it reasonable for us to cooperate. If everyone thinks ethically, each of us will be better able to get more of what we need and want, at a lower cost, than we're able to get when skepticism, wariness, or blinkered self-interest attend interpersonal transactions. It's a mistake to believe we have to choose between the right thing to do and what's best for us. Ethical thinking doesn't require that we always put others' interests before our own; it doesn't require altruism. Nor does it invariably require us to make sacrifices for others—or even to compromise. Ethical thinking requires us to take into account the self-interests of *all* persons who might be affected—*including* ourselves. Participation in ethical thinking is more likely to serve and protect my interests than rejecting cooperation and relying on myself alone.

4. *It's in every person's interest to develop his or her individuality.* We have seen that autonomy makes an invaluable contribution to each person's attainment of true individuality, a condition in which he or she can genuinely flourish as a unique human being. As noted previously, ethical thinking requires people to form their own personal conceptions of the good. Such conceptions are necessary for both the individual and collective task of deliberating the consequences of pursuing different courses of action and choosing which to prioritize. Such conceptions are formed through autonomous choice. Like thinking autonomously about what is good (better, best) for oneself, ethical thinking at the exploration and negotiation levels affords

each of us the opportunity to determine which actions, conditions, experiences, and so forth in fact hold value, whatever our previous beliefs, attitudes, and desires might have been. I should think ethically because it's the best way for me to determine what is best for me. It helps me identify the desires I would have if I were in possession of all relevant information and were thinking clearly and reasoning soundly.

The fact that people find ethical thinking unappealing doesn't mean they don't have a good reason to engage in it. Each person has the potential to improve her character.[4] "Character" is the set of dispositions and habits that result from striving continuously to make ethical decisions. People who practice ethical thinking become ethical thinkers. Because ethical thinkers are likely to grow as well in terms of personal autonomy, a person faced with the choice between striving to fulfill her potential for characterological maturation and leaving it underdeveloped has a good (self-regarding) reason for choosing the former.

5. *Ethical thinking reveals the value in empathy.* Philo, the first-century Hellenistic Jewish philosopher, said, "Be kind, for everyone you meet is carrying a great burden." The pain that accompanies unfulfilled or imperfectly fulfilled need goes far toward explaining many of the attitudes, habits, motivations, and behaviors we find objectionable in others (and in ourselves). Disagreements are a universal response to the perception that one's needs are being frustrated or will be frustrated by having to yield to someone else's wishes. If we can learn to empathize with others who, like us, carry with them the burden of past and present emotional pain, thinking ethically will be easier to commence and sustain. If we can comprehend what's important to each other, deliberating together over conflicting goods and choosing which to prioritize will liberate our thinking from the clutches of psychological egoism.

Historically, of course, few cultures, communities, and societies have found it possible, or have even considered it desirable, to cultivate among their members the ability and willingness to empathize beyond the natural boundaries of kin, clan, and nation-state.[5] The point here, though, is that I might find there is more value for *me* in acting to alleviate or mitigate another's pain than in ignoring it, even if the other person's condition is only slightly improved as a result. By asking us to adopt the ethical point of view and to comprehend (empathize with) each other, ethical thinking may reveal the personal satisfaction of seeing others find relief in feeling understood and in being confirmed in their personhood, even if we can do little to meet their other pressing needs. Showing benevolence toward others—willing their good—costs little, but it can yield rich personal satisfactions for all concerned. If the Scottish "moral sense" philosophers of the 18th century—David Hume, Frances Hutcheson, Thomas Reid, and Adam Smith—were right, all of us have an innate disposition to empathize with others.[6] The possibility that I will find benevolence to be worth the price I pay for showing it gives me a reason to think and act ethically.

6. *Ethical thinking is just as rational as "rational" choice-making.* Thinking rationally is usually conceived as consistently deciding and acting in a way that is beneficial for or advantageous to the decision maker/actor (whether she is thought of as maximizing her contentment, or "satisficing" it, or something else). But defenders of rational thinking often conflate two very different propositions. One is the factual claim that people are strongly motivated by self-interest—by their desire to fulfill their desires. This is "psychological egoism." The other is a normative or prescriptive principle— "rational egoism"—which states that everyone should always do what's best for himself or herself. Proponents of the latter often seize on the former to bolster their argument. It's easy to see why rational egoism appeals to people (especially considering that the winners in a society are usually the ones who make the rules): it's easier, it's more "natural," for us to choose the action that is most likely to result in the best outcome for ourselves.

The normative principle of rational egoism, however, does not follow logically from the psychological principle. We don't have to accept the unwarranted conclusion that, because the behavior of human beings is influenced by psychological egoism, we ought to be guided in our thinking, choosing, and acting by our interest in fulfilling the desires we happen to have. Ethical thinking takes account of the interests and desires of *all* persons. Because it requires this, ethics *encompasses* what is in each person's "rational self-interest." (Indeed, it helps each ascertain what that self-interest consists in.) By situating the individual's choice-making within the context of everyone's entitlement to equal consideration, ethics helps temper and tame instrumental "rationality."

Moreover, human beings also have, as a product of our evolution as social creatures, a psychological disposition to cooperate with others, to help them, care for them, even sacrifice for them. Although this source of motivation might not be as powerful as psychological egoism (because it's the product of evolution at the level of the group, not the individual, where the survival instinct has been coded for in our genes), we seem to have a strong disposition nevertheless toward what we might call "psychological benevolence." Better known as reciprocity, or psychological reciprocity, it provides motivational support for a normative principle we might call "rational benevolence."

7. *Ethical thinking enacts the principle of reciprocity.* In *Democracy and Disagreement*, Amy Gutmann and Dennis Thompson argue that citizens in a democracy must accept the moral principle of *"reciprocity,"*[7] which consists of a commitment "to seek fair terms of cooperation for its own sake."[8] Fair cooperation for its own sake is one way of expressing the commitment to show others equal concern and respect by crafting political outcomes that are mutually beneficial. In public discourse, reciprocity means accepting that we "owe one another an effort" to provide "reciprocally acceptable reasons" for our political prescriptions.[9] We have a duty to offer such reasons—considerations that anyone can recognize as relevant and valid—even if ultimately we discount their force or reject them completely.[10]

Why should we give one another reciprocally acceptable reasons? Recall the traditional practice of cooperative "barn-raising." Historically, putting up a barn required more resources and labor than a typical family could marshal for this task. Barn-raising was a response to this need. Members of the community helped erect their neighbors' barns. Because each member was entitled to recruit others for help, the favor eventually would be returned to each participant. Barn-raising is a practical expression of the principle of reciprocity. As Elizabeth Anderson observes, "no participant is a net burden on others over the course of an entire life, since each farmer receives and gives in turn."[11] The ethical principle of reciprocity reminds us that we all have reason to support whatever produces the best consequences for everyone. It is supported by a motivational counterpart: *psychological* reciprocity, which disposes people to cooperate for the benefit of everyone in their primary social groups. Psychological reciprocity helps each of us recognize that we have a stake in a practice of mutual responsiveness to each other's needs and in cooperating with them to meet both their needs and our own. By adopting the ethical point of view and striving for mutual comprehension, we can extend the boundaries that define "our group" to include members of other groups. In turn, this will activate the motivational influence of psychological reciprocity and, along with it, the ethical reciprocity we have inherited from our predecessors.

8. *Ethical thinking is essential for determining whether our own self-interest justifiably may take precedence over the self-interests of others.* In *On What Matters*, Derek Parfit argues (as I have done) that right and wrong are specified by moral rules that, when generally accepted, "optimize" good—they promote the best overall consequences.[12] On this view ("Kantian

rule consequentialism"), ethical rules "optimize" the good. I take this to mean that, as I have put it, having those rules and following them tend to produce the best consequences, all things considered, from the "point of view of anyone." For Parfit, then, the justification for (rules-level) ethical principles is that following them usually will generate the best ("optimal") consequences. Parfit argues further that rules-level principles that produce the best consequences are ones it would be unreasonable for anyone to reject (hence his addition of "Kantian" to "rule consequentialism"). It would be unreasonable for anyone to reject basic ethical rules because we all have reason to support whatever produces the best consequences. Because the rules "optimize" the good—produce the best consequences—they do so for "anyone," including me. Therefore, I have reason to accept and follow them.[13]

But even if we have a reason for accepting and following an ethical rule, why not break it if it seems that doing so actually would produce better consequences? If in a given situation it makes sense to ask this question, that is because disagreement or uncertainty exists about whether the rule should apply and people should follow it. Parfit's response is to argue that I do *not* have reason to satisfy my own desires or preferences for their own sake, that is, simply because they're mine. The mere fact that an action would promote the satisfaction of some desire is *never in itself* a reason to perform that action. Desire-satisfaction is not a reason because we have no reason to satisfy a desire *irrespective of what the desire is for.* Whether we have a reason depends on the inherent good or value of what we want to do—not because we happen to desire it.

Parfit believes the good of one person is no more important (nor is it less so) than the good of any other person, and that therefore we lack justification for favoring our own interests over those of our fellows. He calls this the "axiom of personal impartiality." I must think *ethically* in order to determine whether the benefit I would gain from pursuing my own interest outweighs the cost to others in terms of their interests. Parfit believes we have reason to accept the "axiom of personal impartiality," and hence to engage in ethical deliberation: it is in *everyone*'s interest. If it's in everyone's interest, then it's in *my* interest as well.

IS IT ENOUGH?

Appearances to the contrary notwithstanding, ethics lies at the heart of our way of life, the way of life we call democratic and want to think of as democratic. Practices like civility and honesty in interpersonal interactions, institutions like free markets and democratic government, and more tangible goods—such as a habitable environment, a safe food supply, or an economically skilled citizenry—depend on people recognizing the indispensable value these shared goods hold for everyone. Participation in public ethical thinking can help us rediscover that our personal well-being depends on the well-being of the community or society of which we are members.

The willingness to think and act ethically—with "enlightened self-interest"—requires, though, that we discern the fundamental *relationality* of human beings. It means seeing that individuals aren't discrete, independent social "atoms," but are creatures situated in social contexts that together form an endless web of connections. Humanity is one vast ecosystem in which even the smallest actions send out ripples that can have far-ranging consequences. The fact that ethics is a socially constructed concept in our common language and way of life shows we understand that human beings are not discrete, separate, or unconnected "atoms" needing little of what others have to offer. Intuitively, we know it makes more sense to think of ourselves as "nodes" in dense networks of relationships that link everyone to everyone else.

If we can accept that "nodes in dense networks of relationships" is a better metaphor for individuals in society than "social atoms," we can see more readily that ethical thinking has *as much of a claim on our reason* as self-interested thinking does. Indeed, it has more of a claim, because thinking ethically with others leads to the best outcome for everyone, *given* the reality that human beings are social creatures and that conflicts between our values and priorities are inevitable. There is no warrant for privileging the narrowly economic (and ideological and outdated) concept of rational self-interest, with its crude and static concept of human motivation and its subjectivist concept of value. Thinking and acting ethically is perfectly rational from the perspective of socially constituted human individuals for whom connection with other human beings is of fundamental importance.

But do the conditions of contemporary life support our efforts to live good, meaningful lives? Or do they undermine them, making it harder rather than easier to do so? Do they make ethical thinking and action seem a burden and a struggle, something that requires nearly the patience, single-mindedness, and willpower of a saint to accomplish what every one of us should want and be able to strive for? Upon considering the reasons canvassed in this chapter for thinking ethically, would the "average," "typical" person consider them good and sufficient? Would they change her outlook?

Would they alter her priorities? Would they lead her to act with greater concern and respect for her fellow human beings?

Do the reasons we have suffice? Can they compete with the natural inclination we all feel to elevate our own self-interest and to refuse to sacrifice it to the needs, desires, and aspirations of others? Do those reasons even begin to approach the kind of motivation William James had in mind when he spoke of the need for a "moral equivalent of war"—for a shared purpose that can elicit from us the same willingness to sacrifice, and the same self-restraint and self-discipline that a threat to our national independence does, but that is guided by an overriding commitment to the individual flourishing of all?

The answer, I believe, is clear: they do not.

TWELVE

Ethical Heroism

LIBERALISM, ETHICS, AND PURPOSE

Since the 17th century, the leitmotif in Western political thought has been that of "liberation." Enlightenment thinkers sought to free humanity from necessity, hardship, and adversity.[1] Their vision was a vision of the world progressively liberated from the ills of ignorance, a new world in which the constraints imposed by nature would be replaced by the free choice of rational human beings.[2] In the Enlightenment worldview, history is the story of continuous improvement in human life made possible by our ability, through science, reason, and the primacy of individual happiness, to control the conditions of our existence and to turn them to human benefit.[3]

From the standpoint of economics and social policy, a key element of Enlightenment thought has been that, because wealth is a necessary condition for efforts to eliminate the suffering that has always marked human life, material prosperity must take precedence over most other policy aims (assuming the preconditions of personal freedom, individual and collective security, and social stability are adequately met).[4] Without question, material prosperity is valuable. It lets us turn our time and energy to the development of our capacities for learning, creativity, health, service, and appreciation of the world and of life. It must be given its due, therefore, and not treated lightly or taken for granted.

But material prosperity is only one good among many. It is neither absolute—thoroughly beneficial, without cost or negative consequence—nor is it invariably the highest good, justifiably accorded invariable priority. Indeed, our preoccupation with prosperity has forced other values into positions of chronically secondary importance. Paradoxically, by permitting it to do so we have undermined our efforts fully to realize the Enlightenment aim of liberating all from necessity, hardship, and adversity; from poverty and disease; and from ignorance and irrationality. Is ours a society whose history is a story of continuous improvement in human life? To a remarkable degree, yes. But the material prosperity of many has been purchased at the cost of a substantial loss of value to us all.

Social theories based on Enlightenment thinking and ideas assume that personal freedom, combined with scientific knowledge and technological advancement, will eliminate uncertainty and toil, making us more secure, more confident, more content—happier.[5] Yet we never seem to arrive at the point where we can say to ourselves, "yes, this is where we should be headed, this is what we should be doing, this is what we're here for." Although in many respects life has improved greatly for many people,[6] the question "is this all there is?" always seems apt, always seems to call for an answer, and never seems to elicit a convincing response.

Conceiving the person as a self-contained aggregate of changing desires—for which no standards or criteria exist to assess their relative worth—liberal societies have "renounced every larger goal in favor of the 'private enjoyment of life.'"[7] Because those societies assume that "human beings value little beyond ease, security, and avoidance of pain,"[8] the people who compose them

> deny . . . that life has any other meanings or values or possibilities. [Such people] eat, drink, marry, bear children and go to their grave in a state that is at best hilarious anesthesia, and at its worst is anxiety, fear, and envy, for lack of the necessary means to achieve the fashionable minimum of sensation.[9]

If people can't be "satisfied merely with the opportunity to choose their goals and lifestyles," as Christopher Lasch puts it, and if liberal democracy means little more than the opportunity to seek pleasures of the sort that only money can buy, why should we expect it to elicit our allegiance, let alone the sacrifice we might be called upon to make in order to preserve it? "How can such a paltry vision," as William James put it, "inspire anything but contempt?"[10] Michael Ignatieff sums up our predicament thusly:

> As long as they cling to the myth that history is—or ought to be—a story of the inexorable rise of secular freedom, liberals risk being perpetually surprised and disillusioned by the times they live in. . . . These societies have proved to be just as plagued by myths, fake news,

enthusiasm, and the madness of crowds as more religious and supposedly more credulous regimes of the past.

. . . The most that [liberalism's] social democratic variants . . . have promised is a welfare state that seeks the slow reduction of unmerited suffering, the gradual diminution of injustice, and the increase of prosperity and individual flourishing. These public goals are what Western liberalism at its best has had to offer . . . , but they leave many people yearning for deeper collective belonging and stronger ties to tradition and community. This dissatisfaction leaves a void, which is constantly being filled by non-liberal doctrines. . . . Liberalism . . . has left a hunger for *shared public conceptions about the purpose of life*.[11] (emphasis added)

Ignatieff's contention that "liberalism . . . has left a hunger for shared public conceptions about the purpose of life" brings us, at last, to the connection between ethics and purpose, and hence to the connection between democracy and purpose. Protecting and promoting the well-being of all people presupposes a *conception of well-being*, such as the one implicit in Maslow's hierarchy of needs.[12] Well-being consists in the felicitous fulfillment of all needs in the hierarchy, beginning with the most basic and concluding with those that, when they are met, realize the person's full potential. At the highest level of the hierarchy—"self-actualization"—Maslow reports that people find themselves in search of a "higher goal," something "outside" or "larger" than the more basic goods that contribute to well-being. In order to flourish, people find themselves drawn to altruism and spirituality, which Maslow suggests is essentially the longing to move beyond—to "transcend"—the limitations and finitude of the human condition.[13] Such "transcendence" is the highest and least self-regarding state of human consciousness, one in which we feel thoroughly connected with and integrated into humanity, nature, even the universe as a whole.

Making "transcendence" one's goal, however, is a bit like aiming for happiness. Happiness, it often has been remarked, is the unsought by-product of doing, achieving, and realizing *other* things that have value. Collectively, these things constitute the good for us and contribute to a life lived well. In turn, living life well generates the feeling we call happiness. Similarly, the condition Maslow calls transcendence is a by-product of doing, achieving, and realizing other things having value.

What are the good things that lead to happiness, well-being, and flourishing? How do we recognize them? How do we know they're good? To answer such questions, we require a standard of good. In turn, we can't develop a standard of good without an idea of *purpose*. Is your mobile phone a good phone? It depends—good *for what*?[14] Is knowledge good? It depends—good for what? Is ethical thinking good? It depends—good for what? Judgments of value require a standard, and a standard implies acceptability, adequacy, suitability, or utility for a purpose.

We can't determine whether a thing is good, then, unless we evaluate it in relation to a person's purposes, as an individual and as a human being. In our society, though—shaped as it has been by the ideas of the Enlightenment and political liberalism—the conventional individualist conception of the person doesn't carry with it such a conception of purpose. Hence societies in which atomism and subjectivism are assumed to be true have no purpose beyond creating and sustaining the conditions—physical security, social stability, liberty, material prosperity—that individuals require in order to pursue their personal conceptions of the good. They offer little in the way of direction, guidance, and support for their constituent members as the latter attempt to discern their personal purposes.

Indeed, it is precisely because we offer the individual so little assistance in identifying her own good that, as a society, we find it so difficult to settle on collective goals and to resolve disagreements that arise concerning the kinds of lives we should live as individuals. Because we associate freedom with the notion that whatever we want is by definition good, "freedom" is ethically empty and hence useless to us as a guide to evaluating actions we might take. Because atomism and subjectivism have made the idea of human purpose seem as plural and diverse as people themselves, it now encompasses almost every idea of good, value, and desirability imaginable. But this definition of "purpose" renders the concept essentially devoid of substance. Because there is no agreement about the PPN of "purpose" in this context, the term applies essentially to anything and everything. Which is to say, it applies to nothing in particular—to *no thing* more than any other thing.

MUST LIFE HAVE A PURPOSE? CAN IT?

Historically, the idea of human purpose has been associated with the idea of history moving in a particular "direction"—specifically, in a "positive" direction, toward a better world.[15] According to Rob Goodman, Western civilization has been profoundly influenced by the conviction that

> there is some meaning and point to history, and . . . that despite apparent confusion, even chaos, in human events, nevertheless those events

are going somewhere and indicating something. [This mode of thought] is deeply appealing and deeply consoling.[16]

Kant believed that human beings find it unbearable to imagine history without a purpose. We would be paralyzed if we didn't act as if it does. "If man did not believe that he must live for something," wrote Tolstoy, "he would not live at all."

In fact, though, writes Mark Edmundson, most of us "live for our personal desires. We want food, sex, money, power, prestige. . . . We want to live forever in the flesh, or for as long as possible." Perhaps

> there can be something bleakly noble in affirming ourselves as fundamentally Darwinian creatures who live to sustain our existences with as little pain and as much pleasure as possible. [But this is a] mere existence based on desire, without hope, fullness, or ultimate meaning. . . . Is this all there is to life?[17]

Maybe it is. And maybe, in a world in which people devote so much of their time and energy to satisfying the desires they happen to have and to expressing the feelings, warranted or not, they happen to have, it makes little sense to try cultivating a participatory ethical consequentialism that takes as its purpose the improvement of each human life so that everyone progresses toward, achieves, and flourishes in his or her individuality. Perhaps John Gray is right in suggesting we embrace precisely the aspiration that Edmundson considers "perhaps bleakly noble." The expansion of scientific knowledge and the technological skills it has made possible have allowed a human-centered worldview to emerge that, in Gray's view, has fostered an ill-founded confidence—even arrogance—in human beings. A great many people today, at least in the technologically advanced countries, "think they belong to a species that can be master of its destiny."[18]

> Humanism . . . means [believing] that, by using the power given us by scientific knowledge, humans can free themselves from the limits that frame the lives of other animals. . . . [H]umankind can shape its own future.[19]

Central to the doctrine of humanism, in Gray's view, is the "inherently utopian belief that humans are not limited by their biological natures and that advances in ethics and politics are cumulative" (although susceptible to setbacks), and that "they can alter or improve the human condition in the same way that advances in science and technology have altered or improved living standards."[20] He denies this proposition, arguing that human nature is an inherent and permanent obstacle to cumulative ethical or political progress. The idea of humanity taking charge of its destiny

> makes sense only if we ascribe consciousness and *purpose* to the *species*. But *humanity has no such thing*.[21] (emphasis added)

We thus find ourselves suspended between a fading Christianity and a scientism that "promises . . . the species will become immortal."[22] In Gray's view, the idea of humanity taking charge of its destiny is wishful—even magical—thinking. Societies founded on a faith in unrealistic progress "cannot admit the normal unhappiness of human life."[23] Although science enables humans to *fulfill* our needs, it does nothing to *change* them. And because it does not change our needs, it does not alter what we value—security, power, wealth, status—or how much we desire it. The dispositions and drives that served the species well as it adapted to the harsh conditions of primitive life not only remain with us, but in the circumstances of the modern world they have become weaknesses and defects.

Our old proclivities—tribalism and aggression, envy and greed, seduction and sexual conquest, jealousy and status-seeking—have not been bred out of us. Instead, they impel us to modern applications that do more harm than good. "The Good," Gray concludes, is "a makeshift of hope and desire, not the truth of things. Values are only human needs, or the needs of other animals, turned into abstractions. They have no reality in themselves."[24] Gray does not deny that progress is possible, if "progress" is conceived as the reduction of suffering. He concedes that progress does in fact occur: ". . . Anaesthetic dentistry is an unmixed blessing. So are clean water and flush toilets. . . ." It is faith in (permanent) progress, he argues, that is a superstition. "Improvements in government and society are . . . real, but they are temporary. Not only can they be lost, they are sure to be." In this regard, we can, and should, accept Gray's admonition. There is no guarantee that we will not lose much, or even all, of the progress humanity has made.

CAN HUMANISM SUFFICE?

Like others who've pondered Gray's perspective, Terry Eagleton is more inclined to the view that the future is not yet written. We might live indefinitely on a knife edge, always in danger of falling past the tipping point that will lead to our destruction. But that we have managed thus far *not* to fall owes to the fact that the capabilities that allow us to annihilate each other are closely linked to those which allow us to die for one another, tell magnificent jokes, and compose symphonies somewhat beyond the capacity of a snail. The Fall from Eden was a fall up, not down—a creative, catastrophic swerve upwards into culture, comradeship, and concentration camps. . . . This is a tragic condition, but not a nihilistic one.[25]

As Gordon McCabe points out, the definition of humanism that Gray offers is better understood as *trans*humanism. Humanism is the belief in the possibility of human improvement, while transhumanism is the belief that humans can transcend their animal nature. Moreover, McCabe continues, humanism should not be conflated with utopianism or perfectibility. According to McCabe, Gray believes that

the secular view . . . of incremental improvement in the human condition through education and political action . . . must of necessity be utopian . . . But it does not: trying to make things better is not the same as believing that they can be made perfect.[26]

The unattainability of human social and political perfection does not entail the impossibility of progress. Nor does humanism assert that progress is certain or irreversible, only that it is possible and should be pursued.

Gray is right that human beings have never shown they are able and willing, as a species, to understand their own nature well enough to modify it in a sustainable fashion. It is foolish to imagine that we have domesticated our nature and improved our institutions sufficiently to conclude that we have crossed a threshold beyond which progress will continue, with no substantial backsliding ever. We are nowhere near attaining either goal, and even if we had reached them we would remain at continuous risk of reverting to our most troublesome beliefs, attitudes, and behaviors.

But human beings, we must remember, are needy.[27] Until we meet all of each person's most important needs, we won't know whether we can bring our evolved nature under better control. We won't know whether we can consistently think and act ethically. We won't know whether we can build and sustain institutions that support our ethicality. The behaviors Gray rightly decries are a symptom of human neediness. Nothing will be accomplished simply by eschewing ideals, aspirations, and hopes. Letting go of these, or being more "realistic" about them, depends on fulfilling people's needs. We cannot simply adjure people to tend their own gardens, to just be, and to just see. One cannot "just see" when under the influence of hunger, pain, grief, frustration, despair, or rage.

PURPOSE AND SPIRITUAL NEED

Human beings, Eric Voegelin believed, are by nature curious—inquisitive to the point of being afflicted with "a restless questioning, a seeking of meaning."[28] There may be a limit, of course, to what we can know. There may be "truths that lie beyond the reach of finite human knowing—irreducible mysteries corresponding to our questions—spiritual questions—about the ultimate whys and wherefores of existence." This possibility troubles us, as a species and as individuals.

Historically, asking questions about the ultimate purpose of life and providing answers to them has been the province of religion. For Tolstoy, "the idea of an Infinite God, of the divinity of the soul, of the union of men's actions with God . . . are ideas without which there would be no life. . . ." Since the 18th century, though, religion has declined steadily in importance, increasingly falling short as a credible source of answers. It has ceded authority to scientific materialism, the cornerstone of liberalism's conceptual foundation. In science some have sought consolation of the sort that in earlier times religion might have provided them, though for most it has proved an inadequate substitute.

Voegelin believed that the crisis of Western culture, whatever else it might be, is at bottom a crisis of fundamental *spiritual* disorientation.[29] In his view, order and disorder in both personal and political life are always rooted in responses to spiritual experience.[30] Spiritual needs are bound to arise, he says, because every human consciousness by nature seeks an understanding of the ultimate meaning of itself and everything else, including the primary origin and purpose of things: "Spirituality is inherent to the human condition . . . [It is the expression of] the primal and primordial aspirations that underpin the search for meaning.[31]

Because meeting their spiritual needs is so important, people suffer if they stop believing that, in Richard Niebuhr's words, "life is a critical affair."[32] Modern ideologies and mass political movements—liberalism included—do not generate and sustain this feeling. Although they attempt to "perform an essentially religious function," they fail to deliver the experience that people long for. In the case of liberal societies, at least, this is by design—in order to protect the individual's freedom to meet her needs as she deems best, societies such as ours refrain from shaping public life in a way that supports any particular approach to fulfilling them.

It seems clear, however, that those needs can't be met solely through exercising the freedom to choose one's personal goals and lifestyles. In 1940,

George Orwell wrote that the world's democracies operate as if "human beings desire nothing beyond ease, security, and avoidance of pain." In contrast, fascists knew that men and women wanted more than

> comfort, safety, [and] shorter working hours . . . They also, at least intermittently, want struggle and self-sacrifice. . . . Whereas capitalism and even socialism . . . have said to people, 'I offer you a good time,' [fascists have] said to them, 'I offer you struggle, danger, and death,' and as a result . . . a whole nation flings itself at [their] feet. . . . Fascism and Nazism are psychologically far sounder than any hedonistic conception of life.[33]

The persistence of religion and the religious aspects of modern secular ideologies show that people's spiritual needs remain strong. The recent recrudescence in the United States and Europe of nationalistic popular sentiments with authoritarian overtones suggests that Orwell's analysis remains apposite in the 21st century.

Like Voegelin, David Brooks recognizes that we live in a secular age.[34] This doesn't mean people aren't religious; many are. It means, he says, that "there is no shared set of values we all absorb as pre-conscious assumptions. In our world, individuals have to find or create their own meaning." Although human beings have the right and responsibility to give meaning and shape to their own lives, it is not easy to do so. Usually, Brooks writes, individuals aren't able to create their own lives "from the ground up. People . . . lack the foundations upon which to make the most important choices." This has led to a "pervasive sadness."

Moreover, writes Fenton Johnson, "the cornerstones of secular culture— money, sex, and power"—are the "three great obstacles" to the kind of meaning the present age desperately needs.[35] Where "Buddhism teaches how to recognize and defend against human weakness, capitalism focuses our intelligence and creativity on exploitation of human weakness—for money, sex, and power." Quoting Milton Glaser, Johnson asks, "in a culture where every image or idea can and will be used for commerce, how can anything remain sacred?" And if nothing sacred remains, "when we are barraged with messages equating personal worth with material wealth, why not cut every ethical corner? Why be honest, or keep promises? Why be fair? Why consider the consequences for others of our actions?"

The problem with modern substitutes for religion—liberalism, capitalism, socialism, and their variants—is they attempt to do for the modern and postmodern eras what religion did for the premodern era: connect our emotional experience of life—our pattern-seeking, sense-making, feeling, longing, needing, and desiring selves—with the vast and mostly incomprehensible universe of time and space of which we seem to be such an insignificant and ephemeral part. As Ken Wilber points out, although modernity brought with it the benefits of political liberalism, it "allowed a powerful monological science to colonize and dominate the other spheres (the aesthetic-expressive and religious-moral) by denying them any real existence at all."[36] The Enlightenment eliminated subjective experience from an all-encompassing materialist, scientific understanding of the world:

> Entire interior dimensions—of morals, artistic expression, introspection, spirituality, contemplative awareness, meaning and value and intentionality—were dismissed by monological science because none of them could be registered [by external observation—by separating ourselves from them and standing outside them] . . . This was the disaster of modernity.
>
> . . . If we [reduce] compassion to serotonin, joy to dopamine, cultural values to modes of techno-economic production, moral wisdom to technical steering problems, or contemplation to brain waves, we collapse quality to quantity, interior to exterior, depth to surface, dignity to disaster. The result is what Weber famously called "the disenchanted world" and Mumford memorably called "the disqualified universe": a world with no quality or meaning at all. . . .[37]

A PURPOSE FOR THE PRESENT: ETHICAL HEROISM

Half a century before Thomas Jefferson immortalized the phrase "life, liberty, and the pursuit of happiness," Richard Cumberland, a 17th-century cleric and philosopher, wrote that promoting the well-being of our fellow humans is essential to the pursuit of our own happiness.[38] Similarly, and shortly before America's declaration of independence from Britain, Adam Ferguson, one of the Scottish "moral sense" philosophers (a group that included Adam Smith), declared that "courage and a heart devoted to the good of mankind are the constituents of human felicity."[39] More recently, David Brooks has written that, in willing the good for others, "each person brings unity to his or her fragmented personality . . . [and purifies] the full personhood in himself."[40] In turning away from a self-centered life, we "find [our] perfection in communion with other whole persons." We demonstrate our goodwill toward others by thinking ethically with them. We find it personally gratifying to do so. Moreover, in thinking ethically with others, we work toward achieving our own individuality and flourishing. Thinking ethically with others is thus a constituent of a life lived well, and hence a key to the eventual achievement of happiness.

Notice that Ferguson believed goodwill—"a heart devoted to the good of mankind"—is one of *two* "constituents of human felicity." The other element is *courage*. Why courage? First, because it is never easy to swim against the tide of the social, economic, and political ideas, norms, values, and practices of one's own time and place. To think ethically in a world relentlessly devoted to self-interest, personal gain, and individual advantage—a world in which goodwill toward others and the demonstration of respect for their individuality and genuine concern for their ability to flourish are vanishingly rare—is to swim against an overwhelming tide of contrary sentiment and inclination.

Second, courage is for us today an indispensable virtue because liberalism exploits and reinforces the powerful motivational principle of psychological egoism. Liberalism makes "no difficult demands on human nature. . . . It presuppose[s] no motivation other than self-interest and nothing more in the way of self-development than normal instrumental rationality.[41] Liberalism assumes our natural self-centeredness, making it doubly hard to think and act ethically.

Third, we need courage in trying to think and act ethically because our evolved human nature has other priorities:

> The vast majority of people, regardless of country or creed or time period, want only to live their lives and protect their families, to be left alone . . . Order, not righteousness, is our most cherished value, no matter what we tell ourselves.[42]

Finally, the contemporary world has no compelling conception of courage that might connect it with ethical thinking and action. Hemingway argued that World War I discredited words like "honor" and "sacrifice."[43] The heroic ideal of the prewar era became identified closely "with unthinking obedience and the glorification of war as an end in itself."[44] It was "conscripted into the service of militarism, jingoism, imperialism, and racial purification." Cut loose from its religious origins, "the defense of the strenuous life degenerated into a cult of sheer strength."[45] As a result, "in our time the heroic ideal is so closely associated with the cult of power" that for many people it seems to imply that, if I am powerful enough, merely by believing a thing to be true I can make it so.[46]

Yet making sacrifices in the service of some "higher cause" is an important and enduring human need. This need has been systematically neglected in the age of material abundance. Contemporary ideologies (and even most religions) have no place for altruism and self-sacrifice. They offer us no *heroic* vision of life. But the opportunity to live such a life is precisely what we need. William James understood that the need to live valorously is an ineradicable feature of human nature:

> Peace-loving people [have] overlooked the importance and legitimacy of [needs for hard work, struggle, aggression, and danger], treating them as atavistic impulses . . . On the contrary, . . . the need to participate in shared communities of risk and high purpose [is] inextinguishable. "Martial virtues [are] absolute and permanent human goods." If they [cannot] be realized in some other way, they [will] continue to be realized in war itself.
>
> . . . Men and women [achieve] dignity only when asked to submit to an arduous discipline imposed by some "collectivity"; and "no collectivity is like an army for nourishing such pride." . . . The only alternative to [armed conflict] is a "moral equivalent of war" [that makes] the same demands on people in the name of peace, satisfie[s] the same taste for self-sacrifice, and elicit[s] the same qualities of devotion, loyalty, and ardor.[47]

To some degree and at least some of the time, we all want to live heroically. We know in our bones what that means. The hero is the principled, courageous, and determined protagonist of stories we've been told throughout our lives. Heroes are people, often ordinary,

> who prevail in extreme circumstances [and] dramatize a sense of morality, courage, and purpose often lacking in our everyday world. Heroes do what is good, just and right; and even though they may be ambiguous or flawed characters, they often sacrifice themselves to show humanity at its best and most humane.[48]

HEROISM AND THE ETHICAL FRONTIER

"As we have slowly and surely attained more progress," writes Andrew Sullivan,

> we have lost something that undergirds all of it: meaning, cohesion, and a different, deeper kind of happiness than the satiation of all our

earthly needs. . . . We are a species built on religious ritual to appease our existential angst, and yet we now live in a world where every individual has to create her own meaning from scratch. . . . We've forgotten the human flourishing that comes from a common idea of virtue, and a concept of virtue that is based on our nature.[49]

Ethically and politically, we have arrived at a frontier. We have pushed on so hard and for so long in search of personal freedom and happiness that we've forgotten that these aspirations are inseparable from the task of building and sustaining community. Now we must relearn the wisdom

> that a person can be a person only in community. . . . If we are to grow as persons . . . , we must consciously participate in the emerging community of our lives, in the claims made upon us by others as well our claims upon them. Only in community does the person appear in the first place, and only in community can the person continue to become.[50]

As Wendell Berry puts it, "[We] create one another, depend on one another, are literally part of one another . . . All who are living as neighbors here . . . are part of one another, and so cannot possibly flourish alone. . . ."[51]

The frontier before us is an ethical one, and we must now cross into it. The quest on which we must embark is to build and sustain communities in this new territory—communities that value and practice public ethical dialogue and deliberation—that will enable us to reverse the malign effects of atomism and subjectivism, consumerism, and the other unintended consequences of the Enlightenment project of liberating humanity from the grip of ignorance, poverty, and disease. It is this quest that will help us construct a standard of virtue rooted in our profoundly social and interdependent nature, and that will make it possible for each of us to flourish in his or her individuality.

To cross the ethical frontier and enter into a new land of human aspiration and effort, we will require the courage and boldness of heroes. The journey ahead will demand the commitment to purpose and the strength of character that are the foundation of any heroism. Our success is not guaranteed. Indeed, we will never succeed completely. Ethical progress will always be resisted and, from time to time, even undone, by those who place their perceived self-interest above the interest we all have in becoming autonomous and ethical thinkers who seek the well-being and flourishing of all. The evil that is egoism cannot be defeated—it can only be held in check. We must keep it from overwhelming the good and the right while recognizing that it serves these values precisely by opposing them. Being human, we will always fall short. But being human, we must keep trying. What matters is that we never cease our effort—unfailingly and unflinchingly, with goodwill toward all—to seek what is best for ourselves and for others alike. Our mere survival may depend on making, for the first time, a conscious, concerted, sustained effort to think and to live ethically.

There are no better words with which to remind ourselves of what is at stake than those spoken by Abraham Lincoln a century and a half ago, in a time of even greater ethical and political crisis:

> The dogmas of the quiet past are inadequate to the stormy present. The occasion is piled high with difficulty, and we must rise with the occasion. As our case is new, so we must think anew, and act anew. We must disenthrall ourselves, and then we shall save our country. . . . The fiery trial through which we pass will light us down, in honor or dishonor, to the latest generation. . . . We—even we here—hold the power and bear the responsibility. . . . We shall nobly save, or meanly lose, the last best hope of earth.[52]

It will be hard. As John Adams said, "All great changes are irksome to the human mind, especially those which are attended with great dangers and uncertain effects."[53] To which we might add, though, in recognition of the difficulty of the challenge before us, the words of Thomas Paine: "We have this consolation with us, that the harder the conflict, the more glorious the triumph."[54]

THE END OF ALL OUR SEARCHING

"It is not unreasonable," wrote E. F. Schumacher, "to treat life and the world as having meaning [and] significance, which we ought to attempt to comprehend."[55] Granted, "this requires an act of faith. But so does the assumption that it has *no* meaning or significance, only material existence." Faith, as Schumacher used the term, is not the same as belief. As Alan Watts explains,

> belief . . . is the insistence that the truth is what one would believe or wish it to be . . . Faith . . . is an unreserved *opening of the mind* to the truth, *whatever* it may turn out to be. Faith has no preconceptions; it is a plunge into the unknown. Belief clings, but faith lets go . . . Faith is the essential virtue of science, and likewise of any religion that is not self-deception.[56] (emphasis added)

With faith—an "unreserved opening of the mind to the truth, whatever it may turn out to be"—we could accept that we cannot know everything. With faith, we could accept that we control precious little, including our ultimate fate.

Conceiving of culture as a collection of criterionless individual choices among available ways to satisfy desire is to cheat ourselves of those elements of life that make us, both individually and collectively, unique—and uniquely human. The best remedy for a culture that, instead of helping us cheat death, has turned us fearful and faithless, is to give our constant, careful, and critical attention to the practices of individuality, autonomy, ethics, and democracy—not democracy as we practice it today, but democracy understood as the public form of ethical thinking and living. Democracy understood in this way can help us cope with our mortality by drawing us out of our isolation, by allowing us to share our fears, by enabling us to construct knowledge as we search open-mindedly for truth, and by multiplying our power to act for the good. Above all, democracy so conceived can help us rebuild our faith in the possibility of human purpose in this "disenchanted world," this "disqualified universe."

Spiritual needs lie at the very heart of the good life. As Ken Wilber so eloquently puts it:

> When spiritual connection is joined with the pursuit of ethical and aesthetic goodness, and when these combine with political freedom and justice, we will come finally to rest, finally to peace, finally to a home that structures care into the cosmos and compassion into the world that touches each and every soul with grace and goodness and goodwill, and lights each being with a glory that never fades or falters. . . . We are called, you and I, by the voice of the good, and the voice of the true, and the voice of the beautiful, called exactly in those terms, to witness the liberation of all sentient beings without exception.[57]

To be fully human, we must attempt to transcend the merely human, all the while accepting that we likely never will. This, too, is part of our nature, a trait evolution has favored. What we do—for good or for ill—we do "naturally." But we must attempt to transcend our own nature in full knowledge and acceptance of the inherent and characteristically human limitations and weaknesses of that nature. We do not exist independently of the universe. It is up to *us* to know good and to choose it over bad.

To discover and to create good; to think and live ethically in the face of uncomprehending or hostile opposition, even from family and friends; to do so courageously, even heroically, when it is so much easier, so much safer, to pursue the course of least resistance—is this not enough to sustain us as we sail inexorably into the unknown? Human beings before us have found inspiration in similar aims. Putting words into the mouth of Ulysses, Tennyson wrote that

> death closes all: but something ere the end, some work of noble note, may yet be done . . . Come, my friends, 'tis not too late to seek a newer world. Push off and, sitting well in order, smite the sounding furrows; for my purpose holds to sail beyond the sunset, and the baths of all the western stars, until I die. . . . That which we are, we are: one equal temper of heroic hearts, . . . strong in will to strive, to seek, to find, and not to yield.

To strive, to seek, to find: the True, the Good, the Right—for all life, including the great web of being in which we are embedded; for life today, for our successors tomorrow, and for theirs the day beyond that. And so on and so on, for as long as life requires.

Afterword

The thoughts I have offered in this book are far from definitive, and for two reasons. First, the human world is not static. Although in some important ways human beings and their circumstances don't change, in other equally important ways they do—constantly. Whatever we think and write in the present is unlikely to remain germane and perspicacious in the long run. Second, none of us can see clearly and understand thoroughly the "whole story" of the human situation, even during the thin slice of time and space we occupy over the course of a lifetime. Our personal perspectives are partial and hence incomplete—they encompass an extremely narrow and highly selective range of perception, experience, and thought. Each of us views life and the world through psychological, cultural, historical, and other "lenses" that affect our interpretations of both our interior and exterior experience that bend, color, limit, and obscure the phenomena that leave impressions on our minds. Such knowledge as we can acquire of the world we must construct through dialogue, by adding, comparing, and integrating our various personal views.

For the foregoing reasons, I hope readers will treat this book as one person's observation in a conversation to which all of us must contribute. Moreover, I hope they will understand that what I offer here is not just an assessment of politics. It is also an act within politics, a personal appeal to take action in recognition of the great challenge before us. It is becoming more and more difficult to see how our present situation ends peacefully and democratically, let alone progressively. The strain on people, especially those of modest means (or none at all), is growing. The hammer continues its backward arc, loading more potential for explosive discharge.

Meanwhile, the best among us, though not lacking in conviction, seem to believe we have the time and the room to maneuver by democratic political means back to safety. In my darkest moments, I worry the die already has been cast. But even if it has not been, I wonder whether we will recognize the point, if it comes, at which we must act swiftly and decisively, lest we sink back from our fleeting day in the democratic sun into the dark condition that has been the norm in most places for most of history.

We do not possess the advantages enjoyed in the 1960s—by people who protested war, inequality, oppression, and malfeasance—of a press able to call out those in power for their dissembling, mendacity, and manipulation; of a legislative branch and judiciary that in the end proved responsible and responsive to calls for essential change; of an electoral system not systematically distorted in favor of a political tribe and its ignorance and authoritarian tendencies; and of a citizenry secure and stable enough to consider facts that do not fit their worldview. Things seem (as perhaps they always are) on the cusp of falling apart. Can we prevent that from occurring? Is it too late? What will we do if worse comes to worst? How much more discontent, frustration, and anger can we take? It is long past time, is it not, for some collective soul-searching?

I want to express my appreciation to Bridget Austiguy-Preschel, Nitesh Sharma, Larry Goldberg, and especially to Kelly Somers, whose superb editing made this version of the manuscript so much better than it was previously. I owe a special debt of gratitude to Hilary Claggett, for grasping the importance of the topic and seeing the value of my contribution to it; to Brian Sullivan, for his indispensable comments and suggestions on previous versions; and to Janette Hartz-Karp for her constant support and encouragement. Finally, thanks to all who take the trouble to read and consider the thoughts I've tried to express here.

Notes

PREFACE

1. Sullivan, Andrew, "The Poison We Pick," *New York Magazine,* February 19, 2018, http://nymag.com/intelligencer/2018/02/americas-opioid-epidemic.html.

2. Will, George F., *Statecraft as Soulcraft: What Government Does* (New York: Simon & Schuster/Touchstone), 1983, 18.

3. Diggins, John P., *The Lost Soul of American Politics: Virtue, Self-Interest, and the Foundations of Liberalism* (New York: Basic Books, 1984), 250.

4. I use the term "liberal" to mean "having to do with liberality—the quality of being open, generous, permissive, devoted to freedom." I don't use it in the contemporary American sense of "left of center" on the spectrum of political attitudes and dispositions.

5. Needleman, Jacob, *The American Soul: Rediscovering the Wisdom of the Founders* (New York: Tarcher/Putnam, 2002), 195.

INTRODUCTION

1. Anna Grzymala-Busse, quoted in Edsall, Thomas B., "Democracy Can Plant the Seeds of Its Own Destruction," *The New York Times,* October 19, 2017.

2. "Perfectly rational citizens might choose an alternative to democracy. For example, today's pragmatic, nonideological authoritarianism offers 'personal benefits' like shiny consumer products and 'collective dignity' in the form of aggressive nationalism." Traub, James, "Democracy Is Dying by Natural Causes," *Foreign Policy,* March 1, 2018, https://foreignpolicy.com/2018/03/01/democracy-is-dying-by-natural-causes.

3. Pinker, Steven, *Enlightenment Now: The Case for Reason, Science, Humanism, and Progress* (New York: Viking, 2018).

4. Sullivan, Andrew, "The World Is Better Than Ever. Why Are We Miserable?" *New York Magazine*, March 9, 2018, http://nymag.com/daily /intelligencer/2018/03/sullivan-things-are-better-than-ever-why-are-we-mise rable.html.

5. Deneen, Patrick J., *Why Liberalism Failed* (New Haven, CT: Yale University Press, 2018).

6. "Liberalism," *Stanford Encyclopedia of Philosophy*, revised January 22, 2018, https://plato.stanford.edu/entries/liberalism. Liberals were generally critical of traditional institutions and practices, such as hereditary privilege, an official state religion, and monarchy. John Locke, often regarded as a key founder of liberalism as well as scientific empiricism, argued that each person has a natural right to life, liberty, and property, and that government may not violate these rights but must honor the social contract, according to which people voluntarily place themselves under the authority of government by giving their consent to be governed. It was out of this sentiment that liberals sought to replace traditional authorities with the institutions of representative democracy. Locke, John, *Two Treatises on Government, Second Treatise*, Chapter 2, Section 6, https://www.gutenberg .org/files/7370/7370-h/7370-h.htm.

7. Applebaum, Anne, "A Warning from Europe: The Worst Is Yet to Come," *The Atlantic Monthly*, October 2018. See also Fisher, Max, "The Weaknesses in Liberal Democracy That May Be Pulling It Apart," *The New York Times*, November 3, 2018.

8. Sullivan, "The World Is Better Than Ever. Why Are We Miserable?"

9. Nationalism is one of the few responses to loss of other viable identities that is still available to people in Western mass societies. Unfortunately, so are racism, anti-Semitism, and other forms of sectarianism.

10. Bell, Daniel, *The Cultural Contradictions of Capitalism* (New York: Basic Books, 1976).

11. Hall, Robert E., *This Land of Strangers: The Relationship Crisis That Imperils Home, Work, Politics, and Faith* (Austin, TX: Greenleaf, 2012).

12. Brooks, David, "The Blindness of Social Wealth," *The New York Times*, April 16, 2018, https://www.nytimes.com/2018/04/16/opinion/face book-social-wealth.html.

13. See, for example, Chua, Amy, *Political Tribes: Group Instinct and the Fate of Nations* (New York: Penguin Press, 2018). For a critique of Chua's book, see Rosen, Lawrence, "Are Our Politics Really 'Tribal'?" https://www .the-american-interest.com/2018/05/21/are-our-politics-really-tribal.

14. We are not talking here about *pluralism*, the view that the good (value) is constituted of a variety of distinct values that cannot be reduced to a "common denominator" like pleasure or happiness. Individual and collective efforts to discriminate among putative values—to order and prioritize them, to reject some and embrace others—are indispensable to adaptation, growth, and progress. Every community and every individual needs to embrace the difficult task of working toward a sound judgment about how to resolve a conflict between competing goods. But subjectivism is another matter altogether. It is pluralism's *reductio ad absurdam*. Though pluralism conduces to the ability of persons and communities to make genuine choices, subjectivism has the opposite effect: it turns all choice into arbitrary selection. Criterionless choice—choice without reference to goods, ends, purposes, etc.—is not genuine choice; it is a simulacrum thereof.

15. Value subjectivism also drives clarity and rigor from our political talk. It renders superfluous the goals, norms, and methods of clear and sound reasoning. One consequence is that we "talk past one another," proceeding down separate paths that never converge. Another is that we deceive ourselves, imagining that our views rest on firmer ground than in fact exists. At its worst, subjectivism licenses us to dispense with public justifications for our political goals altogether. It permits us to give our emotions, no matter how inappropriate or extreme, a blank check, and thereby permits deployment of any rhetorical device whatsoever—including the ceaseless reiteration of outright falsehoods—in order to realize our political objectives.

Finally, because subjectivism forces us to conjure up rhetorical pseudo-reasons that we can use in the emotionally high-stakes debates we have with others, it drives our real—and often valid—concerns and wants underground. We feel it's unsafe and imprudent to reveal the actual, often publicly inadmissible factors that drive our emotions. Subjectivism lets us dress up anger, self-righteousness, impatience, bigotry, ignorance, and arrogance as pseudo-reasons, then allows us to substitute them for genuine reasons that might help us resolve conflict.

16. Ignatieff, Michael, "Are the Authoritarians Winning?" *The New York Review of Books*, July 10, 2014.

17. MacIntyre, Alasdair, "How to Be a North American," Publication No. 2-88 (Washington, D.C.: Federation of State Humanities Councils, 1987).

18. MacIntyre, Alasdair, *After Virtue: A Study in Moral Theory* (Notre Dame, IN: University of Notre Dame Press, 1981), 2.

19. MacIntyre, *After Virtue*, 8.

20. Here is a comment in response to a blog post dated April 12, 2018, that illustrates this point: "When I got far enough along in a career to be

present when major decisions were made, I was appalled at the practices of those in charge. Those successful in climbing a hierarchy had no concept of the wide consequences of their actions. On the other hand, they were very careful of the narrow consequences. 'How will the person over me react this afternoon on hearing what I do? Will I benefit in some other way?' completely drowned out consideration of 'What result will this have on the responsibilities I was put in this job to carry out?' This is particularly insidious when the sense of power and entitlement that increases with higher status becomes a group marker. All the powerful people like force, so they will use more force than anybody else. The benefit is being accepted as a member of the high-status group" (http://www.ianwelsh.net/the-push-for -war-with-syria-and-russia/?utm_source=feedburner&utm_medium=feed &utm_campaign=Feed%3A+IanWelsh+%28Ian+Welsh%29).

21. Fuller, Robert W., *Somebodies and Nobodies: Overcoming the Abuse of Rank* (Gabriola Island, BC: New Society Publishers, 2004), 11. See also Fuller, *All Rise: Somebodies, Nobodies, and the Politics of Dignity* (San Francisco: Berrett-Koehler, 2006); and Fuller and Gerloff, Pamela A., *Dignity for All: How to Create a World without Rankism* (San Francisco: Berrett-Koehler, 2008).

22. Needleman, Jacob, *The American Soul: Rediscovering the Wisdom of the Founders* (New York: Tarcher/Putnam, 2002), 5.

23. Schumacher, E. F., *A Guide for the Perplexed* (New York: Harper & Row, 1977), 132.

24. Douthat, Ross, "Free Speech Will Not Save Us," *The New York Times*, May 26, 2018, https://www.nytimes.com/2018/05/26/opinion/sunday/free -speech-nfl-protests-trump.html?emc=edit_th_180527&nl=todayshead lines&nlid=573176760527.

25. Will, George F., *Statecraft as Soulcraft: What Government Does* (New York: Simon & Schuster/Touchstone, 1983), 82.

26. Johnson, Fenton, "A Skeptic Searches for an American Faith," *Harper's*, September 1998.

27. Will, 163.

CHAPTER 1

1. Pettit, Philip, "Three Conceptions of Democratic Control," *Constellations*, vol. 15, no. 1 (2008), https://www.princeton.edu/~ppettit/papers /2008/Three%20Conceptions%20of%20Democratic%20Control.pdf.

2. Schumpeter, Joseph A., *Capitalism, Socialism and Democracy* (New York: Harper Torchbooks, 1984).

3. Downs, Anthony, *An Economic Theory of Democracy* (New York: Harper & Row, 1957).

4. Buchanan, James, and Tullock, Gordon, *The Calculus of Consent: Logical Foundations of Constitutional Democracy* (Ann Arbor, MI: University of Michigan Press, 1962).

5. Lasswell, Harold, *Politics: Who Gets What, When, How* (New York: P. Smith, 1950).

6. Elster, Jon, "The Market and the Forum: Three Varieties of Political Theory," in *Foundations of Social Choice Theory*, Jon Elster and Aanund Hylland, eds. (Cambridge: Cambridge University Press, 1986), 104–132. See also Pettit, 2008.

7. For an illuminating example of how the market mentality pervades our thinking about matters of public concern, see John Doble, *A Factory Mentality: The Consumer Mindset in American Public Education* (Dayton, OH: Kettering Foundation, 1998).

8. Inglehart, Ronald F., "How Much Should We Worry?" *Journal of Democracy*, vol. 27, no. 3, July 2016, http://pscourses.ucsd.edu/ps200b /Inglehart%20How%20Much%20SHould%20we%20Worry.pdf.

9. Illing, Sean, "Is American Democracy in Decline? Should We Be Worried?" https://www.vox.com/2017/10/13/16431502/america-democracy -decline-liberalism. Other observers are concluding that the United States is no longer a democracy. See, for example, Mounk, Yasha, "America Is Not a Democracy," *The Atlantic Monthly*, March 2018. See also Johnson, Rossarian, "Study by MIT Economist: U.S. Has Regressed to a Third-World Nation for Most of Its Citizens" (review of Temin, Peter, *The Vanishing Middle Class: Prejudice and Power in a Dual Economy*, Cambridge, MA: MIT Press, 2017), https://www.themaven.net/theintellectualist/news/study -by-mit-economist-u-s-has-regressed-to-a-third-world-nation-for-most-of -its-citizens-Sb5A5HZ1rUiXavZapos30g.

10. Sandel, Michael, "America's Search for a New Public Philosophy," *The Atlantic Monthly*, March 1996, 58.

11. Will, George F., *Statecraft as Soulcraft: What Government Does* (New York: Simon & Schuster/Touchstone, 1983), 27.

12. Andersen, Kurt, "How America Lost Its Mind," *The Atlantic Monthly*, September 2017, 79–80, https://www.theatlantic.com/magazine/archive /2017/09/how-america-lost-its-mind/534231.

13. Turner, Frederick Jackson, "Contributions of the West to American Democracy," in *The Frontier in American Life* (New York: Henry Holt, 1920). Reprinted in Billington, Ray Allen, *Selected Essays of Frederick Jackson Turner* (Englewood Cliffs, NJ: Prentice-Hall, 1961), 79–80.

14. Lukes, Stephen, *Individualism* (London and Oxford: Blackwell, 1973).

15. The individual is made sovereign in two ways: by being afforded the maximum amount of freedom compatible with the justifiable interests of all other persons, including exercise of their rights; and by entitlement to cast a vote that is worth no more and no less than the single vote to which every other person is entitled.

16. Siedentop, Larry, "Two Liberal Traditions," in *The Idea of Freedom: Essays in Honour of Isaiah Berlin,* Alan Ryan, ed. (Oxford: Oxford University Press, 1979).

17. *Christian History*, September 1988, https://christianhistoryinstitute.org/magazine/article/puritan-critique-of-attitudes-toward-money.

18. Epstein, Joseph, *Ambition* (New York: Dutton, 1981).

19. The historian Christopher Lasch believed that Emerson is often misunderstood as a radical individualist. Lasch, Christopher, *The True and Only Heaven: Progress and Its Critics* (New York: Norton, 1991), 268. He maintained that Emerson understood the importance of "sociability" and that there are "great wrongs which must be revised." Moreover, Emerson wanted people to become more self-reliant so they could "meet each other as equals." Perhaps Lasch was correct in this assessment. Even so, it is one thing to believe that an individual living in the social and economic conditions of the early 19th century might be spurred to greater self-reliance by denying him charity, and quite another to believe that in the early 21st century.

20. Emerson, Ralph Waldo, "Experience," in *Essays* (second series), 1844, http://transcendentalism-legacy.tamu.edu/authors/emerson/essays/experience.html.

21. Apparently, though, Emerson thought otherwise: "[D]o not tell me . . . of my obligation to put all poor men in good situations. Are they my poor? I tell thee, thou foolish philanthropist, that I grudge the dollar, the dime, the cent I give to such men as do not belong to me and to whom I do not belong." Emerson's language might be a bit dated, but his sentiment is not. The world abounds with people so lacking in compassion, generosity, and even basic goodwill that they won't part with the loose change in their pockets. Emerson, Ralph Waldo, "Self-Reliance," in *Essays* (first series), 1841,

http://transcendentalism-legacy.tamu.edu/authors/emerson/essays/selfreliance.html.

22. Bellah, Robert N., Madsen, Richard, Sullivan, William M., Swidler, Ann, and Tipton, Steven M., *Habits of the Heart: Individualism and Commitment in American Life* (Berkeley and Los Angeles: University of California Press, 1985).

23. This is true other things being equal. Here we are assuming that nothing changes from an earlier point in time to a later point except the passage of time itself.

24. Statements to the effect that something has value (is valuable, is good) involve truth-claims about the thing in question. In contrast, a statement to the effect that "Person A desires (or feels positively disposed to) X" does not involve a truth-claim about the thing desired, but only about the person who desires it. To assert that something like retribution is *valuable* (has value, is desirable, is good, etc.) is to state, in the form of a factual proposition, that R possesses some characteristic or feature that *anyone* could accept as a warrant or justification that supports choosing it. In contrast, the fact that I *desire* R or feel favorably disposed to it is not a *reason* for me to choose it. See Freeman, Samuel, "*Why Be Good?*" (review of *On What Matters*, by Derek Parfit), *The New York Review of Books*, April 26, 2012, 52–54. Still less is it a reason for others who have no desire for R. If *you* have no desire for R, my desire cannot count as a reason for you to desire it. It follows that there are, and can be, no reasons for saying that one person's choice is better than or superior to anyone else's. The objects of their choices are mere desiderata, different only in the degrees of intensity with which they are desired.

25. As Amy Gutmann and Dennis Thompson point out, it is logically possible that conflict ultimately might be unresolvable because "there may be reasonable disagreement all the way down." But *until someone actually demonstrates* that no justifiable deliberative resolution can ever be achieved, there is no reason to believe the disagreement is unresolvable. Gutmann, Amy, and Thompson, Dennis, "Democratic Disagreement," in *Deliberative Politics: Essays on Democracy and Disagreement*, Stephen Macedo, ed. (New York and Oxford: Oxford University Press, 1999), 268.

26. MacIntyre, Alasdair, *After Virtue: A Study in Moral Theory* (Notre Dame, IN: University of Notre Dame Press, 1981), 8.

27. Value subjectivism also drives clarity and rigor from our political talk. It renders superfluous the goals, norms, and methods of clear and sound reasoning. One consequence is that we "talk past one another,"

proceeding down separate paths that never converge. Another is that we deceive ourselves, imagining that our views rest on firmer ground than in fact exists. At its worst, value subjectivism licenses us to dispense with public justifications for our political goals altogether. It permits us to give our emotions, no matter how inappropriate or extreme, a blank check, and thereby permits deployment of any rhetorical device whatsoever—including the ceaseless reiteration of outright falsehoods—in order to realize our political objectives.

Finally, because subjectivism forces us to conjure up rhetorical pseudo-reasons that we can use in the emotionally high-stakes debates we have with others, it drives our real—and often valid—concerns and wants underground. We feel it's unsafe and imprudent to reveal the actual, often publicly inadmissible factors that drive our emotions. Subjectivism lets us dress up anger, self-righteousness, impatience, bigotry, ignorance, and arrogance as pseudo-reasons, then allows us to substitute them for genuine reasons that might help us resolve conflict.

28. Andersen, Kurt, 2017.

29. Brooks, David, "Anthony Kennedy and the Privatization of Meaning," *The New York Times*, June 28, 2018, https://www.nytimes.com/2018/06/28/opinion/anthony-kennedy-individualism.html.

30. Mill, John Stuart, "Of Individuality, as One of the Elements of Well-being," in *On Liberty*, 1859, https://www.utilitarianism.com/ol/three.html.

31. Edmund Phelps defines "flourishing" as "using one's imagination, exercising one's creativity, taking fascinating journeys into the unknown, and acting on the world. . . ." Phelps, Edmund S., "What Is Wrong with the West's Economies?" *The New York Review of Books,* August 13, 2015, http://www.nybooks.com/articles/archives/2015/aug/13/what-wrong-wests-economies. See also Nussbaum, Martha, *Frontiers of Justice: Disability, Nationality, Species Membership* (Cambridge, MA: Belknap Press of Harvard University, 2007).

32. See, for example, Norton, David L., *Personal Destinies: A Philosophy of Ethical Individualism* (Princeton, NJ: Princeton University Press, 1976). See also Rasmussen, Douglas, "Human Flourishing and the Appeal to Human Nature," *Social Philosophy and Policy,* December 1999, https://www.researchgate.net/publication/231787803_Human_Flourishing_and_the_Appeal_to_Human_Nature. See as well Veatch, Henry Babcock, *Rational Man: A Modern Interpretation of Aristotelian Ethics* (Bloomington and London: Indiana University, 1962); and Den Uyl, Douglas J., *The Virtue of Prudence* (New York: Peter Lang, 1991).

33. Greater personal development leads to greater individuality because human beings are most alike at the level of their basic—hence shared—needs, for example, for food and water, sleep, shelter, relief from pain, physical safety, routine, stability, affection, a feeling of belonging, and so forth. Humans reveal their uniqueness as they move up the "hierarchy" of needs to those that emerge when more basic needs are met: material comfort, mastery, self-governance, knowledge, wisdom, creativity, self-expression, beauty, music, art, character, service, generosity, empathy, meaning, purpose, commitment, etc.

34. Consider the sophistication of contemporary advertising, both commercial and political, especially when aided by the tools of metadata analysis.

35. Note what happens if you try to disagree with others' political, religious, or lifestyle views, especially if those views happen to be at odds with those endorsed by groups, organizations, or governments having enormous power and resources.

36. Ten, C. L., *Mill on Liberty* (Oxford and London: Clarendon Press, 1980).

37. Mill, 1859.

CHAPTER 2

1. Benn, S. I., and Weinstein, W. L., "Being Free to Act and Being a Free Man," *Mind,* vol. 80 (1971), 311; and "Freedom as the Non-restriction of Options: A Rejoinder," *Mind,* vol. 83 (1974), 435.

2. Connolly, William, *The Terms of Political Discourse* (Princeton, NJ: Princeton University Press, 1993), 32–35.

3. Benn and Weinstein, 1971, 1974.

4. Mill, John Stuart, *On Liberty* (1859) (New York: Penguin, 1974), 68–69. See Casey, Gerard, "One Very Simple Principle," 2009, https://philosophynow.org/issues/76/One_very_simple_principle. See also Oliveira, Jorge Menezes, "Harm and Offence in Mill's Conception of Liberty," http://www.trinitinture.com/documents/oliveira.pdf.

5. This is a static view, of course. Society may act subsequently to restrict my freedom in reaction to my abuse of it. In practice, this happens continually. The burgeoning of laws and regulations in contemporary society is a symptom of this phenomenon. People see no reason arising from their understanding of what they are free to do for taking into consideration the consequences of their actions for others.

6. Day, J. P., "On Liberty and the Real Will," *Philosophy*, vol. 45, no. 173 (July 1970), 177–192.

7. Nowell-Smith, P. H., "Ifs and Cans," in *Free Will and Determinism,* Bernard Berofsky, ed. (New York: Harper & Row, 1966), 322–339.

CHAPTER 3

1. This is true of action performed because she regards it as an obligation or her duty just as much as it's true of action that's in her self-interest.

2. See Dagger, Richard, "Education, Autonomy, and Civic Virtue," in *Higher Education and the Practice of Democratic Politics,* Bernard Murchland, ed. (Dayton, OH: Kettering Foundation, 1991). As Dagger points out, because the factors that affect us may be internal (overwhelming needs or desires, coping mechanisms that produce dysfunctional behavior or distorted perceptions, etc., as well as prevailing social beliefs, attitudes, and customs), autonomy is sometimes regarded as self-*mastery* or self-*control*. This implies the existence of a "lower" self composed of needs, sensitivities, inclinations, feelings, and desires that we should be able to constrain, suppress, or even eliminate. It also implies a "higher" self whose job it is to make the best possible decisions. The autonomous person, on this view, is the one who achieves self-mastery by holding in check the impulses of the lower self in order to follow the dictates of the higher self. As Dagger rightly observes, though, to think in this way is to misconceive autonomy. It misconceives autonomy because it leads to self-denial and hence to the opposite of well-being and flourishing. The idea of self-mastery, he writes, "is much like the relationship between master and slave, with the higher self called upon to exercise strict control over the lower," often interpreted as a person's "impulses," "appetites," or "baser instincts." But appetites and impulses, like emotions and desires, are natural to human beings. So the attempt to rise above and master them can easily become a form of self-denial.

What, Dagger asks, is the alternative? It would be better to conceive the autonomous person as one who (1) recognizes and understands the appetites, emotions, and inclinations that motivate her, and (2) has developed the ability to reconcile the *values* to which her appetites, emotions, and inclinations correspond with the values she autonomously chooses, so that the two sets of values coexist with the greatest degree of harmony possible (recognizing that conflicts between values always involve trade-offs). This view of autonomy comes closer to self-*integration* or self-*realization* than to self-denial. If autonomy is self-mastery, it is like the craftsman's mastery—of a musician over his instrument and music, or of an athlete over her sport and its requirements—not the mastery of the slaveholder over the slave. As Dagger says, "if autonomy is self-mastery, . . . it is mastery *of* self, not mastery *over* self."

3. For example, many people believe human beings always act in their self-interest, as this is usually (and narrowly) defined. They look out for themselves first and foremost, pursue advantage over others, care little for anyone beyond their family and closest friends, and so forth. This "common sense" understanding of human motivation resembles the social science theory of psychological egoism. Evidence is substantial and growing, however, that psychological egoism doesn't always determine how we act. See, for example, Tomasello, Michael, *Why We Cooperate* (Cambridge, MA: MIT Press, 2009), and Keltner, Dacher, *Born to Be Good: The Science of a Meaningful Life* (New York: Norton, 2009).

4. Blackburn, Simon, *Think: A Compelling Introduction to Philosophy* (Oxford: Oxford University Press, 1999).

5. Not only are beliefs about what a person ought to do conventionally formed, so are beliefs about what is, about what exists, about what is factually true. It's difficult to understand why people act as they do unless their actions are explicable in terms of rules that are familiar to us. Suppose you had never seen a game of golf, and you saw someone walking around outside swinging a long, slender stick at a small white spheroid (and periodically swearing, breaking it in two, or flinging it into a pond of water). At the very least, you wouldn't be able to make sense of what he was doing, and you might even think he was seriously disturbed. Like games, social practices provide the word-concepts we draw on in order to think and act. A person takes the action she does because she has a reason to do so, and her reason is the value or satisfaction to be gained by performing the action. But that value has to be comprehensible in order for the reason to make sense to us (and to her as well).

6. Simons, Daniel J., and Shabris, Christopher F., "Gorillas in Our Midst: Sustained Inattention Blindness for Dynamic Events," *Perception,* vol. 28, no. 9 (1999), 1059–1074.

7. David Kolb, following Dewey (and Piaget and Lewin) posits a "learning cycle" in which "deep learning"—learning that yields thorough comprehension—emerges from a sequence of experience, reflection, abstraction, and active testing. In contrast, what Jennifer Moon terms

"surface learning" involves little or no reflection. Moon, Jennifer, *Reflection in Learning and Professional Development* (London: Kogan Page, 1999), 123.

8. It appears we are "hardwired" by evolution to resist changing our minds. We couldn't function if we didn't take a great deal for granted. See, for example, Popova, Maria, "The Backfire Effect: The Psychology of Why We Have a Hard Time Changing Our Minds," http://www.brainpickings.org /index.php/2014/05/13/backfire-effect-mcraney. A brief, popularized version of how attention to framing and small cues make it more likely for a person to do something that is different from what he or she normally would do can be found here: http://www.frbsf.org/community-development/files /reid_behavioralecon.pdf.

9. Moon, 1999.

10. For example, many people believe human beings always act in their self-interest, as this is usually (and narrowly) defined. They look out for themselves first and foremost, pursue advantage over others, care little for anyone beyond their family and closest friends, and so forth. But this "common sense" understanding of human motivation resembles the social science theory of psychological egoism, for which contrary evidence is substantial and growing. (See, e.g., Tomasello, 2009, and Dacher, 2009.)

11. The following summary of current views on human mental dispositions owes to Carcasson, Martin, "Why Process Matters: Democracy and Human Nature," *The Kettering Review*, vol. 34, no. 1 (Fall 2017).

12. Haidt, Jonathan, *The Righteous Mind: Why Good People Are Divided by Politics and Religion* (New York: Pantheon, 2012).

13. Mezirow, Jack, "How Critical Reflection Triggers Transformative Learning," in *Fostering Critical Reflection in Adulthood: A Guide to Transformative and Emancipatory Learning,* Jack Mezirow and Associates, eds. (San Francisco: Jossey-Bass, 1990), 5, 12.

14. Open-mindedness is a cultivated habit of guarding against the subconscious bias described in Mlodinow, Leonard, "Most of Us Are Biased, After All," *The New York Review of Books*, April 4, 2013, 58–61. Open-mindedness is also a requirement of genuine choice.

15. As a person matures, her personal interests, dispositions, and circumstances usually stabilize. Her environment may continue to change, of course, but it is likely to do so less rapidly than it did when she was younger. Hence, if during her maturity person A has periodically resubjected her beliefs and values to critical reexamination in light of the available evidence and her enhanced knowledge and experience, there is no reason to insist

that she must continue to do this as frequently or comprehensively as would be warranted for a young person just acquiring the ability to think critically about the beliefs and values she has absorbed while growing up.

16. Brandt, Richard, *Ethical Theory* (Englewood Cliffs, NJ: Prentice-Hall, 1959), 173. See also Hare, R. M., *Moral Thinking* (Oxford, UK: Clarendon Press, 1981).

17. Limitations on and distortions in her thinking may result from duress, by unmet or poorly fulfilled physical or emotional needs, poor education, social norms with which she has been inculcated, and so forth.

18. A person reasons "properly" if she reasons in accordance with the best standards of argumentation available and she is alert to conceptual imprecision, incoherence, contradictions, and errors of deduction or inference.

19. A person deliberates when she weighs reasons for and against a proposition, or weighs the advantages and disadvantages, costs and benefits, etc. of each option for action that is open to her.

20. This is not at all to say that a person's freedom—her liberty in particular—is necessarily or always enhanced by an increase in her knowledge, including self-knowledge, or in other characteristics such as self-motivation, self-control, etc. Freedom from external constraint must be extensive enough for individuals to choose actions and ways of life that may seem "willful, perverse, and even consciously irrational."

CHAPTER 4

1. "Incommensurable" means incapable of being reduced to a more basic common denominator (principle, value, standard, etc.) in terms of which comparison and a judgment of relative worth or importance can be made.

2. Wollheim, Richard, "John Stuart Mill and Isaiah Berlin: The Ends of Life and the Preliminaries of Morality," in *The Idea of Freedom: Essays in Honour of Isaiah Berlin,* Alan Ryan, ed. (Oxford: Oxford University Press, 1979), 253–254.

3. Mill, John Stuart, *On Liberty* (1859), Currin V. Shields, ed. (New York: Prentice-Hall, 1956), 7. See also Lee, Eugene, "John Stuart Mill's *On Liberty,*" http://www.victorianweb.org/philosophy/mill/liberty.html.

4. Dworkin, Ronald M., *Taking Rights Seriously* (Cambridge, MA: Harvard University Press, 1977).

5. Kovesi, Julius, *Moral Notions* (London: Routledge & Kegan Paul, 1967).

CHAPTER 5

1. The duty to treat all other persons with respect and goodwill has been justified in a number of ways. One way is to argue that it follows from the right of each human being to be treated with dignity. Another is to argue that the duty is rooted in the recognition that each person is of the same (incalculable, "infinite") worth. A third is to argue that it has a foundation in some universally shared characteristic: physical weakness, frailty, vulnerability, or mortality; fallibility or imperfectability; dependence or need (e.g., to be protected, cared for, loved), and so forth. My own candidate is our shared "subjectivity," our experience of sensations, emotions, needs and desires, thoughts (e.g., the thought that "I" am), and similar "qualia" (https://plato.stanford.edu/entries/qualia).

2. Sign in a shop window: "Good. Fast. Cheap. Pick two."

3. Kidder, Rushworth M., *How Good People Make Tough Choices: Resolving Dilemmas of Ethical Living* (New York: HarperCollins, 2003).

4. Many disagreements are never resolved. In the short term, we often have to settle for managing, tempering, or containing them. In the long term, if they no longer consume a great deal of time and energy, it's usually because they are simply outgrown or left behind as circumstances change and new generations arise for whom they are unimportant.

5. "Rightness" theories actually come in two basic forms: those that emphasize the importance of *rules* and those that focus on particular *actions*. For present purposes it's not necessary to get into the details of this distinction.

6. Care ethics is generally attributed to Carol Gilligan and Nel Noddings, *Internet Encyclopedia of Philosophy*, http://www.iep.utm.edu/care-eth.

7. Much depends on how we define our terms. Is murder ever right or even excusable? No, because *by definition* murder is wrong; it is *in*excusable, *un*justifiable killing. *Killing* may be excusable, but *murder* is a conclusion that no excuse or justification for killing is available. Redefining a rule (e.g., stipulating that murder is unjustified killing) as absolute doesn't change the underlying fact that we may encounter a situation in which a person ought to be excused from following the rule, or would be justified in not following it.

8. Suppose an issue were to arise in which the value of free speech conflicts with the value of political equality. One side argues that it's so important to protect the constitutional right to free political speech that limits must not be placed on how much money corporate "persons" may donate to

candidates' election campaigns. The other side argues that failure to establish limits allows donors to buy access to candidates both before and after they are elected to office, thereby vastly increasing the political power of well-funded political groups at the expense of less well-funded and less well-organized groups such as ordinary citizens. Although the Supreme Court decides that, from a constitutional perspective, the value of free speech is a more important value (even for corporate "persons") than political equality in an ostensible democracy, the supporters of the conflicting values continue the debate in other settings, both public and private. Eventually, though, having appealed to every political and moral principle and value they can think of, they exhaust the reasons for their respective positions. They remain locked in a contest of wills that seems likely to go on indefinitely. With no more reasons to consider on either side, the rules level of ethical thinking has nothing left to offer them. What do they do now?

9. Hare, R. M., *Moral Thinking* (Oxford, UK: Clarendon Press, 1981).

10. Janna Thompson, whom I mention further on, makes a similar argument. Thompson, Janna, *Discourse and Knowledge: Defence of a Collectivist Ethics* (London and New York: Routledge, 1998). See also Parfit, Derek, *On What Matters* (Oxford and London: Oxford University Press, 2011).

CHAPTER 6

1. This is a contested proposition, of course. Deontologists deny it, consequentialists accept it. See, for example, Brandt, Richard, *A Theory of the Good and the Right* (Amherst, NY: Prometheus, 1998); Hare, R. M., *Moral Thinking: Its Levels, Method, and Point* (Oxford, UK: Clarendon Press, 1981); Glover, Jonathan, ed., *Utilitarianism and Its Critics* (New York: Collier Macmillan, 1990); Goodin, Robert E., *Utilitarianism as a Public Philosophy* (Cambridge: Cambridge University Press, 1995); and Singer, Peter, *Practical Ethics* (Cambridge: Cambridge University Press, 1993).

2. Indeed, I would argue that the implicit prediction and expectation that following a rule will produce the "best" outcome is precisely what makes a rule seem to be self-justifying.

3. Why does "right" lead us to "best" (i.e., "most good")? Being our most general term of approbation, the word-concept "good" subsumes all that is

"right." (Everything that is right is also good, but not everything that is good is also right.) It's unsurprising, then, that when we reach an impasse in our effort to identify the right response in a given ethical dilemma, we should look for guidance to the most general evaluative word-concept available to us: "good."

Put in terms of Wittgenstein's theory of meaning (as elaborated by Kovesi, Julius, *Moral Notions* (London: Routledge & Kegan Paul, 1967), when we inquire into the purpose, point, or need (PPN) of the word-concept "right," we discover that "right" exists to help us identify, approve, adopt, maintain, and secure compliance with those rules, principles, and values we believe people should let guide their actions, both for their own sake and for the sake of others. If we then ask the further question of *why* people must allow these to guide their actions, we may answer that the word-concept "right" exists to help us—all of us—to live well: to survive, thrive, flourish, live contentedly or happily, and so forth (given the inescapable fact that human beings must, and inevitably will, live in each other's company).

This is almost exactly the purpose, point, or need of "good": to identify, recommend, and approve those things—objects, conditions, experiences, actions, and so on—that contribute to the ability of human beings to live life well: to survive, thrive, flourish, live contentedly or happily, and so forth. Because "right" is an element of "good," disagreements over what is right invariably lead us to the more general word-concept "good." Ultimately, "right" is a matter of what is best—of what contains the "most good."

4. A person reasons "properly" if she reasons in accordance with the best standards of argumentation available and she is alert to conceptual imprecision, incoherence, contradictions, and errors of deduction or inference.

5. A person deliberates when she weighs reasons for and against a proposition, or weighs the advantages and disadvantages, costs and benefits, etc. of each option for action that is open to her.

6. Limitations on and distortions in her thinking may be whether brought on by duress, by unmet or poorly fulfilled physical or emotional needs, or by social norms with which she has been inculcated.

7. Here I make two assumptions about human psychology: that people generally prefer outcomes that yield a higher level of satisfaction to those that yield a lower level, and that they usually would prefer the consequences of decisions made in the ideal conditions of autonomous choice to the consequences of decisions they otherwise would make. John Rawls makes a similar assumption, which he calls the "Aristotelian principle": in general, people will prefer activities that are more challenging to develop and

exercise because, in general, those activities produce greater satisfaction than less complex, less challenging activities. (See O'Meara, William, "The Aristotelian Principle in Mill and Kant," *Athens Journal of Humanities and Arts*, January 2015, https://www.atiner.gr/journals/humanities/2015-2-1-1-OMeara.pdf.) A rational, self-determining person ought to prefer what she *would* prefer, were she choosing in the conditions required for autonomous choice, because her "de facto" (actually existing) desires usually will yield less value—a lower level of satisfaction—than the choices she *would* make, were she to consider all the relevant information, examine the issue open-mindedly, and reason about it soundly.

8. It is important to bear in mind that participants' desires may not be judged *unilaterally* by *any* participant in ethical thinking at this level. Person A is not entitled to second-guess person B's desires and declare that they are *not* her autonomously formed (i.e., "hypothetical") desires. Person B must reach this conclusion herself (though ideally it will be the conclusion she shares with her fellow deliberators). Person A may and should help B form and identify her hypothetical desires, even by challenging her existing ("de facto" desires) and the feelings that accompany them. But B remains the ultimate judge of the desires she would choose to have, were she choosing in the conditions optimal for autonomous choice. Again, though, if she is thinking autonomously and adopts the ethical point of view, she will prefer the option or course of action that will achieve the best consequences for others as well as for herself, that is, that will have the best consequences for *all*.

9. For each of us, other human beings are both a resource of incomparable value and a source of contention and disagreement that impedes everyone's ability to live life in a way that realizes the most good for him or her as an individual, *given* the inescapable fact that we must, and inevitably will, live in each other's company.

10. Impartiality does not mean, of course, that we must agree to a course of action that treats them identically. Differential treatment might be permitted, if it would produce the best consequences for all. But the burden of justification falls on those who favor it.

11. In John Rawls's *A Theory of Justice*, the ideal decision maker is also a group: all of us, who are placed behind the "veil of ignorance" in the "original position." In practice, we must rely on the group of all actual persons constituting the relevant community (which ultimately and currently is the human species, but which may expand to successor species and non-hominid species). Because actual participation of all actual persons is in

most cases impossible, the next-best option would be a random sample of the population. See Briand, Michael K., *Practical Politics: Five Principles for a Communtiy That Works* (Chicago and Urbana: University of Illinois Press, 1999).

12. Difference theorists, feminists, and others allege that rationality and dispassion tend to favor persons who are more cerebral, analytical, or intellectual, to the disadvantage of those who are more spontaneous, emotional, passionate, etc. According to Lynne Sanders, disadvantaged people in particular have relatively little experience or skill, and hence inclination, for engaging in highly linear, abstract, formal discourse (Sanders, Lynne, "Against Deliberation," *Political Theory*, vol. 25, no. 3, 1997, http://faculty.virginia.edu/lsanders/SB617_01.pdf). But ethical dialogue and deliberation about what is good and best—dialogue in particular, as we will see—are entirely compatible with forms of communication such as testimony, storytelling, parables, anecdotes, and expression of emotions. Adopting the ethical point of view requires equal concern and respect for all persons and their needs, concerns, beliefs, values, and priorities. Allowing for and even encouraging such ways of communicating help participants meet that requirement.

CHAPTER 7

1. Viewing the world from the perspective of others is often called "perspective-taking." The requirement to do so sometimes is called the principle of reversibility. It is captured in the maxim "Put yourself in the other person's shoes" and similar formulations.

2. By "subjectively equal" I mean that others' feelings and desires exert on me the same motivational "pull" that my own feelings and desires do. Understanding them intellectually does not produce the same qualitative effect as comprehending them imaginatively and trying to appreciate them as if they were my own, as if I were experiencing the same motivational appeal that others experience in response to them.

3. Friedman, Maurice, "Healing through Meeting," *Tikkun*, vol. 3, no 2 (March/April 1988), 33.

4. Sympathy, like compassion, is "feeling *with*"—that is, to some substantial degree experiencing the same emotion when witnessing it in someone else or feeling it when imagining circumstances that typically evoke it. Unfortunately, sympathy is often regarded as *over*identification, a blurring of healthy psychological boundaries between the person and others.

5. As with any human capacity, trait, or attribute, the ability to enter imaginatively into the minds of others varies across individuals. (See, e.g., Szalavitz, Maia, "How Not to Raise a Bully: The Early Roots of Empathy," *Time*, April 17, 2010, http://content.time.com/time/health/article/0,8599,1982 190,00.html.) When it comes to empathy, most of us are of "average" ability. A small percentage of us have a great deal of ability. A similar small percentage have relatively little of it. But all of us can improve our ability to empathize and sympathize. Moreover, we know certain things about all human beings from our *own* experience. The more we can learn about others, the better able we become at seeing things from their perspective. This is not so much an affective or emotional exercise as it is an intellectual one. See, for example, Colby, Kim, Ehrlich, Thomas, Beaumont, Elizabeth, and Stevens, Jason, *Educating Citizens: Preparing America's Undergraduates for Lives of Moral and Civic Responsibility* (San Francisco: Jossey-Bass, 2003).

6. Braman, Donald, and Kahan, Dan M., "Overcoming the Fear of guns, the Fear of Gun Control, and the Fear of Cultural Politics: Constructing a Better Gun Debate," *Emory Law Journal*, vol. 55, no. 4 (2006), 570.

7. Gutmann, Amy, and Thompson, Dennis, "Moral Conflict and Political Consensus," *Ethics*, vol. 101, no. 1 (1990), 76.

8. Watson, George, "The Fuss about Ideology," *The Wilson Quarterly* (Winter 1992), 135.

9. Friedman, 1998.

10. Rokeach, Milton, *The Nature of Human Values* (New York: Free Press, 1993).

11. Nationalism is one of the few responses to loss of other viable identities that is still available to people in Western mass societies. Unfortunately, so are those old standbys: racism, anti-Semitism, and other forms of sectarianism.

12. For an insightful discussion of this phenomenon in contemporary politics, see Klein, Ezra, "How Politics Makes Us Stupid," April 6, 2014, http://www.vox.com/2014/4/6/5556462/brain-dead-how-politics-makes-us -stupid.

13. Burkhalter, Stephanie, Gastil, John, and Kelshaw, Todd, "A Conceptual Definition and Theoretical Model of Public Deliberation in Small Face-to-Face Groups," International Communication Association, 2002, 408–409.

14. See the discussion and references in Briand, Chapter 6, especially 106–109.

15. Evidence of our ability to comprehend one another abounds. (See, e.g., Gaitskill, Mary, "On Not Being a Victim," *Harper's*, March 1994. See also, Anderson, Elijah, "The Code of the Streets," *The Atlantic Monthly*, May 1994.) To be sure, some human motivation is (at least currently) largely beyond our comprehension. We find it hard to understand, for example, the psychopath, the obsessive, and the paranoid—even the child and (especially) the adolescent. The motivational states of fanatics and of persons with severe intellectual impairment are scarcely more accessible to us. Nor can we readily grasp what it is like to be a victim of Alzheimer's disease or a person in a persistent vegetative condition. The subjective lives of nonhuman species—dolphins, dogs, dromedaries—remain opaque to us, as do the worlds of the simplest sentient creatures. For most of the ethical and political questions we need to answer, however, the subjects we need to comprehend are human beings not fundamentally different from ourselves.

16. Brooks, David, "The Limits of Empathy," *The New York Times*, September 29, 2011, http://www.nytimes.com/2011/09/30/opinion/brooks-the-limits-of-empathy.html?r=1&nl= todaysheadlines&emc=tha212.

17. Brooks is correct that "people who are empathetic . . . are more likely to make compassionate moral judgments." When we comprehend another person's motivations, we are likely to soften any prior judgment we might have made concerning their beliefs, attitudes, or actions. As the old aphorism has it, "to understand is to forgive." Placing a person's motivations in the context of her past experience and her present circumstances makes them seem less unreasonable—more understandable—in the sense that we can see how anybody, even ourselves, might be motivated as she is. People who have a strong emotional need to disapprove what another person has done or wishes to do will find it difficult to empathize, and hence to forgive.

18. Justice is a value distinct from compassion, benevolence, etc. Recall the saying, "Temper justice with mercy."

CHAPTER 8

1. Bogen, James, and Farrell, Daniel M., "Freedom and Happiness in Mill's Defence of Liberty," *Philosophical Quarterly,* vol. 28, no. 113 (October 1978), 325–338.

2. Wollheim, Richard, "John Stuart Mill and Isaiah Berlin: The Ends of Life and the Preliminaries of Morality," in *The Idea of Freedom: Essays*

in Honour of Isaiah Berlin, Alan Ryan, ed. (Oxford: Oxford University Press), 267.

3. It is also a "networked process"—a process that is highly interdependent with the other "individual self-processes" that are under way contemporaneously.

4. An account of human needs like Maslow's is exactly what Mill needed to ground his theory, but it was unavailable to him. He wrote that, "of all the difficulties which impede the progress of thought, and the formation of well-grounded opinions on life and social arrangements, the greatest is now the unspeakable ignorance and inattention of mankind in respect to the influences which form human character" (Mill, John Stuart, *The Subjection of Women* (1869), 40, http://www.gutenberg.org/files/27083/27083-h /27083-h.htm). Fortunately, in the present era the research and theorizing of Maslow, Max-Neef, Kohlberg, Csikszentmihalyi, and others has reduced that ignorance somewhat by shedding considerable (though by no means complete or definitive) light on what is good for human beings.

5. Wollheim, 264.

6. The Aristotelian principle states that, as a matter of observable fact, people tend to choose more complex pursuits rather than less complex ones. That is, people tend to place more value on what requires time and effort to appreciate. This doesn't mean people always or necessarily prefer, say, attending the symphony, playing chess, or discussing philosophy to eating and drinking or lounging in the sun. It means that, as more basic needs are readily and consistently met, people begin to desire ways to satisfy "higher" human needs. Mill concedes that a life of simpler pursuits might actually lead to more contentment, because they are more easily satisfied. But he argued that *those who have experienced the higher and lower pleasures will prefer the former,* and for that reason *the higher pleasures are more desirable.* Mill points out, moreover, that certain conditions must be met before comparing a "lower" pleasure, X, and a "higher" pleasure, Y, in order to conduct a valid test of their relative desirability. Experimentation must be real experimentation. The experimenters must be "equally acquainted with and equally capable of appreciating and enjoying both"; they must be "equally susceptible to both classes of pleasure" (Haksar, Vinit, *Equality, Liberty, and Perfectionism,* Oxford: Oxford University Press, 1979, 201). In other words, they must think autonomously about the goods they must choose between.

7. Wollheim, 266.

8. And as we know, there is nothing about achieving a particular chronological age that by itself imbues a young person with the abilities, knowledge, and skills needed to develop, thrive, flourish, and live productively, contentedly, happily, and so on.

9. Searle, John R, "Can Information Theory Explain Consciousness?" *The New York Review of Books*, January 10, 2013.

10. Putnam, Hilary, *Reason, Truth, and History* (Cambridge: Cambridge University Press, 1981).

11. Kovesi, Julius, *Moral Notions* (London: Routledge & Kegan Paul, 1967).

12. Putnam, 207ff.

13. The same goes for sound and color.

14. Connolly, William, *The Terms of Political Discourse* (Princeton, NJ: Princeton University Press, 1993), 32–35.

15. Maslow, Abraham H., *The Farther Reaches of Human Nature* (New York: Viking Press, 1971).

16. See, for example, Schwartz, Shalom H., "Basic Human Values: Theory, Measurement, and Applications," *Revue Française de Sociologie,* vol. 47, no. 4 (2006).

17. No account of value based on human needs will ever provide definitive information about what will in fact be good for creatures in the future who differ from us, whether they are members of a substantially altered homo sapiens or of a successor species of intelligent life we are unable even to imagine.

18. Significantly, Maslow did not claim that *all* human beings pursue the same *ends*. Even if people have the same needs, they usually have multiple options for fulfilling them.

19. A more nuanced theory of human needs, perhaps, is the "human scale development" devised by Manfred Max-Neef, Antonio Elizalde, and Martin Hopenhayn. But they, too, contend that human needs are the same in all human cultures and in all historical time periods. What changes over time and between cultures is the variety of ways in which people seek to meet their basic needs. Along with Lawrence Kohlberg, Mihali Csikszentmihalyi, and others, they have shed considerable (though by no means complete or definitive) light on what is good for human beings.

20. Maslow believed a good society is one that creates and sustains an environment—physical, social, cultural, ethical, commercial—that through its ideals, priorities, institutions, practices, norms, and habits encourages and supports the development of human potential (the realization of each person's *"individuality"*). Meeting our needs as human beings is not easily

accomplished. Historically, people have confronted barriers and impediments thrown up by the conditions into which they were born: scarcity, ignorance, poverty, conflict, oppression, selfishness, coercion, fear, danger. A good society helps people overcome such barriers and impediments to meeting their needs.

21. See Goble, Frank G., *The Third Force: The Psychology of Abraham Maslow* (Richmond, CA: Maurice Bassett Publishing, 1970), 101–102.

22. Mill, J. S., *Utilitarianism*, 1863, Chapter 2, https://www.utilitarianism.com/mill2.htm.

23. Ten, C. L., *Mill on Liberty* (Oxford and London: Clarendon Press, 1980), 78–79.

24. Wollheim, 253.

25. Ten, 253–254.

26. Ten, 82.

27. Quoted in Ten, 122.

CHAPTER 9

1. The Veil of Ignorance is Rawls's way of ensuring that people treat each other ethically—that is, as persons entitled to equal concern and respect. By excluding knowledge of their particular identities, Rawls seeks to accomplish what Hare and others call achieving impartiality by adopting the moral (ethical) point of view.

2. Choosing without comparing and contrasting is a bit like trying to decide what color to paint a room and being given a choice between two root colors—say, pure blue and pure yellow—without being able to consider the full range of tints, shades, and tones in between (and without knowing what the room will be used for, who the primary user will be, how much natural light the room gets at what time of day, in which season, etc.). If we can rule out pure blue and pure yellow, the question becomes, How much blue and how much yellow will produce the best result? Similarly, if the choice is between value X (say, individual freedom) and value Y (say, community harmony), we need to consider what combination of X and Y will yield the best consequences in the situation, S (given all the relevant details of S). A sensible response would be to consider hypothetical examples of situations in which X and Y *would* produce the best consequences, and then "work inward" from those examples.

3. Because the number of factual variations of the prototypical and antitypical cases—any number of which might have no substantial bearing on

our judgment—easily could become unmanageable, it might be necessary for participants jointly to predetermine the variations to be deliberated.

4. Thompson, Janna, *Discourse and Knowledge: Defence of a Collectivist Ethic* (London and New York: Routledge, 1998).

5. Pages 32–37 in Thompson are worth reading in their entirety, especially page 37, where she argues that Habermas's consensus theory of truth fails to explain *how* consensus is achieved, and hence is *compatible* with a theory of an individual reasoning to the right conclusion. She says that if an ideal observer could not justify his conclusion to *others*, there would be reason to wonder about the "knowledge" he had arrived at or the way he came to it. It is not clear, she says, that his knowledge or ability to know was *dependent* on discourse with others. This stands in contrast to her own theory, in which ethical knowledge is *necessarily* collective (i.e., constructed "polylogically").

6. As noted previously, a critical-level ethical judgment applies to everyone who is or might be affected by an issue and its resolution. It also applies, prospectively, to every relevantly similar person in a relevantly similar situation. Kovesi's contention that judgments are valid from the point of view of "anyone" is a way of saying that prospective applications are valid for every *relevantly similar* person in a *relevantly similar* situation. That's not *every*one—it's "anyone." That is, judgments are only prima facie valid for everyone; not everyone will be relevantly similar and in relevantly similar circumstances.

7. Again, the Jainist fable of the blind men and the elephant reminds us that, as individuals, our ability to understand and appreciate reality, including (especially) reality as experienced by others, is limited. But it also suggests that, given the right method and proper motivation, we can make progress toward a correct conclusion that will resolve our disagreement. In principle, consensus is at least possible, and in practice it is something that, in the right conditions, can be approximated sufficiently to make it a reasonable aspiration.

8. It is no solution to reject self-consistency and argue that what is right is whatever one believes at a particular point in time for any particular situation, because the private language argument applies to this move as well.

CHAPTER 10

1. Limitations on and distortions in her thinking may result from duress, by unmet or poorly fulfilled physical or emotional needs, poor education, social norms with which she has been inculcated, and so forth.

2. A person reasons "properly" if she reasons in accordance with the best standards of argumentation available and she is alert to conceptual imprecision, incoherence, contradictions, and errors of deduction or inference.

3. A person deliberates when she weighs reasons for and against a proposition, or weighs the advantages and disadvantages, costs and benefits, etc. of each option for action that is open to her.

4. Viewing the world from the perspective of others is often called "perspective-taking." The requirement to do so sometimes is called the "principle of reversibility." It is captured in the maxim "Put yourself in the other person's shoes" and similar formulations.

5. Judgments in cases of disagreement between identifiable persons or between groups directly involved in an attempt to resolve an ethical issue between them apply to *everyone* who is or might be affected. When a judgment in a particular case is *generalized prospectively* beyond the immediate situation, it applies to "anyone"—that is, it applies to everyone as a presumption that can be refuted. This is so because we cannot know prospectively whether a rule in fact will apply to everyone. When it is adopted, therefore, it can apply only to the "typical," "average," or "representative" person, that is, "anyone."

6. As in the previous two stages, saying judgments are valid from the point of view of "anyone" is a way of saying that prospective applications are valid for every *relevantly similar* person in a *relevantly similar* situation.

7. Gutmann, Amy, and Thompson, Dennis, *Democracy and Disagreement* (Princeton, NJ: Princeton University Press, 1996), 81ff.

8. Mansbridge, Jane, "Deliberative and Non-Deliberative Negotiations," HKS Faculty Research Working Paper Series RWP09-010, John F. Kennedy School of Government, Harvard University, 2009, http://nrs.harvard.edu/urn-3:HUL.InstRepos: 4415943. See also:

Warren, Mark E., and Mansbridge, Jane, "Deliberative Negotiation," in *Negotiating Agreement in Politics*, Jane Mansbridge and Cathy Jo Martin, eds. (Washington, D.C.: American Political Science Association, 2013), https://scholar.harvard.edu/files/dtingley/files/negotiating_agreement_in _politics.pdf.

Naurin, Daniel, and Reh, Christine, "Deliberative Negotiation," in *The Oxford Handbook of Deliberative Democracy,* Andre Bachtiger, John S. Dryzek, Jane Mansbridge, and Mark E. Warren, eds. (Oxford and London: Oxford University Press, 2018).

Susskind, Lawrence, Gordon, Jessica, and Zaerpoor, Yamin, "Deliberative Democracy and Public Dispute Resolution," in *The Oxford Handbook of Deliberative Democracy,* Andre Bachtiger, John S. Dryzek, Jane Mansbridge, and Mark E. Warren, eds. (Oxford and London: Oxford University Press, 2018).

9. Fisher, Roger, and Ury, William, *Getting to YES: Negotiating Agreement without Giving In* (New York: Penguin Books, 1981).

10. Fisher, Roger, Ury, William, and Patton, Bruce, *Getting to YES: Negotiating an Agreement without Giving In* (New York: Penguin Books, 1991).

11. Fisher and Ury (and others) employ the acronym BATNA (best alternative to a negotiated agreement). I have amended it to reflect my emphasis on ethical thinking.

12. Braman, Donald, and Kahan, Dan M., "Overcoming the Fear of Guns, the Fear of Gun Control, and the Fear of Cultural Politics: Constructing a Better Gun Debate," *Emory Law Journal*, vol. 55, no. 4 (2006), 570–571.

13. Braman and Kahan, 578.

14. Braman and Kahan, 599–602.

15. Braman and Kahan, 596–598.

16. Braman and Kahan, 596–598.

17. See, for example, Fisher and Ury, 1981; Fisher, Ury, and Patton, 1991; and Burton, John, *Conflict Resolution and Prevention* (New York: St. Martin's Press, 1990). See also:

Stone, Douglas, Patton, Bruce, and Heen, Sheila, *Difficult Conversations: How to Discuss What Matters Most* (New York: Penguin Press, 2000).

Ury, William, *The Third Side: Why We Fight and How We Can Stop* (New York: Penguin Books, 2000).

Rosenberg, Marshall, *Nonviolent Communication: A Language of Life* (Encinitas, CA: PuddleDancer, 2015).

Yankelovich, Daniel, *The Magic of Dialogue: Transforming Conflict into Cooperation* (New York: Touchstone, 2001).

Saunders, Harold, *Politics Is about Relationship: A Blueprint for the Citizens' Century* (New York: Palgrave Macmillan, 2005).

18. On the topic of resolving conflict between worldviews, see, for example, Gerzon, Mark, *A House Divided: Six Belief Systems Struggling for America's Soul* (New York: Tarcher/Putnam, 1996); Saunders, 2005; LeBaron Michelle, *Bridging Troubled Waters: Conflict Resolution from the Heart* (San Francisco: Jossey-Bass, 2002); Stone, Patton, and Heen, 2000; Cragan, John F.; and Shields, Donald C., *Symbolic Theories in*

Applied Communication Research: Bormann, Burke, and Fisher (Cresskill, NJ: Hampton Press, 1995); and Clark, Mary, *In Search of Human Nature* (London: Routledge, 2002).

CHAPTER 11

1. The desire for consistency may stem from the discomfort of "cognitive dissonance."

2. The prisoner's dilemma explains, I believe, why Kant argued that the categorical imperative is the only rational rule for regulating interpersonal relations between the socially interdependent creatures that human beings are.

3. These resources have certain features in common: (1) Everyone needs or at least benefits from them. (2) They can't be provided to some people while keeping others from benefiting as well. Although everybody benefits from a public good, at least some people can avoid paying for it. These people get a "free ride." Hence the name "free-rider" problem. (3) Overuse or misuse by some people could diminish its value or even its availability for everyone. This is the "tragedy of the commons." A corollary is the problem of "externalities." It occurs when someone engages in an activity that has an adverse impact on a public good, but can avoid responsibility for that impact. The cost is "externalized," or "socialized": displaced onto others. Air and water pollution, which eventually have to be cleaned up at public expense, are prime examples of externalities. (4) Ownership or control by some people could render access by others impossible or prohibitively expensive.

4. Colby, Kim, Ehrlich, Thomas, Beaumont, Elizabeth, and Stevens, Jason, *Educating Citizens: Preparing America's Undergraduates for Lives of Moral and Civic Responsibility* (San Francisco: Jossey-Bass), 2003. Studies have found a significant correlation between years of higher education and scores on Kohlberg's *Moral Judgment Interview.* The experience of grappling with challenging ethical issues contributes significantly to the increasing maturity of students' moral judgment. This is especially true when the teacher draws attention to important distinctions, assumptions, and contradictions. Much of the positive impact of such instruction may stem from making students aware of their previously unquestioned interpretive schemes, bringing biases to the surface, and illustrating the inherent ambiguity of ethical situations that previously appeared clear-cut.

5. Reinhold Niebuhr believed that "it may be possible to expect a human being to be genuinely selfless and good in his or her family life and personal relationships. But it is simply not in human nature for these virtues to be translated into the larger, impersonal scale of an entire country or an entire world. 'It would therefore seem better to accept a frank dualism in morals' . . . which would 'distinguish between what we expect of individuals and of groups,' since 'the moral obtuseness of human collectives makes a morality of pure disinterestedness impossible.'" (Kirsch, Adam, "The Ironic Wisdom of Reinhold Niebuhr," *The New York Review of Books*, August 13, 2015, 74.) Although there are important differences between individuals and groups, the latter have individual leaders or representatives, and to them ethical principles must apply. Moreover, to an important degree, I would argue, the distinction between the exploration and negotiation levels of ethical thinking accommodates the differences between individuals and groups, with the latter level apt to prove more readily applicable to national and international disagreements. Within a society like the United States, however, with a national culture with which most people identify, people must make the effort to resolve their disagreement first at the rules and exploration levels. On the matter of intergroup conflict, see also Schmookler, Andrew Bard, *The Parable of the Tribes: The Problem of Power in Social Evolution,* 2nd ed. (Albany, NY: State University of New York Press, 1995).

6. Hutcheson, for example, called the moral sense "uniform in its influence," and Hume said it is "the same in all."

7. Gutmann, Amy, and Thompson, Dennis, *Democracy and Disagreement* (Princeton, NJ: Princeton University Press, 1996). See also Gutmann and Thompson, *Why Deliberative Democracy?* (Princeton, NJ: Princeton University Press, 2004).

8. Stephen Macedo, "Introduction," in *Deliberative Politics: Essays on Democracy and Disagreement*, Stephen Macedo, ed. (New York and Oxford: Oxford University Press, 1999), 7.

9. Gutmann and Thompson, in Macedo, 259.

10. "Acceptable" reasons are not considerations that *everyone will* accept, but that *anyone can* recognize as relevant and valid, even if ultimately we discount their force or reject them completely. We do not have to agree on which reasons are the most important considerations, or on how much weight different reasons should be assigned. But we must explain to our fellow citizens why a position we support (or oppose) will benefit not only us, but will prove best for everyone.

11. Anderson, Elizabeth, "Social Insurance and Self-Sufficiency," February 5, 2005, http://www-personal.umich.edu/~eandersn/blog.html.

12. Freeman, Samuel, "Why Be Good?" (review of *On What Matters*, by Derek Parfit), *New York Review of Books*, April 26, 2012, 52–54.

13. I have reason to accept and follow them, not in a hypothetical thought experiment like Rawls's original position, but in the real-world here and now.

CHAPTER 12

1. Lasch, Christopher, *The True and Only Heaven: Progress and Its Critics* (New York: Norton, 1991), 40–49, 42 (footnote). The major figures of the Enlightenment included Diderot, Constant, Hume, Kant, Montesquieu, Rousseau, Adam Smith, and Voltaire. Earlier philosophers whose work influenced them included Bacon, Hobbes, Locke, Descartes, Bentham, and Spinoza.

2. Lasch, 43.

3. Lasch, 119.

4. Lasch, 328.

5. Lasch, 386.

6. See, for example, Pinker, Steven, *Enlightenment Now: The Case for Reason, Science, Humanism, and Progress* (New York: Viking, 2018). See also Pinker, Steven, *The Better Angels of Our Nature: Why Violence Has Declined* (New York: Viking, 2011).

7. Lewis Mumford, quoted in Lasch, 79.

8. George Orwell, quoted in Lasch, 79.

9. Lewis Mumford, quoted in Lasch, 80.

10. Cited in Lasch, 305.

11. Ignatieff, Michael, "Making Room for God," *The New York Review of Books,* June 28, 2018, http://www.nybooks.com/articles/2018/06/28/making-room-for-god-liberalism-religion.

12. Maslow, Abraham H., *The Farther Reaches of Human Nature* (New York: Viking Press, 1971). See also Goble, Frank G., *The Third Force: The Psychology of Abraham Maslow* (Richmond, CA: Maurice Bassett Publishing, 1970).

13. Maslow, 1971. See also Koltko-Rivera, Mark E., "Rediscovering the Later Version of Maslow's Hierarchy of Needs: Self-Transcendence and Opportunities for Theory, Research, and Unification," *Review of General Psychology,* vol. 10, no. 4 (2006), 302–317; and Garcia-Romeu, Albert,

"Self-Transcendence as a Measurable Transpersonal Construct," *Journal of Transpersonal Psychology,* vol. 42, no. 1 (2010), 26–47.

14. Judgments of value require standards, and standards imply acceptability, adequacy, suitability, or utility *for a purpose.* Is this a good phone? Yes, if it helps me stay in touch with other people; if it helps me find my way around an unfamiliar town; if I can ask it questions it will find the answer to; if it's easy to use; if it doesn't cost too much to maintain; and so forth. Why does that matter? Because I value being able to do all these things conveniently and efficiently. Why do I value these things? Because I value the way of life they make possible. Why do I value this way of living? *Because . . .*

15. See, for example, Lasch, Christopher, *The True and Only Heaven: Progress and Its Critics* (New York: Norton, 1991), 40–49.

16. Goodman, Rob, "The Comforts of the Apocalypse," *The Chronicle of Higher Education,* August 19, 2013, http://chronicle.com/article/The-Comforts-of-the-Apocalypse/141117/?cid=cr&utm_source=cr&utm_medium=en.

17. Edmundson, Mark, "Why We Need to Resurrect Our Souls," *The Chronicle of Higher Education,* August 17, 2015, http://chronicle.com/article/Why-We-Need-to-Resurrect-Our/232369/?cid=cr&utm_source=cr&utm_medium=eny.

18. Gray, John, *Straw Dogs: Thoughts on Humans and Other Animals* (London: Granta, 2002), 3.

19. Gray, 4–5.

20. McCabe, Gordon, "John Gray and *Straw Dogs,*" December 8, 2007, http://mccabism.blogspot.com/2007/12/john-gray-and-humanism.html.

21. Gray, 4–6.

22. Gray, 123.

23. Gray, 142.

24. Gray, 197.

25. Eagleton, Terry, "Humanity and Other Animals," *The Guardian,* September 6, 2002, https://www.theguardian.com/books/2002/sep/07/highereducation.news2.

26. McCabe, 2007.

27. Burton, John, *Conflict Resolution and Prevention* (New York: St. Martin's Press, 1990).

28. Hughes, Glenn, "Introduction," in *The Politics of the Soul: Eric Voegelin on Religious Experience,* Glenn Hughes, ed. (Lanham, MD: Rowman and Littlefield, 1999), 3.

29. Hughes, 1.

30. Hughes, 2.

31. Morrissey, Michael P., "Voegelin, Religious Experience, and Immortality," in Hughes, 1999, 13.

32. Cited in Lasch, 79.

33. Orwell, George, "Review of *Mein Kampf*," *The New English Weekly*, March 21, 1940, https://bookmarks.reviews/george-orwells-1940-review-of-mein-kampf.

34. Brooks, David, "The Arena Culture," *The New York Times*, December 30, 2010, review of Hubert Dreyfus and Sean Dorrance Kelly, *All Things Shining* (New York: Free Press, 2010), http://www.nytimes.com/2010/12/31/opinion/31brooks.html?nl=todaysheadlines&emc=tha212.

35. Johnson, Fenton, "A Skeptic Searches for an American Faith," *Harper's*, September 1998, 39–54.

36. Wilber, Ken, *The Marriage of Sense and Soul: Integrating Science and Religion* (New York: Random House, 1998), 55.

37. Wilber, 56. As Wilber notes (p. 86), Kant went beyond the demonstration that monological reason *cannot prove* the existence of spirit, freedom, or immortality to demonstrate that reason could not *dis*prove their existence either.

38. Cumberland, Richard, *A Treatise of the Laws of Nature* (1727) (Indianapolis: Liberty Fund, 2005).

39. Oz-Salzburger, Fania, *Adam Ferguson: An Essay on the History of Civil Society* (Cambridge: Cambridge University Press, 1995), 99–100.

40. Brooks, David, "Personalism: The Philosophy We Need," *The New York Times*, June 14, 2018, https://www.nytimes.com/2018/06/14/opinion/personalism-philosophy-collectivism-fragmentation.html?emc=edit_th_180615&nl=todaysheadlines&nlid=573176760615.

41. Lasch, 78.

42. Coaston, Jane, "Trump, Andrew Jackson, and Ourselves," *The New York Times*, May 2, 2017, https://www.nytimes.com/2017/05/02/opinion/trump-andrew-jackson-and-ourselves.html.

43. Lasch, 360.

44. Lasch, 297.

45. Lasch, 296.

46. Lasch, 294.

47. James, William, "The Moral Equivalent of War" (1910), in *The Writings of William James: A Comprehensive Edition*, John J. McDermott, ed. (Chicago: University of Chicago Press, 1977). Quoted in Lasch, 301.

48. See, for example, "America's 100 Greatest Heroes & Villains: The Top 50 Virtuous Heroes and Top 50 Wicked Villains" (Los Angeles: American Film Institute), http://www.filmsite.org/afi100heroesvill.html.

49. Sullivan, Andrew, "The World Is Better Than Ever. Why Are We Miserable?" *New York Magazine*, March 9, 2018, http://nymag.com/daily/intelligencer/2018/03/sullivan-things-are-better-than-ever-why-are-we-miserable.html.

50. Palmer, Parker J., *To Know as We Are Known: Education as a Spiritual Journey* (San Francisco: Harper & Row, 1993), 57.

51. Berry, Wendell, *The Unsettling of America: Culture and Agriculture* (1977) (Berkeley, CA: Counterpoint Press, 2015), 22.

52. Lincoln, Abraham, "Annual Message to Congress," December 1, 1862, http://www.abrahamlincolnonline.org/lincoln/speeches/congress.htm.

53. Adams, John, Letter to James Warren, April 22, 1776, https://founders.archives.gov/documents/Adams/06-04-02-0052.

54. Paine, Thomas, "The Crisis" (1776), http://www.loc.gov/teachers/classroommaterials/presentationsandactivities/presentations/timeline/amrev/north/paine.html.

55. Schumacher, E. F., *A Guide for the Perplexed* (New York: Harper & Row, 1977), 46.

56. Johnson, 1998, 39.

57. Wilber, 212–213.

Bibliography

Adams, John. "Letter to James Warren," April 22, 1776, https://founders.archives.gov/documents/Adams/06-04-02-0052.

Andersen, Kurt. "How America Lost Its Mind," *The Atlantic Monthly*, September 2017, https://www.theatlantic.com/assets/media/files/theatlantic20170901_compressed.pdf.

Anderson, Elijah. "The Code of the Streets," *The Atlantic Monthly*, May 1994.

Anderson, Elizabeth. "Social Insurance and Self-Sufficiency," February 5, 2005, http://www-personal.umich.edu/~eandersn/blog.html.

Applebaum, Anne. "A Warning from Europe: The Worst Is Yet to Come," *The Atlantic Monthly*, October 2018.

Bell, Daniel. *The Cultural Contradictions of Capitalism*. New York: Basic Books, 1976.

Bellah, Robert N., Madsen, Richard, Sullivan, William M., Swidler, Ann, and Tipton, Steven M. *Habits of the Heart: Individualism and Commitment in American Life*. Berkeley and Los Angeles: University of California Press, 1985.

Benn, S. I., and Weinstein, W. L. "Being Free to Act and Being a Free Man," *Mind,* vol. 80 (1971).

Benn, S. I., and Weinstein, W. L. "Freedom as the Non-Restriction of Options: A Rejoinder," *Mind,* vol. 83 (1974), 435.

Berry, Wendell. *The Unsettling of America: Culture and Agriculture*. Berkeley, CA: Counterpoint Press, 1977 (2015), 22.

Blackburn, Simon. *Think: A Compelling Introduction to Philosophy*. Oxford: Oxford University Press, 1999.

Bogen, James, and Farrell, Daniel M. "Freedom and Happiness in Mill's Defence of Liberty," *Philosophical Quarterly*, vol. 28, no. 113 (October 1978).

Braman, Donald, and Kahan, Dan M. "Overcoming the Fear of Guns, the Fear of Gun Control, and the Fear of Cultural Politics: Constructing a Better Gun Debate," *Emory Law Journal*, vol. 55, no. 4 (2006), 570.

Brandt, Richard. *Ethical Theory*. Englewood Cliffs, NJ: Prentice Hall, 1959.

Brandt, Richard. *A Theory of the Good and the Right*. Amherst, NY: Prometheus, 1998.

Briand, Michael K. *Practical Politics: Five Principles for a Community That Works*. Urbana and Chicago: University of Illinois Press, 1999.

Brooks, David. "The Arena Culture," *The New York Times*, December 30, 2010. Review of Hubert Dreyfus and Sean Dorrance Kelly, *All Things Shining*. New York: Free Press, 2010. http://www.nytimes.com/2010/12/31/opinion/31brooks.html?nl=todaysheadlines&emc=tha212.

Brooks, David. "The Limits of Empathy," *The New York Times*, September 29, 2011, http://www.nytimes.com/2011/09/30/opinion/brooks-the-limits-of-empathy.html?_r=1&nl=todaysheadlines&emc=tha212.

Brooks, David. "The Blindness of Social Wealth," *The New York Times*, April 16, 2018, https://www.nytimes.com/2018/04/16/opinion/facebook-social-wealth.html.

Brooks, David. "Personalism: The Philosophy We Need," *The New York Times*, June 14, 2018, https://www.nytimes.com/2018/06/14/opinion/personalism-philosophy-collectivism-fragmentation.html?emc=edit_th_180615&nl=todaysheadlines&nlid=573176760615.

Brooks, David. "Anthony Kennedy and the Privatization of Meaning," *The New York Times*, June 28, 2018, https://www.nytimes.com/2018/06/28/opinion/anthony-kennedy-individualism.html?em_pos=small&emc=edit_ty_20180629&nl=opinion-today&nl_art=3&nlid=57317676emc%3Dedit_ty_20180629&ref=headline&te=1.

Buchanan, James, and Tullock, Gordon. *The Calculus of Consent: Logical Foundations of Constitutional Democracy*. Ann Arbor, MI: University of Michigan Press, 1962.

Burkhalter, Stephanie, Gastil, John, and Kelshaw, Todd. "A Conceptual Definition and Theoretical Model of Public Deliberation in Small Face-to-Face Groups," International Communication Association, 2002, 408–409.

Burton, John. *Conflict Resolution and Prevention*. New York: St. Martin's Press, 1990.

Carcasson, Martin. "Why Process Matters: Democracy and Human Nature," *The Kettering Review*, vol. 34, no. 1 (Fall 2017).

Casey, Gerard. "One Very Simple Principle," 2009, https://philosophynow
.org/issues/76/One_very_simple_principle.

Clark, Mary. *In Search of Human Nature*. London: Routledge, 2002.

Coaston, Jane. "Trump, Andrew Jackson, and Ourselves," *The New York Times*, May 2, 2017, https://www.nytimes.com/2017/05/02/opinion /trump-andrew-jackson-and-ourselves.html.

Colby, Kim, Ehrlich, Thomas, Beaumont, Elizabeth, and Stevens, Jason. *Educating Citizens: Preparing America's Undergraduates for Lives of Moral and Civic Responsibility*. San Francisco: Jossey-Bass, 2003.

Connolly, William. *The Terms of Political Discourse*. Princeton, NJ: Princeton University Press, 1993.

Cragan, John F., and Shields, Donald C. *Symbolic Theories in Applied Communication Research: Bormann, Burke, and Fisher*. Cresskill, NJ: Hampton Press, 1995.

Cumberland, Richard. *A Treatise of the Laws of Nature*, 1727. Indianapolis: Liberty Fund, 2005.

Dagger, Richard. "Education, Autonomy, and Civic Virtue," in *Higher Education and the Practice of Democratic Politics*, Bernard Murchland, ed. Dayton, OH: Kettering Foundation, 1991.

Day, J. P. "On Liberty and the Real Will," *Philosophy*, vol. 45, no. 173 (July 1970), 177–192.

Den Uyl, Douglas J. *The Virtue of Prudence*. New York: Peter Lang, 1991.

Deneen, Patrick J. *Why Liberalism Failed*. New Haven, CT: Yale University Press, 2018. Cited in Sullivan, 2018. "The World Is Better Than Ever. Why Are We Miserable?"

Doble, John. *A Factory Mentality: The Consumer Mindset in American Public Education*. Dayton, OH: Kettering Foundation, 1998.

Douthat, Ross. "Free Speech Will Not Save Us," *The New York Times*, May 26, 2018, https://www.nytimes.com/2018/05/26/opinion/sun day/free-speech-nfl-protests-trump.html?emc=edit_th_180527&nl =todaysheadlines&nlid=573176760527.

Downs, Anthony. *An Economic Theory of Democracy*. New York: Harper & Row, 1957.

Dworkin, Ronald M. *Taking Rights Seriously*. Cambridge, MA: Harvard University Press, 1977.

Eagleton, Terry. "Humanity and Other Animals," *The Guardian*, September 6, 2002. https://www.theguardian.com/books/2002/sep/07 /highereducation.news2.

Edmundson, Mark. "Why We Need to Resurrect Our Souls," *The Chronicle of Higher Education*, August 17, 2015, http://chronicle.com/article/Why-We-Need-to-Resurrect-Our/232369/?cid=cr&utm_source=cr&utm_medium=eny.

Edsall, Thomas B. "Democracy Can Plant the Seeds of Its Own Destruction," *The New York Times,* October 19, 2017.

Elster, Jon. "The Market and the Forum: Three Varieties of Political Theory," in *Foundations of Social Choice Theory*, Jon Elster and Aanund Hylland, eds. Cambridge: Cambridge University Press, 1986, 104–132.

Emerson, Ralph Waldo. "Self-Reliance," in *Essays*, first series, 1841, http://transcendentalism-legacy.tamu.edu/authors/emerson/essays/selfreliance.html.

Emerson, Ralph Waldo. "Experience," in *Essays*, second series, 1844, http://transcendentalism-legacy.tamu.edu/authors/emerson/essays/experience.html.

Epstein, Joseph. *Ambition*. New York: Dutton, 1981.

Fisher, Max. "The Weaknesses in Liberal Democracy That May Be Pulling It Apart," *The New York Times*, November 3, 2018.

Fisher, Roger, and Ury, William. *Getting to YES: Negotiating Agreement without Giving In*. New York: Penguin Books, 1981.

Fisher, Roger, Ury, William, and Patton, Bruce. *Getting to YES: Negotiating Agreement without Giving In*. New York: Penguin Books, 1991.

Freeman, Samuel. "Why Be Good?" *The New York Review of Books*, April 26, 2012, 52–54.

Friedman, Maurice. "Healing through Meeting," *Tikkun*, vol. 3, no. 2 (March/April 1988).

Fuller, Robert W. *Somebodies and Nobodies: Overcoming the Abuse of Rank*. Gabriola Island, BC: New Society Publishers, 2004.

Fuller, Robert W. *All Rise: Somebodies, Nobodies, and the Politics of Dignity*. San Francisco: Berrett-Koehler, 2006.

Fuller, Robert W., and Gerloff, Pamela A. *Dignity for All: How to Create a World without Rankism*. San Francisco: Berrett-Koehler, 2008.

Gaitskill, Mary. "On Not Being a Victim," *Harper's*, March 1994.

Garcia-Romeu, Albert. "Self-Transcendence as a Measurable Transpersonal Construct," *Journal of Transpersonal Psychology,* vol. 42, no. 1 (2010), 26–47.

Gerzon, Mark. *A House Divided: Six Belief Systems Struggling for America's Soul*. New York: Tarcher/Putnam, 1996.

Gilligan, Carol. *In a Different Voice*. Cambridge, MA: Harvard University Press, 1982.

Glover, Jonathan, ed. *Utilitarianism and Its Critics*. New York: Collier Macmillan, 1990.

Goble, Frank G. *The Third Force: The Psychology of Abraham Maslow*. Richmond, CA: Maurice Bassett Publishing, 1970, 101–102.

Goodin, Robert E. *Utilitarianism as a Public Philosophy*. Cambridge: Cambridge University Press, 1995.

Goodman, Rob. "The Comforts of the Apocalypse," *The Chronicle of Higher Education*, August 19, 2013, http://chronicle.com/article/The-Comforts-of-the-Apocalypse/141117/?cid=cr&utm_source=cr&utm_medium=en.

Gray, John. *Straw Dogs: Thoughts on Humans and Other Animals*. London: Granta, 2002.

Gutmann, Amy, and Thompson, Dennis. *Democracy and Disagreement*. Princeton, NJ: Princeton University Press, 1996.

Gutmann, Amy, and Thompson, Dennis. *Why Deliberative Democracy?* Princeton, NJ: Princeton University Press, 2004.

Haidt, Jonathan. *The Righteous Mind: Why Good People Are Divided by Politics and Religion*. New York: Pantheon, 2012.

Haksar, Vinit. *Equality, Liberty, and Perfectionism*. Oxford: Oxford University Press, 1979.

Hall, Robert E. *This Land of Strangers: The Relationship Crisis That Imperils Home, Work, Politics, and Faith*. Austin, TX: Greenleaf, 2012.

Hare, R. M. *Moral Thinking*. Oxford, UK: Clarendon Press, 1981.

Hughes, Glenn. "Introduction," in *The Politics of the Soul: Eric Voegelin on Religious Experience*, Glenn Hughes, ed. Lanham, MD: Rowman and Littlefield, 1999.

Ignatieff, Michael. "Are the Authoritarians Winning?" *The New York Review of Books*, July 10, 2014.

Ignatieff, Michael. "Making Room for God," *The New York Review of Books,* June 28, 2018, http://www.nybooks.com/articles/2018/06/28/making-room-for-god-liberalism-religion.

Illing, Sean. "Is American Democracy in Decline? Should We Be Worried?" https://www.vox.com/2017/10/13/16431502/america-democracy-decline-liberalism.

Inglehart, Ronald F. "How Much Should We Worry? *Journal of Democracy*, vol. 27, no. 3 (July 2016), http://pscourses.ucsd.edu/ps200b/Inglehart%20How%20Much%20SHould%20we%20Worry.pdf.

James, William. "The Moral Equivalent of War" (1910), in *The Writings of William James: A Comprehensive Edition,* John J. McDermott, ed. Chicago: University of Chicago Press, 1977.

James, William. *The Varieties of Religious Experience.* New York: Macmillan, 1961 (1903).

Johnson, Fenton. "A Skeptic Searches for an American Faith," *Harper's,* September 1998.

Johnson, Rossarian. "Study by MIT Economist: U.S. Has Regressed to a Third-World Nation for Most of Its Citizens," https://www.themaven .net/theintellectualist/news/study-by-mit-economist-u-s-has-regressed -to-a-third-world-nation-for-most-of-its-citizens-Sb5A5HZ1rUiXav Zapos30g.

Keltner, Dacher. *Born to Be Good: The Science of a Meaningful Life.* New York: Norton, 2009.

Kidder, Rushworth M. *How Good People Make Tough Choices: Resolving Dilemmas of Ethical Living.* New York: HarperCollins, 2003.

Kirsch, Adam. "The Ironic Wisdom of Reinhold Niebuhr," *The New York Review of Books,* August 13, 2015, 74.

Klein, Ezra. "How Politics Makes Us Stupid," April 6, 2014, http://www.vox .com/2014/4/6/5556462/brain-dead-how-politics-makes-us-stupid.

Koltko-Rivera, Mark E. "Rediscovering the Later Version of Maslow's Hierarchy of Needs: Self-Transcendence and Opportunities for Theory, Research, and Unification," *Review of General Psychology,* vol. 10, no. 4 (2006), 302–317.

Kovesi, Julius. *Moral Notions.* London: Routledge & Kegan Paul, 1967.

Lasch, Christopher. *The True and Only Heaven: Progress and Its Critics.* New York: Norton, 1991.

Lasswell, Harold. *Politics: Who Gets What, When, How.* New York: P. Smith, 1950.

LeBaron, Michelle. *Bridging Troubled Waters: Conflict Resolution from the Heart.* San Francisco: Jossey-Bass, 2002.

Lee, Eugene. "John Stuart Mill's *On Liberty,*" http://www.victorianweb.org /philosophy/mill/liberty.html.

"Liberalism," *Stanford Encyclopedia of Philosophy,* revised January 22, 2018, https://plato.stanford.edu/entries/liberalism.

Lincoln, Abraham. "Annual Message to Congress," December 1, 1862, http://www.abrahamlincolnonline.org/lincoln/speeches/congress .htm.

Lukes, Stephen. *Individualism.* London and Oxford: Blackwell, 1973.

Macedo, Stephen. "Introduction," in *Deliberative Politics: Essays on Democracy and Disagreement*, Stephen Macedo, ed. New York and Oxford: Oxford University Press, 1999.

MacIntyre, Alasdair. *After Virtue: A Study in Moral Theory.* Notre Dame, IN: University of Notre Dame Press, 1981.

MacIntyre, Alasdair. "How to Be a North American," Publication No. 2-88. Washington, D.C.: Federation of State Humanities Councils, 1987.

Mansbridge, Jane. "Deliberative and Non-Deliberative Negotiations," HKS Faculty Research Working Paper Series RWP09-010, John F. Kennedy School of Government, Harvard University, 2009.

Maslow, Abraham H. *The Farther Reaches of Human Nature.* New York: Viking Press, 1971.

McCabe, Gordon. "John Gray and *Straw Dogs*," December 8, 2007, http://mccabism.blogspot.com/2007/12/john-gray-and-humanism.html.

Mezirow, Jack. "How Critical Reflection Triggers Transformative Learning," in *Fostering Critical Reflection in Adulthood: A Guide to Transformative and Emancipatory Learning*, Jack Mezirow and Associates, eds. San Francisco: Jossey-Bass, 1990.

Mill, John Stuart. *Utilitarianism* (1863), Chapter 2, https://www.utilitarianism.com/mill2.htm.

Mill, John Stuart. *The Subjection of Women* (1869), 40, http://www.gutenberg.org/files/27083/27083-h/27083-h.htm.

Mill, John Stuart. *On Liberty*, 1859, Currin V. Shields, ed. New York: Prentice-Hall, 1956.

Mill, John Stuart. "Of Individuality, as One of the Elements of Wellbeing," in *On Liberty* (1859). New York: Penguin, 1974. https://www.utilitarianism.com/ol/three.html.

Mlodinow, Leonard. "Most of Us Are Biased, After All," *The New York Review of Books*, April 4, 2013, 58–61.

Moon, Jennifer. *Reflection in Learning and Professional Development.* London: Kogan Page, 1999.

Morrissey, Michael P. "Voegelin, Religious Experience, and Immortality," in *The Politics of the Soul: Eric Voegelin on Religious Experience*, Glenn Hughes, ed. Lanham, MD: Rowman and Littlefield, 1999, 13.

Nagel, Thomas. "What Is a Good Life?" *The New York Review of Books*, February 10, 2011.

Nagel, Thomas. "The Taste for Being Moral," *The New York Review of Books*, December 6, 2012.

Naurin, Daniel, and Reh, Christine. "Deliberative Negotiation," in *The Oxford Handbook of Deliberative Democracy*, Andre Bachtiger, John S. Dryzek, Jane Mansbridge, and Mark E. Warren, eds. Oxford and London: Oxford University Press, 2018.

Needleman, Jacob. *The American Soul: Rediscovering the Wisdom of the Founders*. New York: Tarcher/Putnam, 2002.

Norton, David L. *Personal Destinies: A Philosophy of Ethical Individualism*. Princeton, NJ: Princeton University Press, 1976.

Nowell-Smith, P. H. "Ifs and Cans," in *Free Will and Determinism*, Bernard Berofsky, ed. New York: Harper & Row, 1966, 322–339.

Nussbaum, Martha. *Frontiers of Justice: Disability, Nationality, Species Membership*. Cambridge, MA: Belknap Press of Harvard University, 2007.

Olveira, Jorge Menezes. "Harm and Offence in Mill's Conception of Liberty," http://www.trinitinture.com/documents/oliveira.pdf.

O'Meara, William. "The Aristotelian Principle in Mill and Kant," *Athens Journal of Humanities and Arts*, January 2015, https://www.atiner.gr/journals/humanities/2015-2-1-1-OMeara.pdf.

Orwell, George. "Review of *Mein Kampf*, by Adolf Hitler," *The New English Weekly*, March 1940, http://gutenberg.net.au/ebooks16/1600051h.html (most recent update: February 2016).

Paine, Thomas. "The Crisis" (1776), http://www.loc.gov/teachers/classroom-materials/presentationsandactivities/presentations/timeline/amrev/north/paine.html.

Palmer, Parker J. *To Know as We Are Known: Education as a Spiritual Journey*. San Francisco: Harper & Row, 1993.

Parfit, Derek. *On What Matters*. Oxford and London: Oxford University Press, 2011.

Pettit, Philip. "Three Conceptions of Democratic Control," *Constellations*, vol. 15, no. 1 (2008), https://www.princeton.edu/~ppettit/papers/2008/Three%20Conceptions%20of%20Democratic%20Control.pdf.

Phelps, Edmund S. "What Is Wrong with the West's Economies?" *The New York Review of Books*, August 13, 2015, http://www.nybooks.com/articles/archives/2015/aug/13/what-wrong-wests-economies.

Pinker, Steven. "The Enlightenment Is Working," *The Wall Street Journal*, https://www.wsj.com/articles/the-enlightenment-is-working-1518191343.

Pinker, Steven. *The Better Angels of Our Nature: Why Violence Has Declined.* New York: Viking, 2011.

Pinker, Steven. *Enlightenment Now: The Case for Reason, Science, Humanism, and Progress.* New York: Viking, 2018.

Putnam, Hilary. *Reason, Truth, and History.* Cambridge: Cambridge University Press, 1981.

Rasmussen, Douglas. "Human Flourishing and the Appeal to Human Nature," *Social Philosophy and Policy,* December 1999, https://www.researchgate.net/profile/Douglas_Rasmussen/publication/2317 87803_Human_Flourishing_and_the_Appeal_to_Human_Nature /links/56586f0d08ae1ef9297dbc30.pdf.

Rokeach, Milton. *The Nature of Human Values.* New York: Free Press, 1993.

Rosenberg, Marshall. *Nonviolent Communication: A Language of Life.* Encinitas, CA: PuddleDancer, 2015.

Sandel, Michael. "America's Search for a New Public Philosophy," *The Atlantic Monthly,* March 1996.

Sanders, Lynne. "Against Deliberation," *Political Theory,* vol. 25, no. 3 (1997), http://faculty.virginia.edu/lsanders/SB617_01.pdf.

Saunders, Harold. *Politics Is about Relationship: A Blueprint for the Citizens' Century.* New York: Palgrave Macmillan, 2005.

Schmookler, Andrew Bard. *The Parable of the Tribes: The Problem of Power in Social Evolution,* 2nd ed. Albany, NY: State University of New York Press, 1995.

Schumacher, E. F. *A Guide for the Perplexed.* New York: Harper & Row, 1977.

Schumpeter, Joseph A. *Capitalism, Socialism and Democracy.* New York: Harper Torchbooks, 1984.

Schwartz, Shalom H. "Basic Human Values: Theory, Measurement, and Applications," *Revue Française de Sociologie,* vol. 47, no. 4 (2006).

Searle, John R. "Can Information Theory Explain Consciousness?" *The New York Review of Books,* January 10, 2013.

Siedentop, Larry. "Two Liberal Traditions," in *The Idea of Freedom: Essays in Honour of Isaiah Berlin,* Alan Ryan, ed. Oxford: Oxford University Press, 1979.

Simons, Daniel J., and Shabris, Christopher F. "Gorillas in Our Midst: Sustained Inattention Blindness for Dynamic Events," *Perception,* vol. 28, no. 9 (1999), 1059–1074.

Singer, Peter. *Practical Ethics*. Cambridge: Cambridge University Press, 1993.

Stone, Douglas, Patton, Bruce, and Heen, Sheila. *Difficult Conversations: How to Discuss What Matters Most*. New York: Penguin Press, 2000.

Sullivan, Andrew. "The World Is Better Than Ever. Why Are We Miserable?" *New York Magazine*, March 9, 2018, http://nymag.com/daily/intelligencer/2018/03/sullivan-things-are-better-than-ever-why-are-we-miserable.html.

Susskind, Lawrence, Gordon, Jessica, and Zaerpoor, Yamin. "Deliberative Democracy and Public Dispute Resolution," in *The Oxford Handbook of Deliberative Democracy*, Andre Bachtiger, John S. Dryzek, Jane Mansbridge, and Mark E. Warren, eds. Oxford and London: Oxford University Press, 2018.

Szalavitz, Maia. "How Not to Raise a Bully: The Early Roots of Empathy," *Time*, April 17, 2010, http://content.time.com/time/health/article/0,8599,1982190,00.html.

Ten, C. L. *Mill on Liberty*. Oxford and London: Clarendon Press, 1980.

Thompson, Janna. *Discourse and Knowledge: Defence of a Collectivist Ethics*. London and New York: Routledge, 1998.

Tomasello, Michael. *Why We Cooperate*. Cambridge, MA: MIT Press, 2009.

Traub, James. "Democracy Is Dying by Natural Causes," *Foreign Policy*, March 1, 2018, https://foreignpolicy.com/2018/03/01/democracy-is-dying-by-natural-causes.

Turner, Frederick Jackson. "Contributions of the West to American Democracy," in *The Frontier in American Life*. New York: Henry Holt, 1921. Reprinted in Billington, Ray Allen, *Selected Essays of Frederick Jackson Turner*. Englewood Cliffs, NJ: Prentice-Hall, 1961. http://xroads.virginia.edu/~hyper/turner/chapter9.html#foot1.

Ury, William. *The Third Side: Why We Fight and How We Can Stop*. New York: Penguin Books, 2000.

Veatch, Henry Babcock. *Rational Man: A Modern Interpretation of Aristotelian Ethics*. Bloomington and London: Indiana University Press, 1962.

Warren, Mark E., and Mansbridge, Jane. "Deliberative Negotiation," in *Negotiating Agreement in Politics*, Jane Mansbridge and Cathy Jo Martin, eds. Washington, D.C.: American Political Science

Association, 2013. https://scholar.harvard.edu/files/dtingley/files/negotiating_agreement_in_politics.pdf.

Watson, George. "The Fuss about Ideology," *The Wilson Quarterly* (Winter 1992).

Wilber, Ken. *The Marriage of Sense and Soul: Integrating Science and Religion.* New York: Random House, 1998.

Will, George F. *Statecraft as Soulcraft: What Government Does.* New York: Simon & Schuster/Touchstone, 1983.

Wollheim, Richard. "John Stuart Mill and Isaiah Berlin: The Ends of Life and the Preliminaries of Morality," in *The Idea of Freedom: Essays in Honour of Isaiah Berlin*, Alan Ryan, ed. Oxford: Oxford University Press, 1979.

Yankelovich, Daniel. *The Magic of Dialogue: Transforming Conflict into Cooperation.* New York: Touchstone, 1999.

Index

acting: autonomy and, 28, 155 n.5;
beliefs and, 26–27; desire and,
26, 96, 124; freedom and, 28;
reasons and, 26–27, 124; value
and, 27
Andersen, Kurt, 3
Anderson, Elizabeth, 123
Aristotelian principle, 81, 160 n.7,
165 n.6
atomism, 4; problems with, 5–8,
11–12, 125, 130
autonomy, 25–36, 154 n.2; acting
and, 28, 103; authentic self and,
35–36, 58–60, 154 n.2; choice
and, 34, 59–61, 91, 103–103, 154
n.2; deliberation and, 33–34, 156
n.19; desires, hypothetical, and
27–28, 58, 60, 96, 103, 104, 110,
161 n.8; freedom and, 28, 35;
"higher pleasures" and, 35, 91,
103; individuality and, 13–14,
35–36, 58–60, 91; Mill and, 35,
40; open-mindedness and,
33–35; optimal conditions for,
34–35, 58–60, 103–104;
rationality and, 120; reasons
and, 29–30; self-development

and, 35, 91, 120, 129, 154 n.2;
self-interest and, 120, 125

beliefs: acting and, 26–7; desires
and, 26; social construction of,
155 n.5
Bellah, Robert, 8, 73
benevolence, rational, 123
Berlin, Isaiah, 37–39, 90
Berry, Wendell, 139
Blackburn, Simon, 29
Braman, Donald, 68, 111, 113–115
Brooks, David, 12, 75–77, 135–137
Buber, Martin, 67, 72
Buchanan, James, 1
Burkhalter, Stephanie, 74

choice: autonomy and, 34, 59–61,
103–104; optimal conditions for,
34–35, 58–60, 103–104; reasons
and, 8–11; value and, 9–11, 39
coercion, 28–29
comprehension, 65, 69, 73; ability,
evidence for, 164 n.15, n.17;
conflict and, 44, 48–49, 91;
defined, 45, 162 n.1; dialogue
and, 63, 74–75, 115; distributive

123; exploration level, 58, 76–77, 103–105; good and, 50, 85–89, 174 n.14; impartiality and, 34, 37, 49, 59, 61–63, 65, 98–101, 104,124; inclusion and, 104; individuality and, 105; issues in, 48; knowledge and, 82–89, 107, 168 n.5; levels or stages of, 54–56; monological conception of, 63, 96, 98; moral accommodation and, 107; motivation to engage in, 118–124; needs and, 73, 89; negotiation level, 106, 107, 109–110; other-regarding, 45; polylogical conception of, 63, 96, 98–101; principled negotiation and, 108–110; prisoner's dilemma and, 120; process requirements of, 54, 103–104; purpose, point, or need (PPN) for, 43, 61–62, 65, 88–89, 104; rationality and, 117–125; reciprocity and, 46–47, 113, 122–123; respect and, 69–70, 123; rights and, 42–43; rules level of, 55, 105; "successive approximation" and, 98; sympathy and, 162 n.4; trust and, 70, 119; value and, 50, 85–89; well-being and, 46, 88–90, 105

ethics: aretaic view of, 51; axiological dimension, 51; basic requirement of, 6, 46; care and, 50; characterological conception of, 51; dilemmas in, 48; duty, 50–51, 76; empathy and, 75–77, 96–97, 121–122, 163 n.5; internal/intrapersonal, 48;

rightness conception of, 50; rules and, 55; virtue conception of, 50

evaluative statements, 53; factual nature of, 53, 85–86

facts and values, 10, 83–86, 151 n.24
Fisher, Roger, 108–109
flourishing: human needs and, 13, 105, 132; individual, 13, 105, 152 n.31; purpose and, 139
formal element, 83
freedom: autonomy and, 28, 35, 39; as an ethical principle, 20, 40, 43; ethical thinking and, 118; independence and, 21–22, 39; individuality and, 25; negative, 25, 37, 39, 43, 153 n.5; pluralism and, 39; purpose, point, or need (PPN) for, 43; value and, 17, 20, 28, 43
Friedman, Maurice, 67, 72

Gilligan, Carol, 99
Goble, Frank, 89
good: defined, 83; epistemological, 82; for all, 81; harm principle and, 18–19; human needs and, 86–89, 129, 132; meaning and, 83–89; Mill and, 18–19; objectivity and, 10, 38, 79, 82, 85–89, 99–100; ontological, 82, 85; plural nature of, 37–38, 90; properties of, 83–84; purpose, point, or need (PPN) for, 79, 83–85, 89; quantity and quality, 80–82
Goodman, Rob, 130
goodness, concept of, 50
Gray, John, 131–133

About the Author

Michael K. Briand, PhD, is director of the Ethics and Deliberation Project at CivicEvolution. He is author of *Practical Politics: Five Principles for a Community That Works* (1999).